OREGON DUCKS
FOOTBALL

YEARS OF

100

GL⬤RY

1 8 9 4 - 1 9 9 5

AN ILLUSTRATED HISTORY OF
UNIVERSITY OF OREGON FOOTBALL

Written by
Michael C. McCann, John Conrad, Bob Clark,
Paul Buker, Ron Bellamy, Michael F. Sims, Bill Mulflur

Edited By Michael C. McCann

Designed by Lyn Ryse

MCC | MCCANN COMMUNICATION CORP.

Published in Eugene, Oregon
by McCann Communications Corp.
with the authorization and cooperation of the University of Oregon

Copyright 1995
McCann Communications Corp.
All Rights Reserved.

ISBN: 0-9648244-7-7
Library of Congress Catalog Card Number: 95-79214

Editor & Publisher: Michael C. McCann

Associate Publishers:
  A. Michael Hillis
  Dave Heeke
  Steve Hellyer
  Jim Bartko
  Herb Yamanaka

Authors:
  Michael C. McCann
  John Conrad
  Bob Clark
  Paul Buker
  Ron Bellamy
  Michael F. Sims
  Bill Mulflur

Contributing Writers: Sam Obitz, Keith Richard

Assistant Editors: Margaret Marti, Beth McDaniel

Proof Readers: Jennifer McCann, Denise Behrends

Historical Consultant: Keith Richard

Design: Ryse Design
Computer Graphics: G! Graphics

Photo Editor: Ronald L. Richmond

All Photos: Copyright 1995
University of Oregon Department of Intercollegiate Athletics
Used by permission

Contributing Photographers:
  John Giustina, Paul Spinelli, Peter Read Miller, Kevin Morris, Warren Morgan

Corporate Biographers: Irene Gresick, Lynn Bell

Marketing Consultant: Bart Barica

Additional Support Services Provided by:
  Dan Williams, Bill Moos, Dave Williford, Jamie Klund, Dave Whittle, Brady Crook,
  Steve McBride, Joan Garr Hamrick, Greg Byrne, Jennifer McCann, Carmen Maria Garcia,
  Darin Weiss, Tom Barrows and Lainey Barrows.

Scans and Separations: Koke Printing Company
Printed in the USA by: Meridian International, Inc.

Preface by Michael C. McCann

Everyone who had a hand in producing this book has something very special in common: They're staunchly devoted to the on-going success of University of Oregon football. In all, eight writers, four editors, two designers and numerous photographers and University administrators contributed countless hours to the making of **Oregon Ducks Football: 100 Years of Glory.**

But most of the credit goes to the hundreds of Oregon football players and coaches whose efforts made Oregon's first 100 years of football so exciting and memorable. Their courage and heroics will continue to inspire Duck fans for generations to come.

This book had its genesis in a conversation I had in May 1994 with Dave Heeke, Oregon's Director of Broadcasting and Marketing, at the University's inaugural James H. Warsaw Sports Marketing Forum, where we both were invited to speak.

In conjunction with UO Sports Information Director Steve Hellyer, we began formulating a plan to publish a distinguished and definitive history book to help commemorate Oregon's centennial football celebration.

None of us could have imagined back then, more than a year ago, how dramatically Oregon's football fortunes would change in the interim. But changed they have, and what better time to publish this long-awaited work than on the heels of a Rose Bowl Berth and an undisputed Pacific 10 championship?

I hope you enjoy this illustrated history of the first century of Oregon football. It is a history steeped in a tradition of greatness and glory—a tradition that is sure to continue in the century that lies ahead.

September 19, 1995
Eugene, Oregon

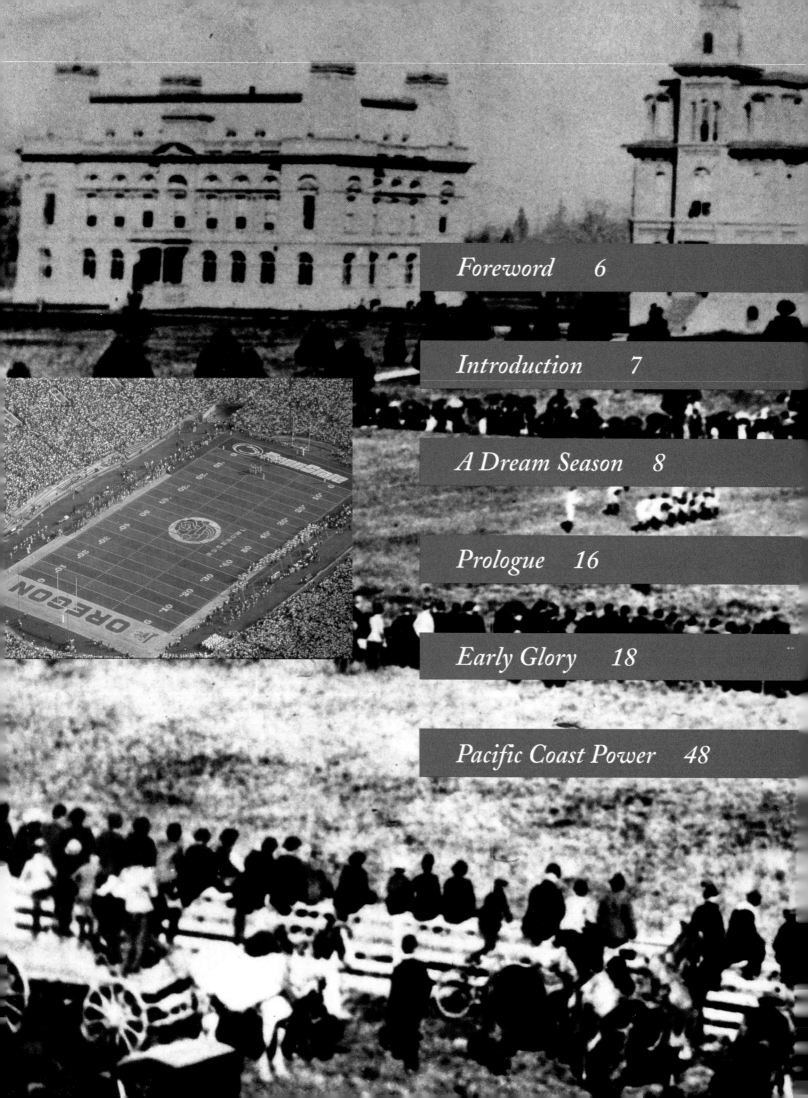

Foreword   6

Introduction   7

A Dream Season   8

Prologue   16

Early Glory   18

Pacific Coast Power   48

CONTENTS

The Len Casanova Era   74

Dawn of the Autzen Age   96

The Rich Brooks Era   114

Epilogue   138

Partners in Excellence   140

Oregon Centennial Football Records   154

Foreword by Bill Moos

A lot can happen in 100 years. The meaning of those events is often determined by a number of small victories that add up to bigger ones—victories that in turn create something more important than the victories themselves. Such has been the case in the first 100 years of football at the University of Oregon.

As the new athletic director for the Univeristy of Oregon, I came here following an outstanding year of victories. It was a year when a goal-line stand and interception became pivotal in creating one of the most memorable Duck football seasons ever; a year when an entire team played with heart in a classic interstate rivalry that resulted in Oregon's first outright Pac-10 championship and a trip to the Rose Bowl.

I mention these events on the playing field, because they are examples of the many victories that have contributed to the bigger triumphs in all aspects of the past 100 years of University of Oregon football. The names and styles of play have changed over the past 100 years, but one thing has remained constant: Commitment has been combined with integrity to create the outstanding century of football detailed in this book.

Those attributes also have created a sense of pride that speaks for the entire university and several generations of outstanding young men who have taken those triumphs on the field into the challenges of the broader fields of life. I truly believe that athletics better prepares men and women to meet those challenges in creative and courageous ways.

As the athletic director kicking off the next 100 years of University of Oregon football, it is my hope to maintain that sense of pride built up in the past 100 years and to see the many victories continue so that new and even larger ones can emerge.

August 31, 1995
Eugene, Oregon

Introduction by Dan Fouts

I t's my pleasure to introduce this authorized history of University of Oregon football. While I am fortunate enough to have played a role in the drama that unfolds in these pages, my love for the school goes far beyond that.

The years I spent at Oregon are among my most memorable ones, and they were made all the more so by the events of this past football season.

Nineteen-ninety-four was a very good year for Dan Fouts, the football fan. My Ducks won the Pac-10 Championship and made it to the Rose Bowl. And my San Diego Chargers were NFC Champs and played the team I followed as a child, the San Francisco 49ers, in the Super Bowl.

While there was no question in the public's mind that I was thrilled to no end about the success of the U of O, there was considerable conversation as to which team I was pulling for in the Super Bowl.

For some, the fact that I played my entire 15-year career for the Chargers was sufficient reason to be ga-ga over the lighting bolts. For others, because I was born and raised a Niner fan and happened to be the son of the team's broadcaster was enough to convince them that there was no other team for me but San Francisco.

But to me, although I was pleased that both San Diego and the Niners made it to the Big Show, deep down inside I really didn't feel all that passionate about either team.

The team I was ga-ga about, the team that made my blood boil, the team that captured my heart was the team that had never left my heart. Yeah, you guessed it . . . the Ducks.

I grew up a Niner fan. I played for the Chargers. I view these statements in the past tense. But when people tell me, "Oh, so you were a Duck!" I am quick to correct them: "I am a Duck!" To me there is no past tense there. Once a Duck, always a Duck.

Why? I'm not totally sure. Maybe it has to do with the people at the school: the professors, aides, coaches administrators, Quacker Backers and alumni.

Maybe it is the campus: the statues, the trees, Deedy hall and Mac Court. Maybe it is Eugene, the Mckenzie River, the coast or Hendricks Park. Maybe it is the weather. Just kidding. Or maybe it is the smell of bread baking at Williams Bakery. It certainly isn't the smell of the lumber mill in Springfield.

I am a Duck, I guess, for all of these reasons. I am proud of my days at the U of O. Proud of the teams I played on in each game. We were hardly ever the favored team and were often out-manned by and underdogs to some mighty impressive competition. But we were never outhustled, nor were we ever embarrassed by the effort we gave.

As the University of Oregon enters its second century of collegiate football, the Ducks have never flown higher. And I, for one, have never been prouder to say: "I am a Duck."

June 5, 1995
San Francisco, California

A PANORAMIC VIEW
OF THE 1995 ROSE
BOWL, WHERE
OREGON MADE ITS
FIRST APPEARANCE
IN 37 YEARS WHEN
THE DUCKS MET
THE PENN STATE
NITTANY LIONS ON
JAN. 2.

A DREAM SEASON

1994

Oregon's Amazing Run for the Roses.

Fall is a beautiful season in the Pacific Northwest. The days are warm. The nights are cool. The air is clean. September 19, 1994, a picture-perfect autumn Sunday with temperatures in the mid-80s, was all of the above.

The beauty of that day was lost on the football coaches gathered inside Oregon's Casanova Athletic Center, however. Rich Brooks and his assistants were smarting from a 34-16 loss to Utah the day before, and their team's 1-2 record carried with it threatening implications. The Center was more like a fortress that afternoon, its occupants bracing themselves for a vicious onslaught of public and media criticism as they prepared for perhaps one final effort to save their team and their jobs.

Unbeknownst to anyone, that day marked the beginning of the most incredible story of the 1994 college football season. An Oregon football team that had been soundly beaten in successive weeks by Hawaii and Utah, and had beaten only Division II Portland State, would go on to win eight of its next nine games to claim the Pac-10 Conference Championship and the Ducks' first Rose Bowl berth since 1958.

Brooks and his assistants agreed to maintain a positive public posture. Rather than apply pressure on the players, they vowed to ease it. They would encourage their players to work hard, have fun and not worry about the public backlash. Most of all, they pledged to stick together.

"We knew expectations weren't being met and our continued employment was in question," then-offensive coordinator Mike Bellotti said. "We just talked about how the cavalry wasn't going to ride to the rescue, there were no free agents out there to sign and what we made out of our situation was up to us. We could blame a lot of things or we could roll up our sleeves and go to work."

The lightning rods for the mounting criticism of the Oregon football program were Head Coach Rich Brooks, defensive coordinator Nick Aliotti and quarterback Danny O'Neil.

Brooks, though he had taken the Ducks to three bowl games in the previous five years, was coming off a miserable 5-6 season in 1993, following a loss to Wake Forest in the 1992 Independence Bowl, where the Ducks had blown a 19-point second-half lead. Right or wrong, public opinion of Brooks was decidedly negative and growing more so by the day.

Aliotti, meanwhile, suffered more and more in comparison to former defensive coordinator Denny Schuler,

who was credited with much of Oregon's success in the late 1980s and early 1990s before leaving the staff after the 1992 season. As the Ducks struggled through 1993 and into 1994, neither the public nor the press had gained confidence in Aliotti as the architect of the UO defense.

O'Neil had been injured as a freshman, had led Oregon to the Independence Bowl as a sophomore and broken the UO single-season passing record as a junior, but those facts went unnoticed by his critics. They pointed out that O'Neil had never brought the Ducks from behind in the second half, had never led the Ducks to a major upset of a ranked team and hadn't even produced a winning season.

No one could have guessed on that sunny September Sunday how the fortunes of these three men would change as the 1994 season continued to unfold.

It didn't happen all at once, but began the following weekend when the Ducks hosted Iowa. It was Oregon's first home game against a Big Ten team since 1980, and the Ducks won 40-18—mostly by not beating themselves. Despite killing themselves with miscues against Hawaii and Utah, they didn't turn the ball over for the first time in two years and were penalized only 26 yards. The Ducks took a 27-12 halftime lead with three second-quarter touchdowns and were never threatened.

"Iowa was a pivotal game in a lot of respects," Brooks

ABOVE: HEAD COACH RICH BROOKS LEADS HIS 1994 CONFERENCE CHAMPIONS ONTO THE FIELD AT AUTZEN STADIUM.

said. "The coffin had been built and the hole had been dug, and there were still people trying to bury me after we won. Had we lost that game, I know what it would have been like, and I'm not sure we'd have been able to overcome that and keep moving forward."

The Iowa game stopped the bleeding, but it was the next weekend in Los Angeles that signaled the start of something special, with the Ducks recording their first stunning upset. O'Neil was out with an infection in his passing hand, and tailback Ricky Whittle and cornerback Herman O'Berry were hurt. Nonetheless, Oregon defeated USC 22-7 in its first victory over the Trojans in the Los Angeles Coliseum since 1971. Backup quarterback Tony Graziani threw for 287 yards, reserve tailback Dino Philyaw turned in 123 yards rushing and a 49-yard touchdown, and freshman cornerback Kenny Wheaton had a big interception and several key tackles.

Before the season, Aliotti nicknamed Oregon's defense "Gang Green," to symbolize a philosophy of playing aggressively and playing together. After the USC triumph, the nickname started catching on, as the Ducks limited the Trojans to 31 yards rushing and sacked USC's quarterbacks nine times. The Ducks staggered slightly the next week, losing 21-7 to Washington State in the Palouse as Graziani was injured in the first half and O'Neil had to play without benefit of any practice time. But Oregon came back the next week to beat Cal at home 23-7, setting the stage for one of the most memorable games in UO history.

It will be remembered not as the game the Ducks upset ninth-ranked Washington 31-20 before a regional television audience and a crowd of 44,134, but as the day O'Neil finally brought the Ducks from behind and Kenny Wheaton made it stand up with a spectacular 97-yard inter-

ABOVE: TIGHT END JOSH WILCOX SHOWED HE WOULD BE A PRIMARY OFFENSIVE WEAPON WITH HIS PERFORMANCE IN OREGON'S 22-7 VICTORY AT USC.

ception return with one minute to play.

Oregon was leading by four points when Washington scored to go ahead 20-17 with 7:44 to play. The game seemed to be unfolding as it had so often—especially against the Huskies—with the Ducks losing their grip down the stretch after playing so gallantly.

But O'Neil led the Ducks 98 yards to regain the lead. He threw for three first downs, ran for another and handed the ball to fullback Dwayne Jones for the 12-yard touchdown run that put Oregon on top 24-17 with 2:40 remaining.

"I finally got it done," O'Neil said. "Not coming from behind is more than something the media has heaped on me. It was a personal thing for me, something I needed to overcome." He later told the media that the performance of Graziani in the USC game made him realize that he could depend on his teammates to help carry the game—that he did not have to do it alone.

But Washington didn't quit. The Huskies, thanks to a key fourth-down pass completion, advanced to the UO 8-yard line with 1:09 to play. They had plenty of time to give the ball to heralded tailback Napolean Kaufman; instead, quarterback Damon Huard threw the ball in the flat toward Dave Janoski. Wheaton timed the throw perfectly, picked it off and raced the length of the field to score one of the most dramatic touchdowns in UO history.

"I was anticipating that pattern and I took a gamble," Wheaton said. "I told myself before the snap that if the receiver

BELOW: THE OREGON DUCK MASCOT CAVORTS ON THE CARPET AT AUTZEN STADIUM.

Kenny Wheaton was very tired.

"My mouth was dry," the cornerback, who'd red-shirted as a freshman, said later. "It's like we were running an hour straight with no rest. That was the most tired I have ever felt in my life."

On that bright afternoon at Autzen Stadium, the Ducks had taken a 24-20 lead over the Huskies, driving 98 yards to a touchdown behind quarterback Danny O'Neil. But now, in the final minutes, the Huskies had mounted a

Kenny Wheaton heads for the end zone against the Huskies.

drive of their own, marching in 11 plays to first-and-goal at the Oregon 8 with 1:05 remaining.

"I thought they were going to score," Oregon linebacker Jeremy Asher said. "I just remember having the feeling that we were going to lose it, and it was really frustrating."

As Oregon used its last time-out, defensive coordinator Nick Aliotti anticipated another pass by Washington quarterback Damon Huard. He called for Oregon's "Falcon" defense, featuring five defensive backs, and called for the blitz.

Meanwhile, Wheaton was remembering some homework he'd done two nights earlier. Studying videotapes of the Huskies at home, he'd noticed that inside the 10, the Husky he was matched against, slot receiver Dave Janoski, typically ran an "out" pattern, running upfield and then cutting toward the front corner of the end zone.

Talking to himself, Wheaton said, "OK, snap of the ball, we're just going to jump the out."

The Oregon blitz never got to Huard. The Washington quarterback dropped five steps back and threw toward Janoski, who had indeed run the out. Expecting it, Wheaton broke for the ball.

"I live on the edge," Wheaton said later. "Either I make the play or the receiver makes the play. On some days, I may lose. If he scores, I look bad. If I make the play, the Oregon Ducks look good. That's all in gambling."

Wheaton struck it rich: Huard's pass loomed large in front of him. "I was like, 'Catch the ball, just catch it,' " Wheaton said. He did, and began sprinting toward the distant end zone. As the crowd roared, as Oregon players and coaches jumped in joy on the sideline, Wheaton raced in front of them to the Oregon 40, cut inside between Huard and another Husky, and didn't stop until he crossed the Oregon goal line with 49 seconds left.

"I saw the goal line far away, and I was thinking of getting to the goal line and calling my mom and letting her know I made a big play," Wheaton said. From the snap of the ball, the play had lasted 16 seconds. Kenny Wheaton's 97-yard interception return saved the game and launched the Ducks into the midst of the Rose Bowl race with four games left. Like Wheaton's sprint to the goal line, it was a race they would win.

Doug Koke

went inside, it might be a touchdown or the safety would have to pick him up. But if it was an 'out,' I was going to make the play."

He did and the standing room-only Autzen Stadium crowd erupted in a celebration that continued nonstop until the gun sounded. The Ducks were 5-3 overall and 3-1 in the Pac-10. If they could pull off yet another upset against Arizona the following week, they would be legitimate Rose Bowl contenders.

Oregon fell behind Arizona 9-0, but its Gang Green defense took over the game in the second half, allowing the eighth-ranked Wildcats only 39 yards after intermission. Matt Belden's field goal cut Arizona's lead to 9-3 in the third quarter, then O'Neil threw a 15-yard touchdown pass to tight end Josh Wilcox for a 10-9 victory that improved Oregon's position to 4-1 in the league and 6-3 overall. Suddenly, the Ducks commanded national respectability with rankings of 17th in the *USA Today*/CNN poll and 21st in the Associated Press.

Now the Ducks found themselves faced with a different challenge. After upset victories in three of their five previous games—four of them against ranked teams—the Ducks would close out the season against three teams they were favored to beat. "Now we just have to take care of business each week," Brooks said. The Ducks had handled adversity. Their skeptics wondered if they could handle success and the pressure of contending for the Rose Bowl.

Oregon answered part of the question by crushing the Arizona State Sun Devils 34-10 in its final home game of the year. The victory also gave the Ducks control of their own destiny, thanks to USC's victory over Washington State. Oregon's ranking jumped to 15th in the AP and 11th in *USA Today*/CNN. Victories over Stanford and Oregon State would put the Ducks in the Rose Bowl for the first time in 37 years.

Stanford fell easily as O'Neil set a UO single-game record with six touchdown passes and Oregon posted a 55-21 victory. The Ducks' fifth straight triumph improved their record to 6-1 in league and 8-3 overall, moving them to within a victory over the Beavers of advancing to Pasadena. Meanwhile, Oregon advanced to ninth in the *USA Today*/CNN balloting and 12th in the AP. The nation awaited to see if Oregon could take the final step to earn a shot at second-ranked Penn State.

"This is what I've wanted ever since I've been at Oregon," Brooks said. "It's down to one game now, and it's

ABOVE: FRESHMAN MATT BELDEN PLAYED AN INTEGRAL ROLE IN OREGON'S SUCCESS AS A PUNTER AND PLACE-KICKER.
BELOW: IN HIS FIRST START SOPHOMORE TONY GRAZIANI LED OREGON TO A 22-7 UPSET OF USC AT LOS ANGELES TO PUT THE DUCKS ON THE ROAD TO THE ROSE BOWL.

great there will be national attention on the Civil War."

The Beavers wouldn't make it easy, though. Oregon State blocked a punt for one touchdown and led until O'Neil's second touchdown pass of the day to Dino Philyaw—a screen pass with 3:43 left to play—gave Oregon a 17-13 victory. The Ducks were not only in the Rose Bowl, they were clear-cut Pac-10 Conference champions, compliments of UCLA's upset of USC.

It was an accomplishment applauded not only in Eugene and around the state but up and down the West Coast and throughout the country. "If I can't go to the Rose Bowl, I'm happy to see Rich Brooks get the chance," Washington Coach Jim Lambright said. "It's a matter of recognizing what he's done there for so long, and it's nice to see him get a chance to get to the very top."

Brooks was voted three national coach-of-the-year honors, including the prestigious Paul "Bear" Bryant Trophy, and was honored by ESPN on national

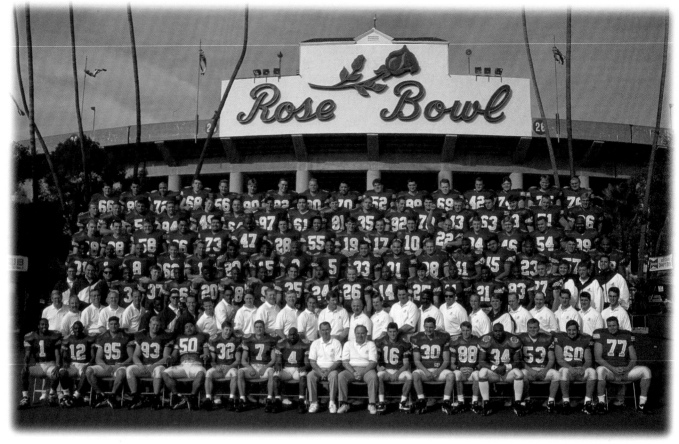

ABOVE: THE 1995 ROSE BOWL TEAM. *Front row (left to right):* KORY MURPHY, DINO PHILYAW, D.J. CABRERA, MARK SLYMEN, SILILA MALEPEAI, JEFF SHERMAN, CHAD COTA, HERMAN O'BERRY, RICH BROOKS, STEVE HELLYER, DANNY O'NEIL, DAN MEADE, ERIC JOHANNSEN, DWAYNE JONES, TIM DEGROOTE, DAVE CUTTRELL, STEVE HARDIN. *Second row:* DR. ROBERT CRIST, ED ELDER, DR. DONALD JONES, DR. KEN SINGER, DEAN ADAMS, EUGENE CHISM, TRAVIS GONZOLEZ, DAVE ZIEMBA, JIM RADCLIFFE, DON PELLUM, JOE REITZUG, BILL TARROW, JOE SCHAFFELD, NICK ALIOTTI, MIKE BELLOTTI, NEAL ZOUMBOUKOS, JOHN RAMSDELL, STEVE GREATWOOD, GARY CAMPBELL, COLLIN HALL, GEOFF GINTHER, MARK PRETO, KEN SMITH, CLAY JAMISON, BOB TOTH, RICHARD SCHLOTFELDT, GARY CLINTON. *Third row:* JEFF WOLGAMOTT, PAT CONRAD, ED GARLAND, DAMERON RICKETTS, BRIAN MCNELY, ROB JOHNSON, KENNY WHEATON, GARY YOUNG, EUGENE JACKSON, DAMIEN FERTITTA, KEVIN PARKER, ERIC WINN, RICKY WHITTLE, MATT BELDEN, LAMONT WOODS, DAMON GRIFFIN, PAT JOHNSON, DAVID COYLE, TADD BRYAN, MATT INSKEEP, TODD KAANAPU. *Fourth row:* ERIC EDWARDS, ALEX MOLDEN, KAON-JABBAR EAST, JOSH PLATT, CRISTIN MCLEMORE, ISAAC WALKER, MARCEL STEWART, BRIAN COLLINS, DANTE LEWIS, PULOU MALEPEAI, BRYANT JACKSON, JOE DONNERBERG, CURTIS MOORE, A.J. JELKS, RONNIE GIPSON, CLAY MAURITSON, DERRICK BARNES. *Fifth row:* RICH RUHL, PAUL JENSEN, ROB WILLIAMS, LEIE SUALUA, TASI MALEPEAI, REGGIE JORDAN, CHAD WILLIAMS, JEROME PERRYMAN, JASON MAAS, RYAN PERRY-SMITH, TONY GRAZIANI, JAIYA FIGUERAS, RYAN EDDY, RYAN KLASSEN, MARK SCHMIDT, DESMOND BYRD. *Sixth row:* CHRIS VANDIVER, JEREMY ASHER, MATT STEEPIN, NICK PAGET, JEFF BRANSON, KYLE STRAIT, BRIAN DUNCAN, MIKE ARMENDARIZ, JED WEAVER, MARTY MURPHY, MATT SCHUETZ, JOHN KIRK, JOSH BIDWELL, STEFAN DEVRIES, MIKE PHELPS, ERIC REID, MITCH SIEGNER. *Seventh row:* CHAD NORMOYLE, CHRISTIAN ANDERSON, PAUL WIGGINS, SEATON DALY, TROY BAILEY, JOSH WILCOX, BLAKE SPENCE, MATT LOFRANO, ANDY PETTY, BOB BALDWIN, MATT REINHARDT, MARK GREGG, DEREK ALLEN, MICHAEL KLEWS, DAVID WEBER, WILLY RIFE.

television. He had become the toast of the coaching profession, but he was quick to share the honors with his players and staff.

The Ducks finished the regular season ranked ninth nationally by USA Today/CNN and 12th by AP. More importantly, they were on their way to the Rose Bowl for the first time since 1957. The Ducks were huge underdogs in '57 to top-ranked Ohio State, and the 1994 Ducks were quickly made 17-point underdogs to second-ranked Penn State. The Nittany Lions featured an offense that averaged 520 yards and 46.7 points per game, with two Heisman Trophy candidates in quarterback Kerry Collins and tailback Ki-Jana Carter.

The trip to the Rose Bowl involved more than just the players and coaches. This was to be the biggest football event in the history of the University of Oregon. The nearly insatiable thirst for tickets led to unparalleled brokering nationwide and prompted UO students to camp outside the Duck Ticket Office for fear of missing out on their allotment.

The pregame parties, included in many of the travel packages, were planned with elaborate detail. For the first time a party was held for every ex-UO football player who could make it to Pasadena. Bob Newland, a former Duck receiver and NFL standout, arranged the party and the turnout was overwhelming. Additionally, more than 10,000 Duck fans, including Rich Brooks, Len Casanova and numerous state officials, rallied at Century Plaza to take part in a simultaneous blowing of duck calls that was billed as "The Quack Heard Around the World!"

On game day, professional golfer and ex-Duck Peter Jacobsen arranged a pregame tailgate party on the golf course adjacent to the Rose Bowl. More than 20,000 Oregon faithful joined in the festivities, which included a giant barbecue, live music and a very loud and spirited rendition of "Mighty Oregon."

The media blitz that preceded the January 2, 1995, contest was unlike any the University had ever experienced. It gave the school an unprecedented "foot in the door" of millions of homes across the country. Radio announcers spoke of the Ducks, newspapers wrote of the Ducks, television personalities commented on the Ducks. From New York City to Miami, Chicago to Los Angeles, the Ducks were becoming the darlings of the college football world.

The players were far from overwhelmed. These Ducks had already performed one miracle in getting to the Rose Bowl, and they believed they had another one left in them. They were a relaxed, even confident, team, and Carter's 83-yard touchdown on Penn State's first play from scrimmage didn't shake that confidence. Oregon came right back and scored on O'Neil's one-yard touchdown pass to Josh Wilcox to tie the score at 7-7.

Penn State scored on fullback Brian Milne's one-yard run in the second period, but the Ducks answered in the third on O'Neil's 17-yard scoring pass to wide receiver Cristin McLemore following linebacker Reggie Jordan's interception.

The Ducks were even with Penn State, 14-14, with 20 minutes to play in the Rose Bowl.

But the roof fell in on Oregon in the second half when the Nittany Lions returned the kickoff 72 yards and Carter ran 17 yards for a touchdown. Soon after, O'Neil was intercepted in UO territory, and Carter ran three yards for another score to put Penn State on top 28-14.

The score became misleadingly lopsided when the Ducks turned the ball over on downs deep in their own territory late in the fourth quarter. A punt would likely have kept the score respectable, but Oregon was still playing to win. Penn State scored again to make it 38-14 before tailback Whittle scored Oregon's last touchdown with 2:44 to play.

The final score was Penn State 38, Oregon 20.

"We're very disappointed," Brooks said afterward. "We played hard, we took our best shot, but we weren't able to take advantage of opportunities we had, and consequently we fell short of what we wanted to do."

The Ducks had plenty to be proud of, however. O'Neil rewrote the Rose Bowl

record book for passing, shattering six individual marks in completing 41 of 61 passes for 456 yards and two touchdowns. He was named co-MVP for his performance, along with Penn State's Carter.

Oregon also earned rave reviews in a Los Angeles press, which had lampooned the matchup before the game.

"These Ducks are unworthy of levity, undeserving of ridicule," wrote Michael Ventre of the L.A. *Daily News.* "They put their hearts and talent on display in bars and living rooms across the land. They exhibited a dynamic, if occasionally errant, offense and a defense undaunted by the challenge of playing a storied team with an icon for a coach in hot pursuit of a national crown. Oregon did OK. They informed the nation they where the champions of the Pac-10 Conference, they accomplished that by playing superb and guts football, and they are to be respected."

Respected, indeed. This was a team that had been picked to finish near the bottom of the conference, yet won the Pac-10 title and gave Oregon its most glorious season in 37 years.

The Ducks finished the year ranked 11th in both polls. Nebraska won the national title and Penn State finished second. But it was Oregon that had written the most amazing story of the 1994 college football season.

ABOVE: RICKY WHITTLE ELUDES THREE PENN STATE TACKLERS.

OPPOSITE: DANNY O'NEIL FIRES A PASS AS HIS LINE HOLDS OFF THE PENN STATE RUSH.

Prologue

From its first game in 1894, to the stunning upsets of 1994, the University of Oregon has enjoyed a remarkably rich football tradition. The Lemon Yellow and the Emerald Green — colors of the native Oregon grape—have stirred the hearts of Duck fans for more than a century. Their choruses of "Mighty Oregon" echo across the Willamette Valley and throughout the world, as the school's proud and loyal following continues to grow.

The roots of Oregon football go back to 1889, when the University's Board of Regents approved a plan to construct a small on-campus gymnasium. John Wesley Johnson, University president, strongly opposed the decision and threatened to resign if the building was funded and built. Nonetheless, the funding was provided, an architect was hired, a contract was let and the gymnasium was completed within the year. Johnson didn't carry out his threat to resign. Instead, he showed his opposition by not proposing to hire a person to oversee any type of physical activity in the gym, or to expend any funds for equipment. The building did not stand unused, however, as students used the gym on their own.

It wasn't that Johnson opposed physical activity. After all, he was an avid hunter and fisherman, and after finishing his degree at Yale in 1861, he returned to Oregon by walking from New Haven, Connecticut to Corvallis. Johnson simply believed the University should not be in the business of providing people with non-academic facilities.

The action that finally prompted Johnson to resign was the board's decision to construct an on-campus dormitory. Johnson denounced the plan because it required him to take on the added burden of providing room and board for individuals he believed ought to be mature enough to take care of their own non-educational needs. In resigning, he did not leave the University faculty altogether, but remained as a professor of Latin.

Hired sight-unseen to replace Johnson was 32-year-old Charles Hiram Chapman, who became the University's second president. Chapman had only recently earned his Ph.D. in mathematics from Johns Hopkins, then considered a "revolutionary" university in the United States. Chapman sent a picture of himself, wearing spectacles, for use with publicity announcing his appointment. Surprised by his bespectacled appearance, board member Blaine Hovey wrote to Chapman that the photograph would not be used as "It is not thought highly for young men to wear glasses."

Chapman wed Alice Hall, a medical doctor who had married into the extended Roosevelt family that included Theodore and Eleanor. The Chapmans believed strongly in the vigorous philosophy of Teddy Roosevelt that both the mind and body had to be developed to full potential if life was to be truly meaningful and enjoyed.

Upon becoming president, Chapman commenced to "freeing" the curriculum by moving away from the concept of rote learning. He also hired new, and generally younger, faculty. Chapman hired Joseph Wetherbee, formerly director of the Salem YMCA, to be the physical director on the campus. Alice Hall Chapman took on the task of organizing classes for female students in the method of Swedish gymnastics. Equipment was purchased, and for the first time, the gymnasium was outfitted and ready for operation. Wetherbee encouraged activities of all sorts—track, baseball, rugby, boxing and gymnastics—allowing the students to work in the gymnasium after classes and without supervision.

Prior to Chapman's presidency, debate had been the only organized student activity sanctioned by the faculty, and at times this activity caused great problems, such as fist fights following debates over continued disagreements.

What else might happen if the faculty approved an extension for more accepted organizations? The two debating societies—one for males and one for females—had weekly columns in the city newspaper. Quite often they attacked the narrow-mindedness of the faculty and openly challenged the pettiness and silliness of several rules established by the faculty and the president, which governed the behavior of students. What would happen, the faculty wondered, if students were able to expand their extracurricular interests with faculty blessing?

The arrival of Chapman and the acceptance of physical activity gave impetus to the long-held desire of many students to have organized athletics. During this period the students voted to have an official school color. They chose lemon yellow, the blossom color of the native plant, Oregon grape or Mahonia aquifolium. In addition, the student body accepted some official cheers or yells.

The next year, in 1893, student's chose emerald green, the leaf color of the Oregon grape, to complement the lemon yellow. At the same time, they voted to call themselves the "Webfoots," a name commonly used to refer to the original white settlers west of the Cascade Mountains. The state of Oregon was unofficially the "Webfoot State" so the Oregon population quite normally assigned that name to the State University—the state's first public university—and the student vote made the name official.

A faculty-approved student publication was also started during this period—a monthly publication named The Reflector. It carried all sorts of articles and news about what other students were doing across the country as well as literary articles and information about student activity on campus. Students used the publication as a mouthpiece to express their opposition to football on campus. Writers called the sport a form of "barbarism" and said it entailed "the brutality and danger of prizefighting." Still, student support remained for a football team, and the next step was to ask the president and the faculty for permission to organize. The president persuaded a reluctant faculty to let the students proceed with their desire to field a football team. Stringent rules were put into place by the faculty: each team member "must have 42 credits earned; he must have a student character above reproach; he must have a standing of 85 percent in each of his studies during the preceding semester; and he must have been a student of the University for at least one year."

To these guidelines another rule was added, stating that the coach had to be a college graduate, and no games could be played after December 1. All games had to be against other college teams and the faculty had final approval of the schedule. Anything might have been acceptable by the students just for the opportunity to field a football team like Stanford and the University of California, but the faculty at the University of Oregon was not about to let things get out of hand.

The stage was now ready for the play—but two more things were needed: a coach and an opponent.

EARLY GLORY

1894

Let the Game Begin

Oregon's first football squad set the tone in a unique and positive manner. "Ours was probably the only UO team that didn't know the word defeat," said Cal Young, Oregon's first football coach. "Of course, we played only one game." That game was a 44-2 triumph over Albany college, and Young, with the victory registered, resigned.

Young, a member of one of Lane County's pioneer families, had learned to play football in 1886, while attending Bishop Scott Academy, a military school in Portland. He was 23 and working in the family meat market when University of Oregon students received the go-ahead to form a team.

"Three or four fellows from the campus came down and asked me to be coach," Young said. "They were students who wanted to play and had heard I knew something of the game, so I thought I'd help them out."

Late in the fall of 1893, Young — "the coacher" — began forming the first team for the University. At many of the workouts, the spectators outnumbered the participants; such was the enthusiasm for the start of the sport.

In the dark days of winter that year, spirits waned. The workouts were strenuous, and there seemed to be no goal toward which to work. Young decided what the team needed was *a game*, and it couldn't wait until next fall. Albany College agreed to be the inaugural opponent, and a date was set: March 24, 1894.

"The home team must pay the expenses of the visitors, hence an admittance fee will be charged," warned a story in the *Eugene City Guard* newspaper. "Those who desire to witness the game can secure tickets at either of the bookstores and at Henderson and Linn's drug stores. Price 25 cents."

The field, now the site of the University's Computing Center and Gilbert Hall, was prepared for the game. There were no bleachers, no grandstands, no seating for spectators, just two long benches for the two teams. Spectators lined the field, or positioned themselves by sitting on the fence, standing on the sidelines, sitting and standing in carriages with the horses still attached, or watching from the roofs of nearby buildings for a favored vantage point. They all witnessed the University's team completely dominate the Albany eleven.

From the warmups it was clear Oregon would have a

size advantage. It had every other edge, too, including its coach, Young, who served as one of the officials.

"We could have won [more] easily," Young said, "but I'd have seen to it that Albany got the benefit of any doubts."

From the time the home team won the toss of the coin and chose to take the football first, there was little doubt about the outcome.

At 3 p.m. on that spring day, a century of football began for the University of Oregon with a 5-yard rush through the middle of the line. Similar gains followed, and six minutes into the game an uncredited Oregon player scored the first touchdown.

Harry Templeton, the fullback, kicked the goal and Oregon was on its way to a 22-0 lead in the first 30 minutes. Then a 10-minute intermission began.

The other Oregon starters were Ted Shattuck at center; guards John Edmundson and Fred Herbold; tackles Fred Templeton and James Linn; ends Roy Hurley and Charles Wintermeier; halfbacks Howard Davis and Clarence Keene; and Frank Mathews, quarterback and team captain.

"We had two substitutes but never used them,"

distinction on the University; and it wishes, figuratively speaking, to place the wreath of laurels on the brow of each member of the football team."

That wreath didn't stay on long.

Young chose not to return as coach for the first fall season, and former Princeton player G.A. Church was named to replace him. A loosely aligned league was formed for the fall of 1894, with Oregon Agricultural College in Corvallis, Pacific University in Forest Grove, Oregon State Normal School and Portland University teams joining the University of Oregon to make up the Oregon College Foot Ball [sic] Association.

A championship would even be decided. Semifinal action saw OAC playing the University of Oregon in Corvallis and Pacific playing Portland, with the winners to meet for the title.

Oregon's first championship hopes ended with a 16-0 loss to OAC. The *Eugene City Guard* account of the game claimed "the University boys had no coaching to speak of before the game, and while individual playing was excellent, the teamwork was open to criticism."

Support during this first full season was somewhat indifferent and unexpectedly shortened. Because a Thanksgiving Day game against Pacific—a scoreless tie—didn't draw enough fans to meet expenses, Oregon's final game of the season against Monmouth was canceled.

Officially, Oregon not only failed to win any of its three games in the fall—it also failed to score a point. But an unofficial game that was supposed to be a game between the UO junior varsity (reserves) and the normal school team from Drain turned into a rout when the UO first team played the first half and held a 52-0 halftime lead. The reserves took over for the second half and the final score was Oregon 64, Drain 0.

Oregon realized the game shouldn't count, and it was never recorded in the official results. So the record remained winless, and as his successors would be for the next century, the coach was blamed for losing. Church wasn't brought back for the next season.

Young said. "Didn't need to. Eleven men were enough."

Certainly for this game.

The rout continued in the second half. Albany's only score came on a safety when Mathews was forced to fall on a kick in his own end zone, making the final score 44-2.

Who could find fault with such overwhelming success? "College athletics at the University of Oregon have always heretofore been visionary, a dream, but the students and friends of the University were forcibly impressed on March 24th that physical feats were no longer Utopias with us but were actual realities," wrote Laura E. Beatie, editor-in-chief of *The Reflector*.

"On the aforementioned date, the football team played against the team from the Albany Collegiate Institute and won a glorious victory," she continued. "And well may we be proud of such a victory when we consider the fact that this is our first physical contest with a sister college."

And what of the worries that the sport was barbaric?

"We are not concerned with these," Beatie wrote. "The University of Oregon football team met the Albany team and beat them, and *The Reflector* wishes to help bestow honor upon those who so bravely and courageously heaped

ABOVE: THE 1895 OREGON TEAM WAS COACHED BY PERCY BENSON AND INCLUDED THE TEMPLEMAN BROTHERS, FRANK AND HARRY.

To Play or Not to Play?

The first question about a second season was whether there would even be one. Again there was opposition to the sport and the *Salem Daily Post* came out strongly in support of banning the game from college campuses.

"The game is little better than the sports of the amphitheater of old or the bullfights of Spain," the *Daily Post* editorialized. "A scientific game like baseball or cricket is all right in connection with universities or colleges, if not carried to excess; but football is on a par with the shinny (field hockey played with a curved stick, a ball or block of wood). White settlers learned this game from the native Americans on the east coast and the game became popular in the schools of the 19th century of the aborigines or the ghost dance of the Sioux."

Cancel football? On the eve of Oregon's only perfect season?

Percy Benson, who had played football at California, was hired as the coach and had several players back from the previous two Oregon teams, including guards Ted Shattuck and John Edmundson, the stalwarts of a defense that allowed only two touchdowns in the four games.

The season began against Oregon Agricultural College, and the increased admission price of 50 cents—double the previous year—seemed well worth it when Oregon beat the Farmers 46-0. An 8-4 victory over Willamette followed in Salem, the game marred by what a newspaper account of the day described as "a slight encounter" between Oregon's Russell Coleman and Willamette's Jay McCormick.

The league format for deciding a championship matched Oregon against Portland and OAC against Willamette; the two winners then paired for the title. If Oregon won its first game, it would meet a team it had already beaten for the championship.

Oregon came through with a 6-4 victory over Portland, a two-point goal after a touchdown deciding the outcome in an era when touchdowns were worth four points. Willamette beat OAC 16-0, and the title match was scheduled for Thanksgiving Day in Eugene.

A crowd of 1,000 turned out to see if Oregon could claim the championship pennant, and their faith was rewarded with a 6-0 victory. The points came midway through the first half when Frank Templeton scored a touchdown on a short run and Harry Templeton kicked the goal.

ABOVE: OREGON'S 1899 TEAM, PICTURED HERE AT MULTNOMAH FIELD IN PORTLAND, PLAYED THE SCHOOL'S FIRST OUT-OF-STATE GAME AT CALIFORNIA. FOURTH FROM RIGHT IS C.N. "PAT" MCARTHUR, FOR WHOM MAC COURT WAS LATER NAMED.

Oregon nearly scored again late in the game, but a disputed fumble near the goal line gave the ball to Willamette. It didn't matter. Oregon was unbeaten, untied and unscored upon, and had a pennant to prove it was a champion. It would be a long time before Oregon would repeat.

The Birth of the Civil War

Two games against Oregon Agricultural College—which years later would be known as Oregon State University—resulted in the only two Oregon victories of the season and hard feelings on the part of fans. It was the beginning of the Civil War.

The second Civil War game of the year was played in Corvallis. University of Oregon fans were roughed up on the sidelines and generally treated so harshly that UO officials considered forbidding future games.

The referee in the game was also attacked by OAC supporters. The action on the field wasn't all football, either. Oregon Coach J.F. Frick protested that one OAC player "was simply registered at the OAC because of his ability as a bruiser," and added that "the prizefighters and other dirty players on the OAC team were decidedly angry with the officials because they would not permit a steal of the game nor an exhibition of dirty football."

Oregon's only other contest of the year—and its only defeat—was against the Multnomah Athletic Association Club of Portland, a major step beyond the original boundaries for football set by the faculty. Permission was granted to play a non-collegiate team because of the influence of prominent political figures who were MAAC members and the potential to make money by playing the postgraduates in Portland.

The team manager later reported a profit of $309.75 from playing MAAC, more than offsetting losses of $35 and $48 for the games against OAC.

Beating MAAC, however, was difficult with its collection of older players, some with college backgrounds, some imported from outside the area. MAAC won the first meeting 12-0, and it would take Oregon 11 more attempts before it could defeat the Portlanders.

A game was also scheduled against Willamette,

but L.H. Van Winkler, manager of the Salem team, called off the trip to Eugene, telegraphing that "from indications it does not look like we could make expenses."

The Civil War Cools Off

The 1897 schedule was even more limited than in previous years, with only a trip to play the Chemawa Indians, won by the UO 10-0, and a home game against OAC. The home field atmosphere lessened the emotion of the rivalry, but OAC went home with a 26-0 victory.

In another attempt to lessen the interstate rivalry, the two schools did away with the idea of repeat games, which had perhaps caused much of the friction in 1896, when Oregon won both encounters.

One Short of Unbeaten

Frank Simpson, a former Cal star, came to Eugene to coach Oregon for the seasons of 1898 and 1899. He compiled a record of 6-3-1 before leaving to coach the Cal Bears in 1901.

Another unbeaten season was marred only by a 21-0 loss to the Multnomah Athletic Association Club. The highlight of the season was a Thanksgiving Day game against Portland University. The two schools had not played since Oregon's 6-4 victory in 1895, the closest call for Oregon in an unbeaten season. The rematch wasn't much of a game. A large crowd watched Oregon rout the visitors 95-0, and it wasn't even that close. Oregon scored virtually at will, while Portland failed to gain a first down.

Oregon players Ralph Starr and Clarence M. Bishop, the two best halfbacks Oregon had before the turn of the century, had a day unlike many who were to follow them in UO lineups. Starr scored eight touchdowns with the longest coming on a 50-yard run. Bishop had six touchdowns, two seventy-yard runs—one for a TD and several other runs of 25 to 40 yards.

1899

The Webfoots Travel South

Oregon's desire to expand its football horizons was in trouble. The football powers of the West Coast were California and Stanford, which had begun playing the game a decade before anyone in the Northwest. What would happen if Oregon ever played one of these schools from the Golden State?

Clifton N. "Pat" McArthur, the student manager of UO Athletics, got permission from new UO President Frank Strong to schedule the first intercollegiate interstate game on the Pacific Coast for November 18, 1899, against California in Berkeley. Simultaneously, Strong gave the

debating teams permission to travel out-of-state and for the music department to have its glee club travel to Washington. These actions indicated a new awareness on the part of the University administration about the possibilities of expanding the educational experience of students, which included the lifting of the faculty ban on fraternities and sororities.

McArthur was the single most important person in getting UO athletics moving forward on all fronts, but especially in football. He served as student manager, the equivalent of the present-day athletic director, with responsibilities that included hiring coaches and paying them; selling tickets; handling promotions, scheduling, fund raising, travel arrangements and accommodations; paying bills and assorted other chores for two years, 1899 to 1901. During this time he challenged the UO to develop itself athletically beyond what it had already accomplished.

Oregon lost to California 12-0, but there was almost universal disbelief that the game had been a mismatch. The San Francisco newspapers promoted the UO team as a worthy and surprisingly strong team, although much lighter than the team from Berkeley. Several of the Oregon players were praised, especially Clarence Bishop, Homer Angell, Richard S. Smith and Fred Ziegler. Angell was noted for his tough play as a 162-pound tackle with the handicap of having only one hand. And as it turned out the California team would furnish two coaches for Oregon in the immediate future.

Their spirits raised and their confidence boosted, Oregon didn't lose again that season. On the way home from Berkeley, Oregon beat Ashland Normal 35-0, a game played to help pay the expenses of having traveled to Berkeley. This contest was followed by a game against the Multnomah Athletic Association Club in Portland which ended 0-0.

All that was left was Oregon Agricultural College, and that turned into "Hayseed Waterloo," as the *Eugene Guard* headlined the results, a 38-0 victory for the University of Oregon.

To avoid a repeat of 1896 when spectators and OAC players had gotten out of control and assaulted both officials and UO fans, a score of deputy sheriffs was present, and the one-sided nature of the contest kept emotions in check. Oregon even forgot about its protest over an OAC player who had enrolled in school just four days before the late-November game. As an OAC official explained, the young man "plans to attend the school in future years as well."

Victory in California

Headlines in the *Portland Oregonian* announced that Clarence Bishop was not going to return for a final season of football. During his years at the UO he had scored 19 touchdowns, and recorded important victories for the track team, winning consistently in the 220 and 880. He was also a class president, vice president of the University of Oregon Athletic Club, as well as secretary and later vice president of the IAAAC.

The football team also lost Homer Angell, a tackle who was always undersized for his position, but was consistently praised in news accounts for his efforts. He also won many 440-yard runs at track meets, was president of the Intercollegiate Debating League and a champion debater. Angell later filled the U.S. House of Representative seat from Oregon's Third District, a seat previously held by McArthur.

The schedule for 1900 again included Berkeley, and once again, McArthur created the atmosphere necessary to give athletics—specifically football—the support he felt was needed to insure future success.

McArthur founded a student government, the Associated Students of the University of Oregon (ASUO), and served as its first student body president. He was the main force in drawing up the ASUO's first constitution, which included a mandatory student fee of $2.50 per student. The money, which was allocated solely to athletics, was of foremost importance to the future of Oregon sports.

For starters, the extra money enabled the football team to return to the Golden State, this time with notable success. The fee was balanced by the proviso of free admission for all enrolled students to UO athletic contests. McArthur also created and was editor of a new student newspaper, *The Oregon Weekly*, which concentrated on the promotion of athletics and other student activities. He did all of this while enrolled as a full-time student and playing a backup role on the football team.

Recalling the 12-0 defeat in Berkeley in 1899, McArthur decided to hire a new coach—the Cal fullback that had caused so many problems for the Webfoots. Peter Kaarsberg had made several long runs against the Lemon Yellow, and his six punts during that game soared for an average of 40 yards each.

With Kaarsburg at the UO helm, the team was fully prepared for Berkeley. But the Stanford team stood in the way and, on November 10 in Palo Alto, the UO team suffered a 34-0 defeat. Nevada had been scheduled to meet Oregon on November 15, but the team from Reno backed out of the game, allowing extra time to prepare for the November 17 game at California.

Practice didn't make perfect, but the game was a surprise. A headline on the sports page of a San Francisco newspaper tells the tale: "Berkeley Rooters Saddened by Oregon. Webfooted Boys Do Not Permit California to Score." The game was a defensive struggle and the UO gained a 2-0 victory over California, becoming not only the first team to beat Cal in Berkeley but also the first visiting team to score points on Cal's home field. The newspaper article concluded, "A little state university with 300 students had outplayed a great state university with 2300 students."

"In intercollegiate athletics, we are supreme in these parts and so must look abroad for our games and meets," the *Oregon Monthly* editorialized.

Again Oregon finished the season strong, recording a scoreless tie against MAAC and a 43-0 victory over the University of Washington. It was the first time Oregon and Washington had met in a football game, and the two schools decided to end their future seasons with the interstate rivalry.

"The competition with the University of Washington was particularly gratifying because of the high quality of sportsmanship that was in evidence on the playing field at all times on the part of the players of both teams," wrote the *Oregon Monthly*.

And what of OAC? The OAC regents did away with football, and the Civil War rivalry was interrupted until 1902.

Four Games in Eight Days

Kaarsburg's contract expired at the end of the 1900 season and was not renewed. But the next coach hired, Warren "Locomotive" Smith, had been a teammate of Kaarsburg on the 1899 California team. Smith, a running back who had scored one touchdown against the Webfoots in 1899, was committed to getting Oregon's football team back on track.

Practice began in late October, and only four players returned from the 1900 team. The faculty and University President Frank Strong wanted to avoid sending the team on more than one long trip away from campus, so games in California were ruled out. If there was to be an out-of-state trip, Oregon wanted to make the most of it. The solution? Four games in one week.

It began with a scoreless tie against Idaho in Moscow. Then came a loss to Washington Agricultural College three

days later, and a loss to Whitman in Walla Walla three days after that.

To help meet expenses—and maybe also to salvage a victory—Oregon also agreed to stop in Pendleton on the way home to play the high school team. The reason was that with a lesser level of opposition, games on consecutive days wouldn't be too rigorous.

Pendleton had a surprise in store for Oregon, however. Instead of a group of high school youths, Pendleton Coach Dave Waddell—a former UO player—had gathered players from the town and surrounding area. It was more of a battle than the University men expected, but Oregon prevailed 12-0. The players had managed to complete four games in eight days, but Oregon ended the season with a 3-4-1 record.

The NIAA is Born

In 1902, eight schools from Oregon, Washington, Idaho and Montana formed the Northwest Intercollegiate Athletic Association. A few weeks later, the University of Oregon decided to join, too. In addition, OAC resumed football that year. The group drew up more stringent rules but didn't set up a central organization to enforce them.

Prince L. Campbell arrived from the State Normal School at Monmouth to become University of Oregon president, and with him came vigorous support for sports. "Athletics are a very important phase of college life," Campbell said. "Physical perfection should precede education because education without physical energy is time and money misdirected."

Oregon students answered the call for support with regular attendance at practices to urge on their classmates. The team responded with three victories three ties and only one loss, a 16-0 decision to the Multnomah Athletic Association Club. The MAAC was the only team to score against Oregon after six consecutive shutouts, though three of them were scoreless deadlocks.

An unbeaten record against collegiate teams was crowned by a 70-0 trouncing of Pacific. On the same day, Oregon's team manager received a telegram from Charles

Johnson, manager of the Washington Agricultural College, challenging Oregon to a game for a mythical Northwest title, if WAC could defeat the University of Washington.

Washington prevailed, but the proposed game with Oregon was never played. Washington wouldn't consider coming to Eugene; Oregon wouldn't travel to Seattle and negotiations to set up a meeting in Portland couldn't satisfy either side.

Oregon Hires a Full-time Coach

Several changes took place in 1903. First, the University students hired a full-time track coach and athletic trainer. William L. "Bill" Hayward began his glorious 44-year career as the school's first employee to be engaged as both a coach and a teacher. The football coaching position, meanwhile, would remain a part-time job, but the decision to hire Hayward would eventually help change that.

As athletic trainer, Hayward had several jobs: to help improve the physical conditioning of UO athletes and serve as "medic"; to invent various protective devices to allow injured players to continue playing; and to make arrangements for the training table and what food would be served. Additionally, he was appointed track coach—the position for which he is most remembered—but his contribution to the success of UO football is well-recorded. He also taught physical education and, for a brief period, coached the basketball team as well.

A second change, and another UO first, was the re-hiring of a former UO coach. Warren "Locomotive" Smith, the Oregon coach from 1901, came back to direct the Webfoots to a 4-2-1 season.

Oregon also played its alumni for the first time in 1903—probably, because it was the first time the Webfoots had enough alumni to play. But whatever the impetus, the University beat the alumni 6-0. Oregon came within two games of another unbeaten season, losing 6-5 to Washington and 12-0 to Multnomah Athletic Association Club in what would become an annual Thanksgiving game.

The Alumni were given three positions on the University's Athletic Council in 1902, and this ignited alumni interest in the football team. Homer Angell and

John Edmundson, two standouts from years past, quit their jobs and volunteered to help Smith whip his charges into shape for the upcoming season. The pair quickly demonstrated the value of having assistants to help the head coach.

A Webfoot at the Helm

For the first time, Oregon would be coached by a former UO football star, Richard Shore Smith. Smith had been UO team captain from 1897-99 and had gone on to play for Columbia University in New York, where he studied law. Upon completing his second collegiate football career, he was recognized as one of the nation's best and earned a spot on the All-America team. He returned to Eugene after completing his law degree, with the intention of going into business. Instead, he was courted by both Oregon and Columbia for their head coaching positions. He decided to stay in Eugene.

The Northwest Intercollegiate Athletic Association, formed only two years earlier, was disbanded, largely because it was ineffectual in governing college sports.

The Northwest was again dominated by Oregon, which defeated Washington 18-0 and Oregon Agricultural College 6-5 on consecutive Saturdays. Five of the eleven positions on an imaginary All-Northwest team were Webfoots. Oregon suffered defeats at the hands of California and Stanford, however, in addition to their annual loss to Multnomah Athletic Association Club, to finish 5-3.

Football Turns a Profit

University of Oregon President P.L. Campbell and several influential alumni wanted to upgrade UO football to the level of Stanford and California, still the perennial West Coast powers, so they hired Michigan graduate Bruce Short as coach with a $620 salary. Ironically, both California and Stanford stopped playing football the following season, opt-

ing for a return to rugby for safety reasons.

Oregon made what would be its last trip to California for several years in mid-October and nearly came away with victories. Against Cal, the Webfoots' Gordon Moores broke away for a 40-yard run that was stopped just short of a touchdown in a game that finished in a scoreless tie. In a 10-4 loss to Stanford, the opponent's touchdown and field goal were both set up by Oregon fumbles.

The biggest victory of the season for Oregon came at the cash register, when 2,000 people showed up to watch the game against Oregon Agricultural College at Kincaid Field. Frank Templeton's touchdown run sealed Oregon's 6-0 triumph, and the large crowd provided gate receipts of $760, which was split between the two teams. It was the most Oregon had ever made from a home game, accounting for most of the $400 profit Oregon football would show for the season.

Clearly, football could make money—even turn a profit—if competition between well-matched opponents was promoted correctly. The newspapers, in carrying stories about the games, began reporting attendance totals, gate receipts and expenses, including the coach's annual salary and the profit for the game. Football was now being accepted as a legitimate form of entertainment for which many people were quite willing to pay.

By the end of the 1905 season, President Campbell, the student manager and the Athletic Council (a group of students, faculty and alumni) decided to look into hiring a football coach on an annual contract. Before then, coaches typically arrived in Eugene a week before the first game and left the day after the last game, having no responsibility beyond November. In the interim, they were also looking for longer-term employment in fields such as business or law.

Hiring Hayward for track had proven extremely successful, as the UO soon came to dominate the sport throughout the Northwest. Moreover, potential profits were now part of the equation. Thus Oregon took the giant step and hired its first full-time football coach, one who would remain on campus throughout the school year. As with Hayward, student body fees would cover the cost of his salary, and the University would pay him to teach. The students would no longer be allowed to hire and fire coaches, as they had in the past, but they would still pay the bills. From then on, the University's president and administration would retain firm control of the school's athletic programs.

The Bezdek Era Begins

Now that football had been elevated to the status of a moneymaking sport, Hugo Bezdek was hired by the

University as Director of the Department of Physical Culture. He would receive a total of $1,500 annually—$1,100 from the University for overseeing the department, and another $400 from the students for coaching. His $400 coaching salary was less than that paid to previous coaches, but the additional $1,100 certainly helped to fill the gap. His total salary package was equal to most regular nine-month teaching faculty salaries. In addition, Bezdek was allowed to hire an assistant football coach, whom the students paid a small salary.

Bezdek proved to be well worth his salary. He went on to become one of the greatest coaches in Oregon football history and was eventually inducted into the College Football Hall of Fame.

Born in Prague on April 1, 1884, Bezdek and his family came to America while he was a small child, settling in Chicago. He was an athlete like few of his generation. By the time he enrolled at the University of Chicago, he had shown sufficient baseball talent to attract the attention of several professional teams. He had few equals as a wrestler, as well, and he helped pay for his college by boxing professionally under an assumed name.

The 5-foot-7, 175-pound Bezdek had never played football until his first fall of college at the University of Chicago when the legendary Amos Alonzo Stagg enticed him to take part in a practice. Within days, Bezdek was in the starting backfield, never leaving it during his four years,

which culminated in 1904 with his being named to Walter Camp's All-Western team, then the highest accolade for a football player not at one of the Eastern institutions.

Bezdek spent a season helping Stagg coach at Chicago, and it was Stagg's recommendation that led to Oregon's hiring of Bezdek. "The best player I ever coached," Stagg often said of Bezdek in the years that followed.

Maybe the best coach Oregon has ever had, too. His innovations made a lasting impact. Players would be provided a training table during the season, funded partially by the student tax being raised to $5.00. Bezdek required all 35 players to learn every position on the field. He put the forward pass into the offense, and his defense was all but perfect. In six games that season under Bezdek, Oregon allowed only 9 points: a touchdown (5 points) by Washington and a field goal (4 points) by the Multnomah Athletic Association Club. The one blemish on the Webfoots' 5-0-1 season was a scoreless tie against Oregon Agricultural College, played in a sea of mud. OAC's longest gain was 2 yards.

Oregon might have won that game, too, except kicker Fred Moullen was held out with an injury, and he was Oregon's most dangerous offensive threat. Moullen scored 21 of Oregon's first 26 points that season on field goals or kicks after touchdowns. His two field goals lifted Oregon over Multnomah Athletic Association Club 8-4 in what newspaper accounts called "one of the greatest games ever played in the Northwest."

Not only was it Oregon's first-ever victory over MAAC, it was the first time in 10 years Oregon had scored against the Portland team. Yes, football with Bezdek was going to be something special. The problem was, Bezdek wasn't going to be around for long—at least, not his first time around.

Bezdek Departs

After one season, Hugo Bezdek had given up the coaching position at Oregon to return to Chicago and attend medical school. He didn't stick with it long and was football coach at Arkansas by 1908.

Oregon, meanwhile, hired Gordon B. Frost, former

Dartmouth star and more recently a successful high school coach in Seattle. In 1906 he took his Seattle High School team to California and defeated Lick High School. From there his team went to Chicago where it beat North Division High School, becoming the official Interscholastic Champion of the United States.

Oregon ran up a 94-5 margin over its first four opponents. The game against Pacific was a 52-0 mismatch, but the defeats of the MAAC (10-5) and Willamette (11-0) proved to be real contests.

The next game against Idaho was the first big-time college football game ever held in Portland. It was played at Multnomah Stadium on a gloomy October day and the Webfoots won 21-5. The game had been promoted by McArthur, by this time a lawyer in Portland, who wanted to prove that the profits of football could be limitless. The total gate receipts came to $2086.05 and the total expenses were $1000. The UO walked away with the profit.

Again the Civil War was a defensive struggle. The largest crowd ever to watch an intercollegiate football game in the state up until then packed Kincaid Field. Over 4,000 spectators came from all over the Willamette Valley, traveling by train and carriage, and a few by automobiles to watch the encounter.

Oregon was forced to play without its talented right end, Gordon Moores, who was injured before the game. And during the game, Dudley Clarke suffered a head injury and the Webfoots were left without his tremendous punting and rushing services for the remainder of the contest. The extent of the loss was later illustrated in Oregon's 6-0 victory over Washington. In that game, Clarke not only hurdled over the Washington line to score the only touchdown of the game, but he also averaged more than 50 yards per punt with one soaring more than 60 yards and another sailing 70 yards-plus. He would later be selected as fullback on the All Northwest team.

Consequently, Oregon Agricultural College prevailed 4-0 after Fred Moullen's drop kick for the tying field goal fell short. The Webfoots' 10-year dominance of the "Farmers" from up north had come to an end. However, the crowd and the profits once again proved that football could be a popular draw as well as a moneymaker for institutions willing to present the entire package.

At the end of the 1907 season, Gordon Moores became the first UO player to be included on what Walter Camp called his "special mention" list. Since Camp almost entirely ignored football west of the Mississippi and Moores was the only player west of the Mississippi River to be on that list in 1907, it was a high honor of recognition.

Bezdek had left Frost with the foundation of a solid team, but the University's commitment to having a full-time coach was abandoned with serious consequences. Frost left at the end of the season, and for the next several years, the "coach-a-year" syndrome would reassert itself on the UO football program.

Picking up Speed and $2,500 in Profit

Success bred more interest in football from both the student body and the alumni. The first practice for new coach Robert Forbes drew 50 players as well as increased pressure to improve the playing field along the east side of

Kincaid Street in Eugene, between 13th and 12th streets.

The field was very wet and soggy because of several underground springs beneath the area. In fact, a game held in the latter part of the season just before the turn of the century was delayed when the only ball used was lost in the mud. The 22 players stretched across the field and poked the mud until a player found the ball. Because of the wet conditions some early Oregon games were moved to Stewart's Field, now the location of the Lane County Fairgrounds.

Back in 1903, UO President P.L. Campbell had recommended a new field be built, with the needed revenue to come from an alumni game against Multnomah Athletic Association Club on Thanksgiving Day. The new playing site, to be called Kincaid Field, was located south of 13th, on land belonging to Harrison Kincaid, a Eugene pioneer, newspaper publisher and Oregon's Secretary of State for two terms.

The University signed a 10-year lease to use the prop-

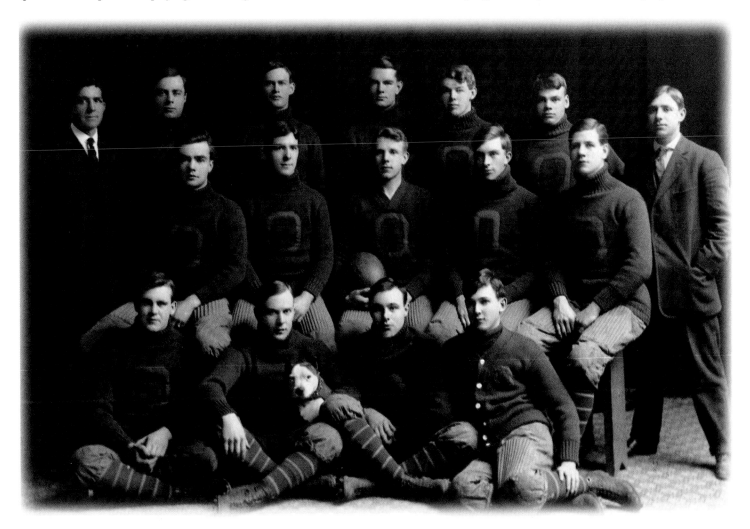

ABOVE: WARREN SMITH *(far right)* COACHED THREE OREGON TEAMS, THE LAST IN 1907. STANDING AT LEFT IS TRAINER BILL HAYWARD. THE DOG'S NAME WAS DUBIE.

erty and was granted permission to make improvements with Kincaid's approval. The entire area had a closed fence, requiring spectators to purchase tickets to see the game. Previously, spectators weren't actually charged admissions, but were asked to donate money as their view was unobstructed from without. Soon after, the alumni led a fundraising campaign, and $1,000 was spent on grandstands to seat 800.

Oregon's enthusiasm and the large turnout of players couldn't prevent it from finishing one game without a full team on the field. Against Idaho, William Main was ejected for slugging an opponent he claimed was holding him. Under the rules of the day, a player wasn't allowed to be replaced during the final 20 minutes. The rule could be waived if the opposing coach agreed, but Idaho's coach would not, so Oregon played the final 20 minutes with only 10 players. Nonetheless, Oregon prevailed 27-21 as Fred Moullen, in his final season, kicked four field goals. He also kicked a pair of field goals in the Webfoots' 8-0 victory over MAAC before a crowd of 4,000 in Portland.

The Northwest Conference, made up of Washington, Oregon, Idaho, Oregon Agricultural College, Washington Agricultural College and Whitman was formed in 1908 as well. The league immediately established a significant rule: Transfer students were not eligible during their first year on a new campus. Eventually the league, with its constitution and rules, would become the model and base of the Pacific Coast Conference.

The Civil War Leaves Portland

Before the season began, students at Oregon and Oregon Agricultural College made a major decision: The rivals would never again play each other in Portland, but instead would go back to playing at campus sites in alternating years.

Portland newspapers protested the decision with outraged editorials, but students were adamant that the games should be played on campus. The 1909 contest was played in Eugene, and Oregon's Earl "Sap" Latourette's 60-yard touchdown run was the highlight of a 12-0 victory over OAC during this 4-1 season.

Oregon's Biggest Rout

Oregon only played Puget Sound once in football and it was obvious why. In the biggest rout in UO football history, Oregon overwhelmed Puget Sound 110-0. Charles Taylor remains in the Oregon record books for scoring 52 points, including seven rushing touchdowns, 14 conversion kicks and one field goal, which was now worth 3 points. His one-game performance was enough to land Taylor on the All-America "Honorable Mention" list compiled by Walter Camp.

The first serious conflict between the football fans of the UO and OAC occurred in 1910 as well, when the Webfoots beat OAC in Corvallis. This was the Hay Miners' second straight loss by a score of 12-0, and as the UO fans were making their way from the OAC campus to the railroad depot for the trip back to Eugene, OAC fans shouted insults at the departing Webfoot supporters. The insults were returned and fights followed, including some inside the railcars where the Farmers' rooters had followed the UO fans. The police were called in to stem what newspapers called "a riot."

Schedule Roulette

The 1911 season was noted more for two games not played and another that was nearly called off than for the other ones that actually took place. Oregon and Oregon Agricultural College didn't schedule each other because of the aforementioned problems in 1910 and the less serious, but still disturbing, problems in 1909.

A home game against Idaho in mid-November was canceled by Oregon after the sudden death through natural causes of Virgil Noland, a freshman lineman on the varsity team. The cancellation caused financial hardship for Idaho, which had planned on playing at Oregon before traveling by train from Walla Walla to Salt Lake City to meet Utah. The gate receipts from the first two games were to be used to defray the expenses. However, Idaho was understanding of

Oregon's decision to cancel the game in the wake of a player's death—that is, until the Webfoots agreed to play a game just days later against the Multnomah Athletic Association Club in Portland.

In actuality, the players would have preferred not to play MAAC either, but prominent UO alum C.N. McArthur strong-armed Oregon into playing the game.

"Some of the cheap sports here (in Portland) are already saying that the Oregon football men are using Noland's death as a cloak behind which to hide from possible defeat at the hands of Multnomah," McArthur wrote to UO President P.L. Campbell. "Of course, this is absolutely untrue, but such talk does an injustice to the men on the team, and also injures the University." Not playing also would have had a financial impact on Oregon and MAAC, a bigger concern to McArthur. MAAC got the better of the disheartened Webfoots 17-6.

The annual meeting with Washington was nearly called off because of concerns by UW officials that there may have been gambling on the outcome. Campbell wired Thomas Kane, UW president, that the game should be played, stating there were "no rumors here in Eugene in regard to anything like systematic betting on the Oregon-

Washington game." If there was, the Sundodgers, as they were known, cashed in with a 29-3 triumph over Oregon.

◆ 1912 ◆

Civil War Renewed

For the second straight year, Oregon didn't have a game scheduled against Oregon Agricultural College. That changed when Oregon was beaten by Washington 30-14. "When (OAC players) read about that, they thought it was a heck of a chance to beat us," said Johnny Parsons, a halfback who was still around four years later to help the UO win a Rose Bowl.

OAC had beaten every one of its opponents except Washington, which the Aggies tied, and the challenge from OAC was awaiting the Oregon team members when they arrived back at the Eugene train station after the Washington loss. "We said 'Bring 'em on,' " Parsons said. "We'd had such a bad licking (in Seattle), we wanted to play somebody right away."

ABOVE: THE 1909 TEAM ON THE STEPS OF ITS FRIENDLY HALL TRAINING TABLE. BILL HAYWARD IS SEATED AT LEFT ON THE BICYCLE.

The Civil War was renewed, but only after the schools agreed to play in Albany. The neutral site was chosen to avoid the problems that had caused the interruption of the series in previous seasons.

Oregon thoroughly dominated OAC, but won by only a slim 3-0 margin. "We should have won 30-0," Parsons grumbled. "It was the worst game I'd ever played in. We did so much and got so little."

The Oregon administration felt the same way about the entire season's 3-4 record, the first losing record in a decade and only the third since Oregon began playing football. What could turn the program back around, the way Hugo Bezdek had done in his sole season as coach in 1906? How about Bezdek himself?

ABOVE: TACKLING DUMMIES WERE A PART OF PRACTICE AS FAR BACK AS 1912.

Bezdek Returns

The 1912 losing season had convinced the University of Oregon and its followers to put an end to its yearly football coach merry-go-round. Only two coaches in Oregon's 20-year football history had returned for a second season, and most of the ones who left did so because they wanted a full-time job. The UO was still bashful about taking the step into big-time football, even though there was ample proof that it could be profitable.

The Emerald, the new and only student newspaper, suggested that Oregon should rethink its hiring practices. "Figures show that in the hiring of coaches it pays, for financial as well as sentimental reasons, to get the best," *The Emerald* editorialized. "If it is a good investment to hire any coach, it is more profitable to hire the best."

Enrollment at the University of Oregon had risen to 691 in 1912, and stronger athletic teams were seen as one of the keys to maintaining and building upon it. Oregon had taken a step in that direction by hiring Hugo Bezdek in 1906. He left the following year to pursue a medical degree, he said, but instead became football coach and athletic director at the University of Arkansas. Would he consider coming back to Eugene? Yes, he would—if the pay was right. Oregon offered Bezdek a two-year contract at $3,500 annually, with the student body paying $2,000 and the University picking up the other $1,500. He would be the

head coach for football, basketball and baseball. For what it was worth at the time, he was also given the title of athletic director, a portfolio without influence. Bezdek wrote back with his acceptance, adding one further question: What would his rank be at the University of Oregon?

"Here I enjoy the title and rank of professor and it has added considerably to the influence of my work," Bezdek wrote. P.L. Campbell turned down Bezdek's implied request, explaining that he could only be an assistant professor because his pay from the University was $1,500, and "rank goes by salary, with full professorship ranging from $1,600 to $2,500." The money paid by the students wasn't counted. Officially he was Assistant Professor of Outdoor Athletics. Bezdek took the job, but his differences with Oregon over money continued throughout his tenure.

Bezdek's football philosophy was simple. "Give me a bunch of boys who can block, and I'll show you an offense," he said. "Give me a bunch of boys who can tackle, and I'll show you a defense." In reality his tactics were often years ahead of his opponents'. Oregon's teams used the forward pass, and they threw different backfield formations at the competition. Bezdek tried to get information about the opponents and then put it to better use than the typically crude scouting reports of the era.

Oregon opened the season with three victories by a

marked the only season in which Bezdek didn't field a winning team at Oregon.

Down by a Shoestring

Oregon ran off four straight victories to start the 1914 season, including a 61-0 trouncing of Willamette that seemed to make up for the loss the previous season. Bezdek again started the second team, and they had the rout well under way when the starters entered the game after halftime.

Oregon still couldn't beat Washington, losing 10-0 in Seattle. The Webfoots mounted only one serious scoring threat, which ended in a missed field goal. A week later, Oregon could manage only a field goal in a 3-3 tie with Oregon Agricultural College, the second straight deadlock in the always-intense rivalry. "That was the hottest thing this side of hell," halfback Johnny Parsons said of playing OAC. "One year, we had a fight and it broke into a free-for-all right on the field."

Oregon claimed the difference in the game was a shoestring that allowed an OAC tackler to pull down Oskar Wiest at the 10-yard line after a 60-yard pass from quarterback C.A. Sharpe. When three plays netted no gain, Shy Huntington kicked the field goal to tie the game.

combined score of 112-9, but the opposition included Idaho, an alumni team and a group of sailors from a Navy ship berthed in Bremerton, Washington. The fourth game was against Willamette, and Bezdek approached it as though it would be another automatic victory, which it had been since Oregon's first season of football. Anson Cornell, the starting quarterback, couldn't play because of an injury, and Bezdek used the second unit for the entire first half. Oregon led 3-0.

The starters were put in at halftime, but they struggled and couldn't come up with a score. The three-point lead seemed safe, however, until Oregon fumbled deep in its own territory and a Willamette player recovered the ball in the end zone for a 6-3 Methodist lead. The Webfoots mounted a late drive toward the end zone, but the final gun ended the threat. For the only time in a 24-game series against Oregon, Willamette had triumphed.

Oregon was almost too late in its comeback again the next week, falling behind Oregon Agricultural College 10-0 in the first half. The 1,500 Webfoot rooters who had taken the train to Albany were wondering why they'd bothered, as the game ended in a 10-10 tie.

Oregon lost 10-7 to Washington the following week, then ended the season with a 19-0 loss to the Multnomah Athletic Association Club. The Webfoots' 3-3-1 record

New Rules and a New Conference

As World War I raged in Europe, the winds of change began blowing through football and intercollegiate athletics. Concerned about the amount of attention Bezdek had brought to football, the UO faculty sought to regain control of sports. A measure to eliminate basketball and limit football to seven games was passed, though too late to affect the nine-game schedule Bezdek had arranged. For the first time, Bezdek had arranged games for his freshmen, since they were no longer eligible to play for the varsity.

The rule barring freshman came from the Pacific Coast Conference, formed the summer prior to the 1915 season by Oregon, Washington, California and Oregon Agricultural College. Stanford was also invited, and joined two years later. Among other PCC rules was one that required transfer students to be on campus a year before playing.

The University further tightened its control of athletics by eliminating preseason training camp for the football team, limiting practice from 4:00 to 6:30 p.m. and requiring that all athletes be enrolled in at least 12 hours of class work. In addition, the athletes had to have passed that many hours the previous semester.

On the field, Oregon's football team also encountered setbacks, losing two of its first three games. Of particular concern was a 28-3 loss to Washington Agricultural College—later known as Washington State University—in which even Bezdek admitted he was outcoached by "Lonestar" Dietz, who had his team use an unbalanced line and several other unorthodox plays to rout Oregon. However, Bezdek would later master and put to use many of WAC's strategies. Oregon wouldn't lose again that season, nor for two more years.

The 1915 Oregon team might have been even stronger, except that outstanding halfback Johnny Parsons had dropped out of school. He returned the next season, when his presence mattered even more than his absence did

in 1915. Although the WAC's victory meant the Pullman team would eventually be chosen to represent the West in the resumption of the Rose Bowl, it was quite a year for Oregon.

For a decade, Oregon had been confined to playing games in the Northwest, but college football was expanding its horizons. OAC traveled halfway across the country to beat Michigan Agricultural College, and Washington knew few boundaries in its scheduling, though the Sundodgers—in the midst of a nine-year unbeaten streak—broke precedent by refusing to play Oregon or OAC.

If he couldn't play Washington, Bezdek looked in the opposite direction and set up a game in Los Angeles against the University of Southern California. Oregon received the go-ahead from the faculty to leave early for the game, and then had to ask for permission to stay late. The game was scheduled for Saturday, November 6, but was postponed because of rain. The faculty relented, allowing the football team to stay until Monday; two days after kickoff was scheduled, Oregon routed USC behind the passing and running of Shy Huntington.

Oregon finished the season with victories over OAC and MAAC, and couldn't wait for the next year with virtually the entire squad eligible to return. So successful was the team that Kincaid Field, enlarged to seat 8,000, couldn't accommodate all the alumni invited back for Homecoming weekend, which culminated in a 9-0 win over OAC. The

ABOVE: OREGON AND OAC BATTLED TO A 3-3 STANDOFF IN CORVALLIS IN 1914. IT WAS THE SECOND STRAIGHT TIE BETWEEN THE SCHOOLS.

alumni wanted a bigger, better facility, and the seeds were planted for a fund-raising campaign that would lead to the building of Hayward Field for the 1919 season.

Rose Bowl Bound

"Mighty Oregon" was played at UO football games for the first time in 1916. The music, written by band director Albert Perfect, replaced "On Wisconsin" which had served as the team song, with local lyrics added to support the Webfoots. Now Perfect's music, married to the words written by a UO sophomore, DeWitt Gilbert, gave UO its own fight song.

Bezdek, no longer basketball or baseball coach, was given a new title: Director of Men's Gymnasium. No money followed the change in title and he was still an assistant professor.

Johnny Parsons, the great halfback, was back in school but unable to play in the opener against Willamette because of injuries. Few noticed. Orville Monteith, playing the other halfback position, ran for touchdowns virtually at will, and Shy Huntington passed and ran for big yardage as Oregon opened the season with a 97-0 rout of Willamette. Then the Multnomah Athletic Association Club fell to the Webfoots 28-0, and Oregon went on the road for its first big test of the season against California in Berkeley.

One of the biggest crowds to watch a game in Berkeley at the time turned out for a contest that would decide supremacy on the West Coast and a berth in the Rose Bowl. Oregon made it obvious which team was better. California used a fake field goal to set up an early touchdown, but Parsons and Hollis Huntington, Shy's younger brother, led Oregon on consecutive marches to touchdowns in the first quarter and an eventual 39-14 victory.

Clearly, Parsons made Oregon a much better team. With his speed and ability to avoid tacklers, he was a scoring threat from anywhere on the field. Moreover, he imparted his personality to the team, wearing a helmet only under protest and cultivating a knack for losing it. He also hated wearing any type of protective pads, despite the risk of injury. "I just kind of slid off to one side and they couldn't catch me with more than a glancing blow," Parsons said.

Indeed, only twice did he miss games because of injuries. But a bigger problem confronted Parsons as Oregon prepared to play Washington for the Pacific Coast Conference championship: Was he even eligible?

Under today's guidelines, there's no question the swift Parsons shouldn't have played in 1916. He'd first enrolled at Oregon in 1911 but didn't play football because of illness. He played in 1912, 1913 and 1914, then dropped out of school in 1915 for financial reasons, he said. The problem wasn't the number of years he'd been in college—he was also 26 years old now—but whether he met academic requirements of the University and the PCC.

Parsons had been enrolled for spring semester of 1915, and PCC rules required that he must have completed 12 credit hours during his last semester of school. However, he dropped out during the term, and thus claimed that it didn't count. Oregon agreed, but Washington protested, because it had obtained proof he had competed in a track meet during April 1915. That was 10 weeks into a 16-week semester, Washington contended, and too late for Parsons to have dropped out without receiving failing grades on his classes.

The Sundodgers were serious about the game, which represented a threat to their nine-year unbeaten streak. If Parsons was going to be allowed to play for Oregon, then Washington wanted to bring back three of its players from past years. On behalf of the league, Dean Cordley of Oregon Agricultural College ruled all four eligible, as long as they were currently enrolled in classes.

With the Washington faculty in an uproar over bringing alumni players back for the varsity, UW Coach Gil Dobie relented and said he wouldn't use any players who might be of questionable eligibility. It was an obvious challenge to Oregon to rule Parsons out, but he played. However, what turned out to be even more pertinent to the outcome of the game was the quagmire of Kincaid Field, which allowed neither team to mount an offense. The game ended in a scoreless tie.

The battle over Parsons continued, however. Another PCC committee declared him ineligible for future league games, which knocked him out of a 12-0 victory over Washington Agricultural College.

Oregon received an invitation to the Rose Bowl, based on its victory over California being more impressive than Washington's triumph over Cal. Oregon was headed for Pasadena. A pair of 27-0 victories over OAC and MAAC

put an exclamation point on the season.

From the day the pairing was made, Oregon was a huge underdog to the University of Pennsylvania, the Eastern representative. Penn's lineup included a trio of All-Americans: fullback Lou Little (later a long-time football coach at Columbia University); end Heinie Miller; and quarterback Bert Bell, who would later go on to fame as commissioner of the National Football League.

"Scared of 'em? We were scared to death of 'em," said John Beckett, an Oregon tackle. "They came out with quite a reputation."

There was no break for Oregon when the regular season ended. Hugo Bezdek was going to do all he could to overcome the formidable odds against his team.

"We practiced every day, in rain and snow, it didn't make any difference," halfback Johnny Parsons said. "We were out on that damn field full of water and sawdust, it was something. We even used a white ball because it got dark too quickly."

There were other hurdles to clear, most notably the lack of money to pay for a postseason trip. The students sold the student-owned University Bookstore to a group of investors to acquire the funds to pay for expenses, including an extra month of salary for Bezdek.

The trip to Southern California could only be made by train, and a week before the game the Oregon players and staff boarded *The Lark*. The highlight of the trip was a stop in San Jose, where student manager Roland Geary got off long enough to buy some bottles of beer, which he brought back for the players.

"It was pretty good beer, too," Parsons said. "The drinking on the way to Pasadena didn't hurt our game a bit. In fact, it probably helped it."

Everything seemed to go Oregon's way. Penn fit right into the role of cocky favorite, while Oregon played the part of the underdog to the hilt.

"I feel that my men will play a game that has never been seen on the Coast, and barring hard luck, it should be a winning game because it is a winning team," Penn Coach Bob Folwell said on the eve of the game. "I am fairly confident because I have a team that would make any coach feel that way about them."

How could Bezdek respond to that? "We ask nothing but a chance to go on the field and play the game," the Oregon coach said humbly. "If we win, then it will be time enough to claim the victory. We are ready."

ABOVE: OREGON, COACHED BY HUGO BEZDEK *(far right)*, PLAYED IN ITS FIRST ROSE BOWL IN 1917 AND DEFEATED PENNSYLVANIA 14-0.

There was a slight controversy before the game when it was reported that R.H. Loomis, a standout player at Washington Agricultural College, met with some of the Penn players at a fraternity convention and provided information on Oregon's offensive plays. Loomis admitted he was asked about Oregon but said he refused to give the information. "Besides, my money is on that team to beat Pennsylvania, so why should I aid the latter?" Loomis said. "The story is untrue."

The irony is that it was Oregon that had advance information on Penn. Bezdek had contacted Amos Alonzo Stagg, his former coach at the University of Chicago, and Stagg was able to provide a scouting report on Penn, which had played Chicago that season.

The smell of upset was in the air. Penn didn't heed the warnings, even the one from Cal Coach Andy Smith, himself a Penn graduate. Smith spoke to the Penn players and told them, "You have one chance out of three of beating Oregon."

On January 1, the odds were even less.

"They never got a chance," Parsons said. "We had the ball most of the time, and we stopped 'em any time they had the ball anyway."

Beckett, the outstanding tackle, was ejected in the first half for clipping, but it hardly deterred Oregon. Shy Huntington passed to Lloyd Tegert for a touchdown, and Parsons ran 40 yards to the 1-yard line to set up another. On consecutive plays, Huntington handed off to Parsons, but he couldn't make it over the goal line.

"It was getting toward the fourth quarter, and after playing all the time and running the ball most of the time, I was just too tired to get it over," the exhausted Parsons said. "That was my biggest disappointment, not making that touchdown."

After those two futile attempts, Oregon players questioned Huntington's play calling as the team huddled for third down. "I know what you want," Huntington barked back. "You want 42."

"It was a play we had used all year," the quarterback said later. "I steamed up through that hole and into the end zone. I could have driven a baby carriage through that hole."

Penn never threatened to score, and Oregon left Pasadena with a 14-0 victory and the respect of the East.

"Not an alibi to our names," said Folwell, the Penn coach. "We ran into a batch of football that was a cross between a zip of forked lightning and the roll of a fast freight. We were licked by a better team. Just let it go at that."

Oregon's heroes in the game were many, and the next day Orville Monteith and Huntington added to the lore of that Oregon adventure. Standing on a sidewalk in Los Angeles, the two Oregon players watched in dismay as a car skidded on wet pavement, struck a man attempting to cross a street and then came to rest on top of the man's body.

Huntington and Monteith rushed to the car and lifted it off the injured man, while others pulled the man out from under the tire.

No Repeat for Webfoots

It was all but impossible for Oregon to repeat its championship season of the previous fall. Fielding a team wasn't easy.

With World War I taking many college-age men into the service, only 20 players attended the first practice. It was, however, at least a workout with Hugo Bezdek as coach; doubts had persisted about his presence almost until the first whistle blew.

An outstanding baseball player in his college days, Bezdek had proved his ability to lead football teams with success at Arkansas and Oregon. That was enough for the Pittsburgh Pirates of the National League, who enticed Bezdek to become manager midway through the 1917 baseball season.

Upon taking the baseball job, Bezdek had assured Oregon he would return to coach football, which didn't begin until October, after professional baseball had concluded its regular season. But in early September, UO President P.L. Campbell received a query from a Portland journalist about reports Bezdek wouldn't be back.

Campbell's responding telegram was brief: "Fully expect him."

It wasn't the full truth. Campbell had twice written to Bezdek, in August and early September, trying to elicit a commitment from the football coach. Finally, Campbell received his answer, with Bezdek's concluding his promise to return by saying, "We'll try to be in the race."

They weren't. An early season 26-3 loss to Washington Agricultural College was Oregon's first defeat in 17 games, dating back to 1915. It prompted Bezdek to appeal for "every able-bodied man who weighs 145 pounds [to come] out in a suit for practice."

The turnout was big, and Oregon defeated its next three college opponents. The highlight was a 21-0 blanking of California, in which Oregon's defense held Cal's star fullback Dummy Wells to zero yards rushing. The season ended with a 14-7 loss to Oregon Agricultural College in Portland. It was to be the last game Bezdek coached for Oregon.

Though his team didn't return to the Rose Bowl, Bezdek did as coach of the Mare Island Marines. The service team asked Campbell to allow Bezdek to coach in Pasadena, and it wasn't a difficult transition for Bezdek. Among Mare Island's players were a half-dozen former Oregon stalwarts, led by John Beckett.

Bezdek knew better than anyone how much talent Mare Island had: Oregon had lost 27-0 to the Marines during the season, the most one-sided defeat of Bezdek's 44 games at Oregon. Bezdek's Oregon teams compiled a 30-10-4 record during his six seasons, with only six of the defeats coming against other college teams.

The Bezdek Era Ends

The first hint that Hugo Bezdek might not return as Oregon's football coach came in a February 7, 1918, letter to P.L. Campbell. From Chicago, Bezdek complained that coaching the Mare Island team in the previous Rose Bowl had so physically drained him that "I find myself in too nervous a condition and unable to think or concentrate."

There were problems in Eugene, too. The war had

ABOVE: COLLEGE HALL OF FAME TACKLE JOHN BECKETT *(No. 1 in center)* WAS NAMED THE OUTSTANDING PLAYER OF THE 1917 ROSE BOWL VICTORY.

drained the University of young men and financial resources were so limited that football itself was in doubt for 1918. Oregon thought Bezdek was making a gracious offer when he said he wouldn't force the University to honor the financial terms of his contract, but Bezdek also had gains to be made by not coming back to Oregon.

The U.S. Army wanted Bezdek to teach physical conditioning to troops; by coincidence, he could be stationed near State College, Pennsylvania, where Penn State was in need of a football coach. By releasing Bezdek from his contract, Oregon freed him to take the two positions in Pennsylvania, neither of which interfered with his summer duties as manager of the Pittsburgh Pirates.

Oregon went ahead with football, aided by a Pacific Coast Conference decision that freshmen were again eligible. For a coach, the University hired Shy Huntington, the quarterback of the 1916 Rose Bowl team. Huntington could never quite repeat the feat as a coach—nor could he ever live up to Bezdek's reputation.

Oregon had its share of success in 1918, notably beating Oregon Agricultural College and Washington. The victory over Washington was a big one for Oregon and the Webfoots weren't even dressed for the occasion. The

Oregon team arrived in Seattle for its season finale on December 1 and discovered that the trunks containing the uniforms were missing, apparently taken off the train during a stop at Portland. Wearing uniforms borrowed from a Naval unit in Seattle, Oregon won 7-0, its first triumph over the Sundodgers since 1907.

Back to the Rose Bowl

In 1919, games were moved from Kincaid Field to Hayward Field, the home of UO football until 1967. During the previous two years the ASUO and alumni poured money into the building of this field. The land had been purchased by the University in the early part of the century with the idea of having all athletics and physical education classes concentrated in the area between 15th to 18th avenues and University to Agate streets. The corner of the area from where Hayward Field is located to the south of where the practice fields were situated had once been an

ancient wetland and a part of the flyway for ducks and geese.

The entire area had to be excavated and a drain field constructed beneath the surface. Tons of gravel and fill were brought in to cover the tile that transported the naturally occurring water, as well as any accumulated water, away and down Agate in a drainage system to the Millrace. The entire area had to be raised above the surrounding area and the football field itself was given a high crown to keep the water moving away from the surface.

The west grandstand was constructed and bleachers were placed around the north end and down the east side of the field. Pilings were placed on the field and lights were located on top of each high post. Grass was planted on the loam that was brought in to complete this major undertaking. The UO football team had a new home. The track team later joined the football squad on Hayward Field in 1921.

As players returned from their military service and University enrollment climbed to 1,700, Oregon's administration began the campaign to lure Hugo Bezdek back as coach. P.L. Campbell wired Bezdek in May that "we are keenly interested in the possibility of your return."

This was followed by another wire to Bezdek in Pittsburgh from Karl Onthank, an aide to Campbell: "Press rumor comes from New York you may return. Hope may be

true. Looks like beginning of new era for state and university. Nearly all old men back in fall. Rest would come if you should. Everyone wants you. Campus in suspense waiting to hear from you."

Bezdek responded in June: "As much as I would like to come back to Oregon, I cannot next fall, owing to my present obligation to Penn State. Sorry more than I can express. Kindly tell all those interested best wishes to all and Oregon."

Even without Bezdek it was a glorious season for Oregon. Many of Oregon's former stars returned to play, including Hollis Huntington, the brother of the coach. Huntington got Oregon started on its second drive to the Rose Bowl by scoring four touchdowns in a 26-6 victory over Idaho.

In the game that would eventually decide the Rose Bowl berth, Oregon jumped to an early lead over Washington, scoring a pair of first-quarter touchdowns behind quarterback Bill Steers. But Steers was injured during the game and the Huskies came back to take the lead 13-12.

Skeet Manerud, the reserve quarterback who would come off the bench to gain more fame later, etched his name in Oregon's book of heroes by running for a pair of touchdowns in the fourth quarter and Oregon won 24-13.

With a host of players out with injuries after that brutal contest, Oregon lost 7-0 to Washington Agricultural College. That left Oregon and Washington tied for first place in the Pacific Coast Conference with one game left; Oregon had to defeat Oregon Agricultural College.

Hayward Field was dedicated in honor of Bill Hayward at the OAC game. Hayward missed the ceremony as he was busy in the locker room tending to the players as the trainer. The second Rose Bowl berth in four seasons was wrapped up with a 9-0 victory as Steers and Manerud alternated at quarterback to lead the offense and Prink Callison led a defensive effort that blanked OAC. The next morning in the newspaper, Hayward read about the dedication of the field. In the excitement of the victory, no one had told him about the honor.

It was back to Pasadena for the Webfoots. And while the UO administration went back to luring Bezdek west, Shy Huntington began preparations for his Oregon team to play Harvard on January 1, 1920.

The 1919 season had been over only a matter of days when Campbell wired Bezdek on December 2: "Athletic Council has unanimously voted to ask you to return to Oregon on full-year plan. All anxious to have you. Are you open to offer?"

Three days later came Bezdek's reply: "Afraid cannot consider offer now. Work has developed to such condition where it requires my presence to see it through. Appreciate Oregon's kind attitude. Very sorry situation is such that I cannot return."

So, wanted or not, Huntington went ahead and coached his team in the Rose Bowl.

The December weather in Eugene was even worse than normal, so Oregon departed for Pasadena two weeks prior to the Rose Bowl and its meeting with Harvard.

"It took three nights and two days to get down there," Skeet Manerud recalled. "We stopped in Medford and they loaded some pears for us. Then we stuck on about as many kids as players on the train. They all got kicked off in San Francisco."

What Oregon wouldn't have given for one more kick in Pasadena or even a point to tie the game. It wasn't a day for the Oregon offense, except for Hollis Huntington's 122 rushing yards in 29 attempts. Oregon didn't complete either of its two passes and not even the famed "Dead Man's Play" could get Oregon in the end zone against Harvard.

"We would tell the official what was happening," Manerud explained. "A player would fall on the ball feigning injury and the quarterback would say, 'What's the matter, ya hit?' That was the signal to throw the ball back to halfback and run like sheep."

Bill Steers, the starting quarterback, gave Oregon a 3-0 lead in the game with a 25-yard drop kick in the second quarter. Harvard answered with a touchdown, but Manerud, the backup quarterback, added a 30-yard drop kick before halftime.

Harvard's 7-6 lead at the break stood up as four subsequent Oregon drop kicks were either blocked or wide of the goal posts. The last attempt by Skeet Manerud was so close to being successful that the scoreboard operator had changed Oregon's point total to 9 before seeing an official rule the kick wide, even as Harvard players slammed their helmets to the turf in frustration that Oregon had apparently taken the lead.

The Crimson could later celebrate the 1-point victory, and Oregon could resume its pursuit of Bezdek. Was a narrow defeat in the nation's only bowl game going to be the coaching finale for Shy Huntington?

On January 3, 1920, Campbell wrote to Bezdek, "We hear splendid accounts of your work at Penn State and of the support you are getting, financial and otherwise. We wish we might figure some way to get you back but don't suppose we can match the opportunities offered you at some Eastern institution.

"Shy has done very well, it seems to me," Campbell added in the letter written just two days after the Rose Bowl defeat, "but of course, everybody would feel much better if you were here. This is no discredit to him."

Dodge and Feint

Athletics were brought under the rule of the new school of Health and Physical Education in 1920. The entire athletic program was placed under the Dean of the School. This loss of autonomy and direct access to the University president introduced new problems for the athletic program.

Shy Huntington was back for his third season as head

coach, but still there remained the shadow of Hugo Bezdek. It wasn't only that Oregon kept courting Bezdek, but that the Penn State coach continually led the Oregon officials into believing he might return to Eugene. "I am very glad to hear you express a hope and a wish that some day I may be able to come back to Oregon," Bezdek wrote prior to the 1920 season. "So do I."

On the field, Huntington's team had a mediocre year, winning three games but going scoreless in the other three to finish 3-2-1. Of the five touchdowns Oregon scored all season, one was a punt return and the other a fumble return. Bill Steers, named All-Coast quarterback, ran the punt back 75 yards against Washington for one of his two touchdowns in a 17-0 conquest of the Sundodgers. Rudd Brown made the 40-yard fumble run for the winning score against Idaho.

A scoreless tie against Oregon Agricultural College was memorable for at least one thing: a crowd of 10,000 watched in Corvallis—the most at that time to witness a game between the rivals.

BELOW: SHY HUNTINGTON *(Standing, far left)* COACHED THE 1919 OREGON TEAM TO ITS SECOND ROSE BOWL IN FOUR YEARS.

Under Fire

The Pacific Coast Conference was dead, disbanded after the previous season. This left Oregon and Oregon Agricultural College without a league because Stanford, California and Washington had gone ahead to form the Big Three.

What was still alive was the debate over Shy Huntington continuing as coach. P.L. Campbell was under siege from both sides, those advocating the University hire a professional coach at any price and those satisfied with a graduate and former player such as Huntington.

As usual, one of the most influential voices was C.N. McArthur. He'd gone from being a Portland lawyer to state legislator, where he served as Speaker of the House, to the U.S. House of Representatives, but he always found time to be involved in the athletic affairs of his alma mater. He was outraged to hear the University had not only sought to lure Bezdek back but had resorted to making a contract offer to Gil Dobie, the former Washington coach then at Cornell.

"I am also astounded to think that our athletic authorities are willing to offer the fabulous sum of $8,500 for a

football coach, a thousand dollars more than the salary of a congressman," he wrote on February 1, 1921.

The next day, a four-hour meeting of the athletic council concluded with a unanimous vote to offer Huntington a new contract, though members acknowledged that the decision came after not being able to come to salary agreement with Dobie.

Hayward Field was reconditioned as the attendance at football games overfilled the grandstands and new bleachers were added raising the capacity to 6000 seats.

"I am more than gratified to know that the vote for me was unanimous," Huntington said. "With this support and the men I now have, I'm not afraid of the Big Three or of the world."

Oregon started off the season by losing quarterback Bill Reinhart to a shoulder injury. He wasn't able to play the rest of the schedule, even though the 5-1-3 season again extended into the New Year.

The team didn't go to the Rose Bowl but instead took a trip to Honolulu for games against the University of Hawaii and Pearl Harbor, an all-star team of service personnel. The trip also served as Huntington's honeymoon, as well as a much-needed respite from Eugene and the constant debate over bringing Hugo Bezdek back to replace him. Faculty legislation had previously required a note from the parents of each player giving permission for the their child to leave the state to play football. The trip to Hawaii required a special note from the parents giving permission for their child to leave the continental United States.

The Bezdek situation reached its apex of ridiculousness on December 6, 1921, when the former coach actually visited Eugene. His Penn State team had finished its season in Seattle playing Washington, and Bezdek took a train to Eugene two days later. Greeted like a returning hero by UO officials at the train station, Bezdek was taken to the campus, where a turnout of 1,500 saluted him with a four-minute ovation prior to his speech to the gathering.

"So I've gone back East," Bezdek said. "Sometimes I wonder if it was a wise move. True, I gained in wealth and maybe some reputation, but still I think of the happy days I had here."

Even Huntington was asked to make some remarks about Bezdek, and he handled the awkward situation very graciously.

"When I came to fill Bezdek's shoes, I had a hard row to hoe," Huntington told the crowd. "Bezdek taught me all

Ready for the Referee's Whistle - - . - - - By GALE.

the football I know and can still teach me more. He is the best coach in the United States, and I hope that Oregon may hope some day to have Hugo Bezdek come back."

1922

Nearly Perfect

Only a 20-0 loss to the Multnomah Athletic Association Club kept Oregon from an unbeaten season in 1922.

The offensive star was kicker-quarterback Hal Chapman, who scored all the points in victories over Whitman and Idaho, and provided Oregon with a 3-3 tie in the season finale with Washington. The Oregon-Washington game was played on Thanksgiving Day after an agreement of the two university presidents.

"I have always felt that our final game with a Northwestern team should be with the University of Oregon," UW President Henry Suzzalo wrote to P.L. Campbell. "I have argued for the establishment of this tradition. I am thoroughly convinced that the universities of Oregon and Washington should maintain the same relations as Stanford and California, Harvard and Yale."

The tradition remained in place for three of the next four years and then faded away.

ABOVE:
THIS NEWSPAPER CARTOON CAPTURES THE NATIONAL MOOD OF OREGON'S CLASH WITH EASTERN POWER HARVARD IN THE 1920 ROSE BOWL.

Huntington Resigns

Oregon started off in grand style, winning its three opening games by a combined score of 96-7. But the opposition was Willamette, Pacific and Whitman, hardly preparation for the Pacific Coast Conference, which had been re-established.

Hal Chapman, named the All-Coast quarterback in 1922, didn't have much help, and didn't make it through the season, suffering a knee injury before the final game. Oregon only scored 17 points in its final five games, with a series of blown opportunities.

In a scoreless tie with Idaho, Oregon twice marched inside the 5-yard line but couldn't penetrate the end zone. In a 13-7 loss to Washington Agricultural College, Oregon

was threatening to tie the game when an interception stopped a drive at the 2-yard line.

Next came a loss to Oregon Agricultural College, which all but sealed Huntington's fate as coach, aided by a season-ending loss to Washington.

Oregon finished eighth in the Pacific Coast Conference at 3-4-1, and Huntington knew his six-year coaching career was over despite a 26-12-6 record.

Three days after the last game, Huntington sent a resignation letter to P.L. Campbell.

"Each year my teams have been with me, but the alumni have not," Huntington said in explaining his decision. "The alumni have carried on a sort of guerrilla warfare. They have demanded a high-priced coach, a Bezdek or a Dobie or a Warner, and not for a moment does it appear to have entered their heads that a hometown boy might possibly be a good coach.

"So without knowing the facts to investigate the

material I have had to work with or looking into my coaching methods, they have watched our games with their thumbs down, and some of them have even wished to see us lose in order that their cries for a new coach might be heard."

There was, of course, an immediate and expected rush to once more lure Hugo Bezdek back to the campus. But this time, there was outright opposition from the faculty, led by long time English Professor Herbert Howe, the UO Athletic Representative to the PCC.

Howe decried the idea of raising $10,000 or more to pay Bezdek, claiming that big alumni funds "are fairy gold. They look all right in the moonshine, but they pay no bills."

Even if the money had been raised, Howe questioned if it would be enough to bring Bezdek back from Penn State, where he had almost total control of the athletic department, something he would never be given at Oregon.

"And lastly, Bezdek does not wish to come back," Howe wrote in an article for *The Emerald*, the student newspaper. "He himself says it is not worth consideration. He can play Harvard every year, he can play in Philadelphia and in New York City, and he can read his name in the metropolitan papers every week. To use his favorite phrase, 'When you're in the big leagues, who wants to go back to the bush leagues?'"

Mediocrity Says it All

Rebuffed in attempts to lure a more prominent coach to replace Shy Huntington, Oregon settled on Joe Maddock, a Michigan graduate and former Utah coach. Oregon's 4-3-2 season was mediocre from start to finish, opening with a scoreless tie against Willamette and finishing with a 6-0 blanking by the Multnomah Athletic Association Club.

In between, Oregon posted a rare victory over Washington, 7-3, but balanced that with a 13-0 loss to Idaho, the first defeat for Oregon in the 23-year series. There was, at least, a victory over Oregon Agricultural College, this one ending 7-3 after Robert Mautz caught a touchdown pass late in the game.

One year was enough for Maddock, who resigned to enter private business. Oregon was back in the hunt for a new coach and ended up with an old one.

1925

Recalled Coach Posts Grim Record

Spend money on a big-name coach? Hire a former player? Bring in a candidate from the East or hire away from a Western rival? Or do none of the above to fill the latest coaching vacancy?

Oregon decided on the latter, bringing back Eugene resident Richard Shore Smith who had coached Oregon's 1903 and 1904 teams and had compiled a record of 8-5-1 for the two seasons. Smith, however, viewed his coaching as a duty and never put the time into the job that he had during his previous stint. This last fling at coaching resulted in the worst record ever: 1-5-1.

It was the third game of the season before Oregon reached the end zone, and the only victory was 13-0 over Pacific. In the other six games, Oregon scored a total of six touchdowns.

Oregon did manage to make a run at Stanford, trailing 14-13 at half time before All-American Ernie Nevers scored three touchdowns rocketing Stanford to a 35-13 triumph.

The season ended—as did Smith's coaching career—with defeats to Oregon's archrivals. OAC beat Oregon 24-13 as a state-record crowd of 22,200 watched the game played on a field described as "much better for water polo than football."

A week later, the Ducks, a word starting to replace Webfoots more and more on the sports pages, took a late 14-12 lead over Washington on a touchdown pass from Louis Anderson to Robert Mautz. But Washington came back to win on a field goal that hit the cross bar and dropped over.

C.N. "Pat" McArthur, the man who had done so much to further UO athletics, died of meningitis in 1925. His death coincided with planning for the new basketball pavilion, so the student body petitioned the UO Board of Regents to name the building in his honor. The name given to the new pavilion was McArthur Court.

C.W. Spears' first Oregon team won seven of nine games in 1930, prompting such scenes as this pep rally outside Villard Hall.

PACIFIC COAST POWER

The University of Oregon began its 33rd year of collegiate football as it had 20 previous ones: In search of a new head coach. President P.L. Campbell died in 1925 and a triumvirate took over the presidency for one year. None of them had a background in athletics. Two were scholars—Henry Sheldon and Karl Onthank—and the other, L.H. Johnson, was an administrator. That didn't stop the trio from finding a suitable candidate to fill Oregon's head coaching job, however. Capt. John J. McEwan, formerly a successful coach at West Point, applied and was hired.

"Cap" McEwan had also been an All-America player at West Point in 1914, in addition to coaching the cadets from 1923 through 1925. The UO gave him a five-year, $3,500-a-year contract for coaching football along with the academic title of Professor of Physical Education.

In establishing the new regime, McEwan adopted the epigram, "The best defense is the best offense." But it proved to be only partly true in 1925. His team came to be known as "The 30-minute men," leading all but two games at half time, only to lose them in the second half. McEwan had a strong first unit, but lacked the substitutes to fully implement the offense he had installed. Among his assistants was former cadet Eugene Vidal, who would later serve in the Roosevelt administration and was the father of author Gore Vidal.

Replanting the Seeds of Greatness

McEwan's 1926 team won only two games, defeating Cal for its lone conference victory and prevailing over Pacific in a nonconference battle. Only Montana and Cal faired worse, and Oregon finished in a tie with Idaho for sixth in the conference.

The Business of Football Comes of Age

By 1927, college football was in a boom period. Players and coaches had become national heroes, attracting growing numbers of fans to large new stadiums. Fans at home followed the action through the advent of the new medium of radio as well as expanded, specialized sports coverage in newspapers and magazines.

Business jumped on the college-football bandwagon, giving rise to concerns about commercialism. A late-1920s Carnegie Report on Athletics at the University of Oregon was commissioned in the wake of concerns about the growth and prominence of athletics on the campus. The concerns cited included the controversial construction of McArthur Court (financed through student fees), the perception of negligent attitudes by athletes toward academics and the acknowledgment that coaches were paid more than professors.

The Carnegie report caused a stir among students, faculty, townspeople and alumni, but had little long-lasting effect. Big-time intercollegiate athletics had arrived at the University, and its football Ducks were on the brink of becoming a Pacific Coast power.

Oregon opened the 1927 season at Hayward Field against Linfield, and for the first time the team was fully attired in the official school colors of emerald green and lemon yellow.

This at the insistence of the student body, who previously had tolerated the use of blue in place of the green. The students also voted to retain "Ducks" as the school's official nickname. Two other alternatives were on the ballot:

Imagine cheering for the "Oregon Timberwolves" or the "Fighting Lumberjacks."

Despite the new look and an initial 7-0 victory over Linfield, it was clear the Ducks were at least a season away from success. The Oregon offense rolled up 31 points to rout Pacific in the second game, but scored only 7 points the rest of the season. McEwan's men fought Idaho to a scoreless tie, then lost to California at Portland's new Multnomah Stadium and to Stanford in Palo Alto. After a 21-7 loss to Oregon Agricultural College, which had started dropping the word "Agricultural" and replacing it with "State," the Ducks closed the season with a 7-0 loss at Washington.

Oregon had duplicated its 2-4-1 record of the previous year, but the winless Pacific Coast Conference campaign meant a drop to 7th place.

The Excitement Returns

In 1928, a sophomore quarterback named John Kitzmiller emerged to lead the Ducks to their first-ever nine-win season, bringing back a level of excitement to Oregon football that had not been felt since the early Rose Bowl years.

Nicknamed "The Flying Dutchman," Kitzmiller was voted All-Coast and quickly established himself as a force to

be reckoned with in the PCC. He also led all PCC scorers with 48 points, the first of which came in a 45-0 romp over Pacific in the season opener. It represented as many points as Oregon had scored during the entire 1927 season.

Kitzmiller was not invincible, however, as Stanford whipped the Ducks 26-12 the following week.

The Ducks rebounded with a 38-6 thrashing of Willamette, then shutout Washington and Oregon Normal in succession before being shut out themselves by Cal at Berkeley. It was the last time the 1928 Ducks would taste defeat, however, as they finished out the season with a six-game winning streak.

Breaking Oregon State College's three-year grip on state bragging rights was in order when McEwan led the Ducks onto Bell Field for the annual showdown. New OSC leader Paul Schissler preached defense as the best offense, but Oregon blanked the Beavers 12-0.

Montana and UCLA fell victim to Oregon next. The Los Angeles school, new to the conference, got a rough introduction to PCC football when Kitzmiller returned an interception 96 yards for a touchdown to highlight the 26-6 Duck victory in the first meeting between the two schools. Despite winning more games than in the previous three seasons combined, early Bay Area losses relegated the Ducks to fourth in the PCC with a 4-2 record.

Oregon capped a season of welcome improvement with a holiday trip to Hawaii, where it split a pair of games with two gritty, determined island teams. After losing 13-2 to a Honolulu town team on Christmas Day, the Ducks

closed out the satisfying 1928 campaign with a 6-0 victory over the University of Hawaii to claim the "Championship of the Mid-Pacific" on New Year's Day.

<hr>

1929

Back in Title Contention

Some preseason writers and observers predicted a conference title for McEwan's resurgent program in 1929, and the Ducks began the campaign with another crushing 58-0 defeat of Pacific. But a disappointing trip to Palo Alto followed as Oregon wilted in the heat of the Peninsula and Stanford rolled to a 33-7 triumph.

However, the Ducks returned to their winning, end-zone-denying ways by clobbering Willamette 34-0 in the second of six shutouts for one of the top defensive teams in the West that year. At Portland, Oregon defeated Idaho 34-7 for its first victory over the Vandals in six years.

Dramatic big plays have always been a staple of the Oregon-Washington series and the 1929 fray at Seattle was no exception. Oregon's Bobby Robinson intercepted a Husky pass at the Duck 5-yard line and raced downfield for what appeared to be a sure touchdown. But Washington end Larry Westerweller, who had been removed from the contest moments earlier, jumped off the bench and ran on to the field to bring down Robinson well short of the goal. Officials awarded Robinson and Oregon a 95-yard touchdown nonetheless. Kitzmiller passed for the other score in the Ducks' 14-0 victory.

The reserves played most of the game the following week back at Hayward Field, as Oregon routed upstart UCLA 27-0. In the final Eugene contest of the year, OSC again was denied the goal line. Robinson scored twice and helped prevent a Beaver touchdown with a flying tackle for a loss within sniffing distance of the goal. Mason then intercepted an OSC pass at the 1-yard line to seal a 12-0 triumph.

The victory ensured Oregon of a 4-1 conference record and a third-place tie in the PCC, but it was also costly: Kitzmiller broke his leg and was out for the three following postseason games.

Hawaii visited Portland in the first of the postseason contests, and Robinson scored Oregon's only points with a

LEFT: HAYWARD FIELD DOUBLED AS OREGON'S FOOTBALL AND TRACK FACILITY FOR NEARLY FIVE DECADES.

ABOVE:
OREGON AND
STANFORD TANGLE
IN A 1926 GAME
AT HAYWARD
FIELD.

65-yard punt return and an extra-point kick.

The Ducks concluded the season with a long road trip, the first stop being San Francisco, where they were the first team that season to score against pesky St. Mary's—the so-called "Notre Dame of the West." Robinson passed 5 yards to Al Browne for Oregon's only points, as the Gaels racked up a 31-6 triumph.

The game was the first of an exciting series between Oregon and the tiny Moraga, California, Catholic college whose football program was elevated to national prominence by colorful coach Slip Madigan during the 1920s and '30s. The 1929 contest was the only one of the series in which either team scored more than three touchdowns. The winner of each meeting took home a handsome Governor's Trophy that bore a bronze rendering of a football player in action, flanked by miniature replicas of the Oregon and California state capitals. The trophy rivalry continued uninterrupted until 1935 and then was renewed for three seasons between 1948 and 1950. St. Mary's dropped football in 1951.

Oregon wrapped up the 1929 season with a cross-country train ride to Miami to meet the then-unheralded University of Florida. It wasn't the first time the Ducks had played in hot weather, as those on the Stanford jaunt could attest, but the subtropical heat of southern Florida was something else. Many of the Oregon men took off their jerseys during the contest and played clad in shoulder pads and moleskins.

The Ducks were minus a number of stars in Miami, including Kitzmiller, Robinson and All-Coast linemen Austin Colbert, George Stadelman, and Charles Williams.

Robinson and Williams, both starters and valuable backfield players, were informed by Florida that they would not be allowed to play in the game because they were black. Wally Shearer threw to Walt Browne for Oregon's only touchdown in the 20-6 upset loss to the Gators.

McEwan had been on a short leash for the past two seasons and his personal problems were interfering with his coaching. UO President Arnold Bennett Hall had fore-warned McEwan prior to the season that he had to shape up or be fired. McEwan's problems persisted, however, and the UO purchased the remaining year of his contract at the end of the 1929 season. McEwan signed on to coach football at Holy Cross.

Winning Ways Continue

With the departure of McEwan, President Hall appointed himself a committee of one to find McEwan's successor. Hall was a product of the Midwest and understood big-time football as it was played in those universities. Coming from Wisconsin to Oregon, Hall brought many new ideas to the campus. His commitment to excellence stretched across the University and led to an expansion of the school, its purpose and mission. Fund raising took a front seat and faculty research was pushed as a main purpose of the University.

Hall was set on landing a high-powered coach and was willing to pay the price to get him. He managed to lure Clarence "Doc" Spears to Eugene on the heels of a successful career at Minnesota, where he had compiled a 28-3-9 record. Spears was a 1915 All-America selection at Dartmouth, where he went on to coach two years later. He left Dartmouth and coached at West Virginia before arriving at Minnesota and improving his overall record to 77-18-13. With Spears, it appeared Oregon had finally dressed for success.

Spears was a great believer in the passing game and Oregon had the talent to build on that belief. He was also a medical doctor, and he signed a UO contract with a salary second only to Hall's. For $11,000—$6,500 from the ASUO as football coach and $4,500 from the UO as a professor of physical education—Oregon alumni and fans finally had the high-caliber coach they had been wanting since Bezdek left in 1917. Spears was given complete authority over football and reported directly to the president; the dean of the School of Health and Physical Education was no longer involved.

Spears was intent on doing things his own way. This immediately became apparent when he had all the grass scraped off Hayward Field and the exposed soil raked constantly. With sprinklers left running for days on end, the field became a quagmire. Spears believed this would give the UO a distinct homefield advantage. The grass would not be restored until 1937 when the UO used federal Works Projects Administration (WPA) funds and ASUO funds to reinstall the turf.

Spears got off to a fast start in 1930, outscoring in-state rivals Pacific, Willamette and Linfield 77-0 in "tuneup" contests. The big test, and the big break, for the Ducks came when they traveled to Chicago for a showdown with Midwestern power Drake in a rare night game at Soldier Field.

Oregon dominated Drake in the school's first-ever intersectional victory, rolling up 16 first downs to Drake's six in a 14-7 victory. Sportswriters gave Kitzmiller his first national recognition, proclaiming him All-America material.

The largest crowd yet to see a football game in the Northwest packed Multnomah Stadium to watch Oregon capture its third straight shutout over Washington. The Ducks prevailed 7-0 in this classic UO-UW defensive battle.

Kitzmiller, Colbert and George Christensen made their last Eugene appearances a week later against UCLA. The Bruins very nearly spoiled the trio's Hayward Field

swan song and Oregon's Homecoming, but Oregon pulled out another 7-0 victory to improve its record to 7-0.

The bubble burst in Corvallis, however, as Kitzmiller sat out most of the OSC game with an injury for the second year in a row. Reserve quarterback Choppie Park led a gutsy Oregon effort, but the Beavers blanked the Ducks 15-0.

The Thanksgiving Day contest against St. Mary's at San Francisco was regarded as Oregon's best effort of the year. But the Ducks fell short in their quest to capture the Governor's Trophy, as Kitzmiller missed a critical point after attempt—his first miss of the year—and the Gaels won 7-6.

Kitzmiller closed his Oregon career as an All-PCC back and a Shrine All-Star player (along with Christensen and Colbert). Everyone who saw Kitzmiller play regarded him as one of the most versatile players in Oregon football history.

In October 1931, scarcely a year after he hung up his lemon and green, *Old Oregon* magazine named Kitzmiller quarterback of its all-time Duck All-Star team based on an alumni survey. The crowning glory came more than three decades later, when he was inducted into the National Football Foundation and College Hall of Fame.

Spears Leads Midnight Express

The 1930 Ducks boasted a strong freshmen team, and its members added to the varsity weaponry of a 1931 Oregon team that again was expected to contended for the

BELOW:

HALFBACKS JAY GRAYBEAL *(left)* AND BOB SMITH WERE TWO OFFENSIVE STARS OF OREGON'S TEAMS IN THE LATE 1930S.

PCC title. Leading the way was the acclaimed "Midnight Express" backfield, a speedy unit paced by quarterback Leighton Gee and running backs Mark Temple as well as sophomores Joe Lillard and legend to be, Mike Mikulak.

The Express-led Ducks opened with four straight victories, three of them shutouts. They easily defeated Oregon Normal 21-6 and Willamette 20-0, then edged Idaho 9-0 in Portland.

In the first of four straight road games, Oregon once again blanked Washington 7-0. Bowerman scored on a school-record 87-yard punt return, and as he ran down the field toward the goal line, 63-year-old Bill Hayward, the track coach, ran parallel to Bowerman shouting at him to keep his knees high. Both men reached the end of the field at the same time.

Bad news came the following week when Lillard was lost from the "Midnight Express" due to charges that he'd once played semi-pro baseball under an assumed name.

The timing of Lillard's departure could not have been worse: Oregon's next opponent was USC, eventual winner of the Helms Foundation's version of a national championship.

Lillard became one of the first two blacks to play in professional football, playing two seasons with the Chicago Cardinals.

Oregon's first meeting with the University of Southern California since 1915 was a brutal one with the Trojans pounding the Ducks 53-0.

Another cross-country journey awaited the bruised UO contingent. At Grand Forks, fumbles and a bad kicking game led to a scoreless tie against North Dakota. It was an inauspicious warmup for a major showdown against New York University, in which Eastern writers had projected the Ducks to be three- or four-touchdown underdogs.

Oregon embarrassed the scribes and the Violets with a 14-6 upset at Yankee Stadium.

After the heady victory at New York, the annual rivalry with Oregon State could have seemed anticlimactic. It turned out to be just that: the season's second scoreless deadlock, on a soupy Hayward Field. Beaver punter Keith Davis let sail long kicks which gave the Ducks poor field position to start most offensive series.

The season ended with a two-game California trip for Spears' road warriors. They defeated UCLA 13-6, then fell to St. Mary's 16-0. The loss at San Francisco gave the Ducks a 6-2-2 overall record, 3-1-1 in the PCC for another third-place finish. It was Spears' last game as coach at Oregon.

The Callison Years Begin

Spears quit and signed a contract with Wisconsin, where he felt more comfortable. After his departure, University alumni and students asked that a young UO graduate be hired to replace the controversial coach. The result was the hiring of Prince G. "Prink" Callison, class of '23, and it proved to be a wise and popular choice. The second-youngest head coach in the PCC at 34, Callison earned three Duck letters between 1920 and 1922. He was named All-Coast center in his junior and senior seasons, and earned the title "60-Minute Man" for his skill and stamina.

After graduation, Callison became head coach at Medford High School, and his teams went unbeaten between 1924 and 1928, winning four state championships.

The University had hired Callison as freshman football coach in 1929, and in his three seasons in that capacity, Callison's teams lost only two games—both to the OSC frosh. Callison's elevation to the varsity coaching ranks also gave Oregon its first-ever all-alumni coaching staff. He was joined by main assistants John Kitzmiller, Gene Shields, frosh coach Irv Schulz and assistant Skeet Manerud. Callison was to be paid $5,500 by the ASUO for coaching football and his salary as an assistant professor of physical education remained the same, $2,500.

The 1932 season also saw Mike Mikulak shine on both offense and defense, where he was characterized by Bowerman as "the original middle linebacker." Legendary "Iron Mike" was a key part of one of the nation's top collegiate backfields as well. When carrying the ball, he was a master at what Gregory tabbed the "cruncher" play, in which he could make his own interference and was never caught off-guard by an opponent.

Mikulak and his backfield mates benefitted from outstanding blocking from Bowerman and future NFL All-Stars Bernie Hughes and Bill Morgan on the front line. Morgan was so tenacious, he played in the 1932 Washington game with both arms in casts.

Optimistic Duck fans welcomed the new Hayward Field east grandstand and a 26-6 season-opening victory over Pacific. At the same time, Santa Clara, Oregon's next opponent, was pulling off one of the Coast's big upsets against California. The Broncos invaded Eugene in high spirits and

allowed the Ducks only one touchdown—an off-tackle run by Stan Kostka. But the 212-pound fullback's scoring romp was all Oregon needed to hold on for the 7-0 victory.

Successive Multnomah Stadium contests were less than successful for Callison's troops. First they fought to a scoreless tie with Washington, then suffered their first-ever loss to UCLA 12-7 the following Saturday. In the traditional OSC battle at Bell Field, Temple broke a 6-6 deadlock by following what observers called "perfect interference" on a 65-yard punt return for the game-winning touchdown.

Duck boosters had reason to celebrate above and beyond the OSC win in early November. Three days after the contest, the state's voters overwhelmingly rejected a ballot measure proposing that the university and OSC be merged into one large university located on the Corvallis campus.

On the first leg of the late-fall tour that year, Oregon endured another long Los Angeles afternoon in losing to USC 33-0. Thanksgiving by the Bay was becoming a tradition, but St. Mary's again spoiled the party with a 7-0 victory at San Francisco.

The Ducks were invited to play Southeastern Conference champion Louisiana State at Baton Rouge in a December 17 exhibition, which would be a forerunner to the Sugar Bowl. A thousand Oregon fans followed the team to Louisiana, where it was so cold that trainer Bill Hayward's famous water wagon and the band instruments froze. Hayward did not want the players to chance getting sick while on the road by drinking the local water, so he took a water wagon filled with what he joking called "Oregon water" on long journeys.

The extreme cold didn't stop Oregon from claiming another major intersectional victory over feisty LSU 12-0. Bowerman recalls the LSU game as the best of his career as a blocking back, a position he later characterized as "fun if you don't mind getting a taste of your own blood from time to time."

After graduation, Bowerman spent a year at Portland's Franklin High School, then returned to Medford where he'd played high school ball under Callison. At Medford, Bowerman coached three undefeated state-championship teams. He then served in World War II with the 10th Mountain Division, attaining the rank of major, before returning to the University of Oregon, where he would follow in the steps of mentor Bill Hayward as track and field coach.

A Co-Championship But No Roses

One of Oregon's most experienced teams ever returned for the 1933 season with 22 lettermen. The Ducks again fielded an outstanding defense, which allowed only 17 points in its first eight games and claimed five shutouts.

First came Linfield, which suffered through a 53-0 defeat at the hands of the Ducks under the lights at Hayward Field. Gonzaga did not fall easily at Spokane but the Ducks held on for a 14-0 victory.

Oregon returned home to face Columbia University, now known as the University of Portland. The Ducks sent the Irish back to the Bluff, winning 14-7, then continued their habit of keeping Washington from the end zone in a 6-0 triumph.

Next, Idaho fell 19-0, then UCLA tumbled to the Ducks 7-0. Utah visited Eugene the following week, but provided little challenge. The Ducks won the first contest between the two schools 26-7. That same day, Stanford upset USC, placing Oregon atop the PCC race and giving Stanford title hopes. The scent of roses, so long missing from the UO campus, again was in the air. An Oregon victory over Oregon State in an Armistice Day clash at Portland would put the championship and a Rose Bowl bid on the line the following week against USC in Los Angeles.

The 1933 Oregon-OSC game was one of the most anticipated in the series up until then. Football fever ran high in Corvallis that year as well. First-year coach Lon Stiner's "Ironmen" had surprised the football world by holding USC to a scoreless tie in Portland using only their 11 OSC starters, without a single substitution. A record 32,000 fans jammed Multnomah Stadium for the Civil War.

Oregon's 13-3 triumph was the Ducks' ninth straight victory spanning two seasons. It kept the Ducks atop the PCC standings with a 4-0 record and set up the USC showdown—with a New Year's trip to Pasadena on the line.

Callison ran his team through grueling workouts in preparation for playing USC in the November heat of Los Angeles. He was confident his players were ready and the Associated Press agreed, picking the Ducks the favorites.

Oregon's high hopes were dashed in the Coliseum, however, as USC defeated the Ducks 26-6. The Southern Cal loss was a heartbreaking one, but the Ducks could take

RIGHT:

BACKFIELD MATES
(Left to right)
JOHN REISCHMAN,
BUD GOODIN,
WALT BACK
AND FRANK
MICHEK OF THE
1934 TEAM.

pride in capturing a share of the PCC championship for the first time since 1919. And a Rose Bowl berth remained a possibility, if California could beat Stanford and Washington beat USC. The Huskies did their part, but Stanford won the Big Game and the bowl bid.

There remained one final goal for the 1933 Ducks: They could still record another nine-win season by defeating St. Mary's in the season finale. Mikulak took a reverse from Bob Parke late in game to score the last touchdown for Oregon and give the Ducks their first Governor's Trophy and their ninth victory with a 14-7 triumph.

Mikulak was named to the All-PCC squad for the second straight year and became the Ducks' third All-American. He joined Bernie Hughes and guard Bree Cuppoletti on the West team for the Shrine game, and played fullback against the Chicago Bears, pro football's 1933 champions, in the first College All-Star Game, which ended in a 0-0 tie.

Mikulak went on to play three seasons with the NFL's Chicago Cardinals, then returned to the University of Oregon as back coach. Don Mabee, who played under Mikulak at Oregon and later became a high school coach, recalled him as "possibly the greatest player Oregon ever had. He was tough, but we respected him and thought the world of him." Mikulak might have made a career of coaching football, but World War II intervened and he retired from the Army as a colonel in 1973.

A Young Squad Overachieves

Graduation took a heavy toll on the Ducks after the 1933 season. Yet, despite the lack of depth, the 1934 Oregon team surprised many by winning six of its first seven games and compiling a 4-2 conference record.

The lone blemish in the Ducks' first seven contests came against Washington in the third game, after victories over Gonzaga and UCLA. The Huskies had neither scored against or defeated Oregon in the previous seven years, so their 16-6 victory was great cause for celebration.

Oregon then completed a three-game Rocky Mountain sweep with road triumphs over Idaho and Utah, followed by a 13-0 victory over Montana at Hayward Field.

In their Homecoming contest with the Beavers, the Ducks were drawn into a fight—literally—when Oregon's All-Coast tackle Alex Eagle and OSC's Jack Brandis had a minor difference of opinion away from the ball. Blows were exchanged and soon both teams joined in the fracas. After some semblance of order was restored, the Ducks claimed a rare second-straight win in the series, edging the Beavers 9-6.

At 6-1, the Ducks were flying high. Even a Rose Bowl berth was possible, albeit a longshot. Then three straight losses in the waning weeks of the season eliminated any such hopes and took much of the steam out of an odds-defying year for the young Ducks. USC handed Oregon its second PCC loss of the year in a 33-0 rout, dropping the Ducks to fourth place in the conference for the season.

Things only got worse when St. Mary's spoiled Oregon's Thanksgiving dinner 13-7. Two weeks later, the Ducks returned to Baton Rouge where LSU awaited to settle a 2-year-old score with its Yankee visitors. The weather was more congenial than during the 1932 visit, but the day ended with a chill when the Tigers edged Oregon 14-13.

The passing game got a boost in 1934, as the 5-yard penalty for incomplete passes after first down was abolished. The rejuvenated passing game and an end-around play developed by Callison enabled sure-footed Raymond "Butch" Morse to score three touchdowns that season. He earned All-America and All-Coast honors, then played in the East-West Shrine and College All-Stars games. He went on to play in the NFL before being drafted into the Army for World War II, and later coached Randolph Field to a shocking 7-7 tie with Texas in the 1944 Cotton Bowl. Eagle was tapped for an All-Coast squad that played in a postseason All-Star contest at Honolulu.

1935

Still in the Middle of the Pack

Oregon's record improved a notch in 1935, but the unhearalded Ducks remained in the conference's fourth spot, despite allowing only 57 points and posting six shutouts. Oregon earned Northwest bragging rights, however, going 3-0 against regional rivals.

Oregon shutout Gonzaga for the fourth straight year, winning 18-0 in the season opener, before the Ducks dispatched Utah 6-0 in preparation for their PCC opener with California. The renewal of this West Coast rivalry with the Golden Bears, abandoned for several years, was played on a muddy Multnomah field in Portland. It turned out to be more of a punting exhibition, with Cal's Floyd Blower blocking a punt by Oregon's Stan Riordan to set up the game's only score in a 6-0 defeat.

The Ducks rebounded to beat Idaho 14-0 but then were trampled by a newly-powerful UCLA team 33-6. Oregon had two weeks to regroup for the Civil War, and the

extra practice time paid off in the form of a fourth straight victory over Oregon State College. With their 13-0 triumph, the Ducks had held OSC to 15 points in five games.

In a similar vein, it was "back to the good old days" in Seattle the following week, as Oregon racked up its sixth shutout of the year in a 7-0 win over Washington. Guard Ross Carter later recalled that jubilant Duck fans attempted to capture the Husky Stadium goalposts, resulting in an hour-long riot on the field. Players from both teams sat together in the stands to take in the crowd's post-game mayhem.

The Ducks closed out the season with an 18-0 victory over St. Mary's. Their 6-3 record would be Callison's last winning-season mark as Oregon coach.

1936

Trying Times Return

Only a dozen lettermen returned for the 1936 season in which the depth-poor Ducks struggled against more well-stocked, experienced units. USC, which used two sets

BELOW: ALL-AMERICA END RAYMOND "BUTCH" MORSE *(right)* CATCHES A PASS FOR OREGON'S ONLY TOUCH-DOWN IN A 1934 GAME AGAINST ST. MARY'S.

of reserves to hand Oregon a 26-0 loss in the third game of the season, was but one example.

Oregon's season-opening 14-0 victory over Portland marked the end of an era. The contest against the Pilots was the last Oregon would schedule against an in-state opponent other than OSC for nearly 60 years.

After the USC loss the following week, the Ducks regrouped and gained more than a measure of respect by tying a powerful Stanford club 7-7 in Palo Alto. Then it was back to Portland for three Multnomah Stadium games, the first of which saw Oregon score its last victory and last point of the year in a 13-0 triumph over Idaho.

Washington State could muster only a field goal against the Ducks, but the Cougars still managed to spoil Homecoming with a 3-0 victory the following Saturday. Washington was next, and Oregon rolled up 10 first downs to Washington's four but had four goal-line drives turned back in a 7-0 heartbreaker.

UCLA and Cal handed Oregon its next two losses, with the Bruins nipping the Ducks 7-0 and the Bears prevailing 28-0.

Worst of all, a five-game unbeaten streak against OSC came to an end with an 18-0 Beaver triumph at Corvallis. The loss was Callison's first in the Civil War—and the Ducks finished the season in the PCC cellar.

Melee Marrs Last Callison Season

Sophomore strength brought new hope to the campus in 1937, though lack of depth and a diverse attack were again seen as handicaps. The newcomers shined in a 26-13 season-opening loss to UCLA, particularly in two long Oregon drives led by Medford sophomore Bob Smith and "Pendleton Jack-rabbit" Jay Graybeal.

The home opener against Stanford was commemorated by the dedication of the new Hayward Field turf, which replaced the combination sand-and-sawdust playing surface that had been in place since the departure of Spears in 1932. Chancellor Frederick Hunter and UO President C. Valentine Boyer oversaw the turf dedication ceremony then sat back and watched one of the season's most thrilling upsets.

Duck tackle Bill Foskitt blocked a point-after attempt to preserve the victory—Oregon's first-ever over Stanford, the only PCC member it had not yet beaten in football.

Next the Ducks rolled to a 40-6 triumph over Gonzaga, highlighted by Jimmy Nicholson's 70-yard interception return to set up a touchdown.

At Los Angeles, Oregon lost 34-14 to USC, but wowed the city of angels with two 70-yard scoring passes—one from Steve Anderson to sophomore Ted Gebhardt, the other from Smith to Graybeal.

The Beavers held onto bragging rights for another year in the mid-season Civil War, but they had to fight for them. The Oregon line kept OSC from scoring until the waning minutes of the 14-0 showdown in Eugene.

It was one of the biggest defensive battles in the series. Two days later however, an even bigger battle would erupt on the streets of Eugene as a result of the Hayward Field contest. OSC students, heady with victory, asked their school's president to cancel Monday classes in celebration of the second-straight win over the Ducks. Despite the president's refusal, a Monday morning caravan of about 100 cars left Corvallis for the UO campus and an impromptu victory parade.

LEFT: BY 1939, HELMETS, SHOULDER PADS AND HIGH-TOP CLEATS WERE STANDARD PARTS OF THE UNIFORMS.

ABOVE: OREGON'S 1939 TEAM IS READY FOR ACTION. (*Left to right*) VIC REGINATO, RIGHT END; ELROY JENSEN, RIGHT TACKLE; MEL PASSOLT, RIGHT GUARD; JIM CADENASSO, CENTER; NELLO GIOVANINI, LEFT GUARD; MERLE PETERS, RIGHT TACKLE; JOHN YERBY, RIGHT END; (*backfield*) BOB SMITH, RIGHT HALF; HANK NILSEN, QUARTERBACK; FRANK EMMONS, FULL BACK; JAY GRAYBEAL, LEFT HALF.

Advance warning came to Eugene just after 11 a.m., and when the procession reached the Eugene city limit, it was greeted by state and local police, who sternly advised the Beaver students to be law-abiding.

According to *Oregon Daily Emerald* and *Oregana* accounts, UO students received word of the invasion from Corvallis from Dean of Students Virgil Earl who helped the law students drape hoses out of Fenton Hall to prepare to meet the crowd.

The Beaver students eventually gave themselves up to the Duck crowd, which hustled them up the butte to restore the "O"—which had been painted orange—to its proper lemon yellow.

The Civil War chaos behind them, the Ducks continued their rebuilding efforts with a 10-6 win over Washington State. California (26-0) and Washington (14-0) handed the Ducks their final conference losses of the year, and the Ducks finished PCC play in eighth place.

The Ducks concluded the season with a 24-6 victory over a tough U.S. Marine Corps squad in sunny San Diego and a 20-6 loss to Arizona. Shortly thereafter, Callison resigned, putting an end to one of the most successful coaching runs in Oregon football history.

Wildcat Coach Gerald A. "Tex" Oliver was hired as the new Oregon leader.

"Oliver Twist" Opens In Eugene

Tex Oliver played at West Point after serving in World War I and then earned a bachelor's degree from USC before going on to coach at the University of Arizona. His contract with the University of Oregon called for him to receive $4,500 from the ASU, $600 from alumni and boosters and a signing bonus of $1,000. He earned the UO portion of his salary as a professor of physical education.

The cerebral Texan, a Phi Beta Kappa key holder, brought many innovations to the Duck program. Mabee recalled Oliver using a metronome in practice to teach backs and ends the proper timing method of shifting. The new style of Oregon football, dubbed "Oliver Twist" by UO publicist Bruce Hamby, included a new, wideopen passing attack. It took some time for the young Ducks to master the new offense in a 4-5 season.

The Ducks opened with two straight victories, dropping WSC 10-2 at Pullman and then nipping UCLA in a 14-12 home-opening thriller.

Bad breaks and big Stanford plays cost Oregon a rare opportunity for a Palo Alto victory. The Ducks led 16-13 going into the final quarter, but the hosts blocked a UO punt for a go-ahead touchdown and quickly added another to make it 27-16.

Fordham came next at New York's polo grounds. The Bronx school that had produced college football's legendary "Seven Blocks of Granite" blocked the Ducks from the end zone in a 26-0 victory. USC treated the Ducks and their fans to a 31-7 drubbing in the Trojans' first Eugene appearance.

The Idaho game was a happier experience for fans, the team and Bob Smith. The shifty, speedy back scored on a 92-yard run from scrimmage—a school record that stood throughout the first 100 years.

Smith's touchdown was the high point of the 19-6 victory over the Vandals. The following week, California brought him and his teammates back to earth with a 20-0 defeat.

Jimmy Nicholson's 25-yard field goal seconds before half time provided the victory margin in a 3-0 triumph over the Huskies at Portland.

The Civil War returned to Multnomah Stadium a week later and the Beavers again prevailed, this time 23-12. Mercifully for all concerned, there was no post-game parade to Eugene.

Back to the PCC's Upper Ranks

Fall 1939 began with war clouds over Europe—ominous for young men of military age—but blue skies over Eugene, where the Ducks opened with a 2-0-1 record and subsequent national ranking. Rose Bowl champion Southern Cal was fortunate to escape the Coliseum with an embarrassing 7-7 tie.

Revenge over Bay Area contingents was in order. The Duck pass defense rose to the occasion in the Portland mud to deny sophomore Stanford quarterback Frankie Albert and his Indians air supremacy in a 10-0 victory. Then it was Cal's turn, and the Ducks mounted an 86-yard drive to claim a 6-0 Oregon victory.

The Ducks were ranked sixth in the country following the Berkeley triumph but were brought down to earth in their final encounter with Gonzaga. The Bulldogs, whipped so often by Oregon, got the last bite in the series with two long touchdown passes and a 12-6 triumph.

A strong defensive effort against UCLA followed but to no avail. Future baseball Hall of Famer Jackie Robinson was called "safe" in the end zone on two long runs from scrimmage, leading the Bruins to a 16-6 victory in the Coliseum. The Ducks then returned to Hayward Field and the win column with a vengeance against WSC. The Cougars absorbed a 38-0 drubbing.

The 1939 Civil War was a wild affair that kept the Eugene crowd on the edge of its collective seat, but a safety sealed the Beavers' 19-14 triumph. In the finale, Graybeal scored all Duck points in a 20-13 loss to Washington.

The Hoffman Award, presented to the team's outstanding player each season based upon a vote of the team, was presented the first time in 1939. Bob Smith was its first recepient.

Smith also played in the 1940 Shrine All-Star contest in San Francisco. Teammates Floyd Rhea (guard) and Dick Ashcom (tackle) were named to the College All-Star team. Graybeal joined tackle Jim Stuart, a Hermiston native, on the all-conference roster.

Rebuilding Year

Graduation depleted Oregon's talent pool for the 1940 season, which began at Hayward Field with a 12-2 victory over San Diego's Marine contingent.

Four close losses followed. Rose Bowl champion Stanford, paced by Clark Shaughnessy's revolutionary "T" formation, blanked Oliver's single-wing attack 13-0. Then Washington kept its own bowl hopes alive with a 10-0 shutout before 30,000 Portland spectators. At Los Angeles, a possible scoring drive was halted at the Trojan 2, and USC prevailed 13-0. The first half of the season ended with a 6-6 tie against lowly Washington State, in which Tom Roblin scored Oregon's only touchdown on a 54-yard run.

The Ducks then regrouped to win three of their last four games against Montana, UCLA, California and OSC.

The season ended on a cheery note at Corvallis, where the Beavers were favored in the annual Civil War showdown. "They were supposed to be so much better than we were, but everything went right for us for a change," said tackle Ed Moshofsky of the 20-0 upset over the third-place Beavers.

Oregon finished the 1940 season as the top defensive squad in the PCC, holding opponents to an average of 168 yards per game.

From High Hopes to War

Sportswriters and Oregon fans had high preseason hopes for a talent-laden 1941 squad. A major rule change that year allowed two-platoon systems and free substitution. And newcomers were allowed to immediately talk with players on the field.

The Ducks took the lead from Stanford twice in the opener but the Indians prevailed 19-15. Three successive victories followed, beginning with a muddy Friday-night contest against Idaho, a 21-7 triumph.

USC fell to the Ducks for the first time since 1915, in a 20-6 showcase for Curtis Mecham's passing and running game. The Duck defense did its part, twice halting Trojan drives. Mecham's performance against the Trojans earned him praise not only from Los Angeles sportswriters but also from Fox Movietone News, which featured him in a newsreel as a "five-star back."

A 19-7 victory over California was a major shot in the arm for Oregon's Rose Bowl hopes. It showed that the 3-1 Ducks were living up to their preseason billing, but losses to UCLA and Washington State took much of the shine off Oregon's luster. A welcome week's layoff followed the WSC contest. Then the Ducks traveled up the valley to a midweek Armistice Day date with Santa Clara.

Bronco assistant coach Len Casanova got his first look at an Oregon team from the bench, and it nearly became the winner's side of the field. Oliver's new man-in-motion play confused the Bronco defense and aided Roblin in completing two touchdown passes to Crish. Santa Clara made an afternoon of it and after falling behind 14-0, the Ducks escaped Portland with a 21-19 victory.

Another gritty effort followed in Seattle, with the Ducks prevailing 19-16.

The Ducks had high hopes of upsetting a Rose Bowl contender in the Civil War, and possibly contending for the bowl bid themselves. Washington and Washington State remained in the title picture as well, but the Beavers recovered an Oregon fumble to seal the 12-7 victory and earn their first PCC title.

"We should've beaten them," said Ed Moshofsky, who started at tackle in three Civil Wars. "We'd beaten them the year before. They had much the same team, and I think we had a better team than we did in '40."

While the Beavers prepared for Pasadena, the Ducks had an appointment in Austin, Texas. The Longhorns had been considered one of the top teams in the nation during the regular season and hoped for a Rose Bowl bid. But as PCC champion and host school, OSC had the option of selecting its opponent and chose Duke; 6-11 Texas didn't even make OSC's short list of potential foes.

Thus an angry Texas team awaited the Ducks. The Longhorns publicly rejected invitations to any other bowl games, opting to concentrate on their meeting with the other Oregon team from the PCC. "When the Longhorns announced their decision . . . it gave followers fair warning the Texans were pointing toward a decisive victory over their Pacific Coast Conference rivals," the Associated Press later reported.

The Texans achieved just that in a 71-7 pasting, Oregon's worst football loss to that point. Dana X. Bible's 'Horns allowed Oregon only one touchdown and point-after and rang up 10 touchdowns of their own.

The next day AP reported that Oregon students and fans were taking the beating in stride: There was no talk of staff "shakeup or reorganization" among fans and no such announcements from UO athletic officials. But by noon Oregon time, the wires were full of far more crucial reports from higher-ranking sources, and the previous day's disaster at Austin had become a matter of mere trivia. It was Sunday, December 7, 1941.

The Ducks were boarding their train in Austin when they learned of the Japanese attack on Pearl Harbor. They were en route to Eugene when they heard of President Roosevelt's "day of infamy" speech and Congressional declarations of war against the Axis nations.

Moshofsky said his memories of that long trip home from Texas are vague, but he recalled "a general realization by all of us fellows" that their lives had suddenly and dramatically changed. America now was engaged in a

Eleven months after the bombing of Pearl Harbor, the University of Oregon football team hosted undefeated UCLA for its homecoming.

The Ducks, severely depleted by World War II officer training program recruitment, had won only one of their first four

Ed Moshofsky

games and weren't given much of a chance against the mighty Bruins.

UCLA was led by All-America and future pro quarterback Bob Waterfield, and seemed all-but certain to claim the 1942 Pacific Coast Conference title.

But what Oregon lacked in experience and depth, it made up for in determination and hustle.

The Ducks stopped the Bruins on their first two drives, then took a surprising quick 7-0 lead in two plays.

First, Tom Roblin took off on a spectacular 51-yard romp. Then single-wing halfback Bob Reynold threw a 29-yard touchdown pass to end Jim Shepard, who carried a UCLA defender on his back for the final four yards of his journey to the end zone.

The Bruins tied the game midway through the third quarter, when Waterfield hit Al Solari to cap a 96-yard march. They were driving for what would have been the go-ahead score in the fourth quarter when

Oregon's defense changed the course of the game.

Oregon defensive end Pete Torchia broke threw the UCLA line and nearly got to Waterfield, forcing him to throw a desperation pass on the run.

Reynolds was waiting for it on his own 5, and after juggling the ball for nearly 10 yards, returned the interception 37 yards.

Reynolds stayed on the field and took up where he left off, breaking loose on a 31-yard run that set up Roblin's touchdown run a few plays later. Roblin finished the game with 151 yards rushing—26 more than the entire Bruins team.

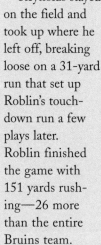

UCLA threatened one more time, but Bill Davis' interception sealed Oregon's 14-7 victory.

UCLA's Bruins were the Ducks' Homecoming guests, and Roblin & Co. spoiled the day for the eventual Rose Bowl representatives. It was Oregon's last civilian football victory until 1945. Two tough contests remained in the 1942 campaign. USC steamrolled the Ducks 40-0 the following week and defending conference champion OSC closed out PCC competition for both schools for the duration with a 38-2 win.

RISING TO THE OCCASION AND TRIUMPHING OVER SEEMINGLY UNBEATABLE ODDS HAVE LONG BEEN HALLMARKS OF THE OREGON FOOTBALL PROGRAM. THE EVENTS OF THAT 1942 WARTIME FOOTBALL SEASON ARE INDELIBLY ETCHED INTO ED MOSHOFSKY'S MEMORY, BECAUSE HE FACED THE GIANTS ON THE FRONT LINE. A THREE-SEASON STARTER, MOSHOFSKY PLAYED TACKLE FOR THE WEBFOOTS. HIS TEAM'S COURAGE AND CONFIDENCE IN THE UPSET AGAINST UCLA ARE QUALITIES HE REMEMBERS PROUDLY.

"WE HADN'T ANY DEPTH," HE SAID OF THE 42 TEAM. "IN ADDITION TO SO MANY FELLOWS HAVING ALREADY GONE INTO THE SERVICE, WE HAD A LOT OF INJURIES—GUYS WITH ARMS IN SLINGS, CASTS, AND SO FORTH. WE LITERALLY DIDN'T KNOW FROM WEEK TO WEEK IF WE COULD FINISH THE SEASON."

THE WIN OVER UCLA WAS THE UNIVERSITY'S LAST CIVILIAN FOOTBALL VICTORY UNTIL AFTER THE WAR'S END. FOOTBALL WAS SUSPENDED IN THE 1943 AND '44 SEASONS. MOSHOFSKY COMPLETED HIS ADVANCED ROTC COURSES, THEN JOINED OTHER WEBFOOTS, BEAVERS, BRUINS, AND MANY MORE IN COMMON CAUSE ON THE BATTLEFIELDS OF EUROPE AND THE PACIFIC.

"IF A PERSON WANTS TO PUT SOMETHING TOGETHER BADLY ENOUGH, HE CAN DO IT," SAID MOSHOFSKY.

THE CAN-DO SPIRIT OF THOSE DETERMINED YOUNG MEN ON A EUGENE FOOTBALL FIELD EXEMPLIFIED THE SPIRIT OF A GENERATION THAT WOULD TRIUMPH IN A GLOBAL WAR AGAINST TYRANNY.

RIGHT: DUCK LOGO, 1943 OREGANA.

global war of survival, and the urgencies of such a war would take many men from the university in the coming months.

Last Season of the Duration

One of the first to go into World War II service was WWI veteran Tex Oliver. Stepping in to fill his shoes as interim coach was former letterman John Warren. Warren was first hired in 1935 out of a successful Astoria High School program to serve as freshmen football, basketball and baseball coach at Oregon.

In his nine years at Astoria, Warren coached the Fighting Fishermen to a 52-11-6 football record and to four state basketball titles. His hoop teams in the early 1930s provided several key members of Oregon's 1939 NCAA champion "Tall Firs," including starting guards Bobby Anet and Wally Johansen.

Warren inherited a team with high hopes for a PCC championship. But depleted manpower due to graduation and the war helped dash title hopes during the last season in which Oregon would field a PCC football team until after the war's end.

Oliver was a familiar sight on the sideline—at least for one game—as the opposing coach in the season opener at Portland. Lt. Cmdr. Tex Oliver, USN, coached an all-star service team, St. Mary's Navy Pre-flight, to a 10-9 victory over the draft-depleted Ducks.

WSC salvaged a 7-0 victory at Pullman, and Washington prevailed 15-7 before a relatively sparse Multnomah Stadium crowd of 15,000. The first of two Duck victories came against Idaho, in an effort sparked by Nowling's two touchdown catches with Bob Reynolds and Roy Erickson sharing quarterbacking duties in the 28-0 victory. Roblin scored the only UO touchdown in a 20-7 Halloween loss to California.

UCLA's Bruins were the Ducks' Homecoming guests, and Roblin & Co. spoiled the day for the eventual Rose Bowl representatives. It was Oregon's last civilian football victory until 1945. Two tough contests remained in the 1942 campaign. USC steamrolled the Ducks 40-0 the following week and defending conference champion OSC closed out

PCC competition for both schools for the duration with a 38-2 win.

"A lot of people had graduated from the '41 team and the war did its part in calling guys away, so that '42 season was a rough one." Moshofsky recalled. "We didn't have a lot of depth anyway, we had guys playing with their arms in slings and that sort of thing."

The War Years

The numbers continued to dwindle. Moshofsky took advanced Army officer-training courses and then went into the service after the 1942 season, as did many teammates and other college men. Small numbers of potential players turned out for practice on the playing fields of Eugene and Corvallis before the 1943 season. It became quickly, painfully evident to coaches that normal football competition would be virtually impossible. Oregon withdrew its program from the PCC with Oregon State following suit a few days later.

Other conference schools with larger enrollments and large, campus-based officer-training programs were able to continue playing ball as they had in peacetime. But UO fans had to settle for an ROTC-based "Armyduck" unit coached by Warren.

The Armyducks went winless through a four-game schedule, dropping contests with Willamette University's Navycats and a Salt Lake Air Base squadron. The Coos Bay-based 104th Cavalry unit took both games of a home-and-home series.

Student demand for varsity-level competition remained. The September 29, 1944, edition of the *Oregon Daily Emerald* featured an open letter to Warren on the subject: "What happened to football? A traditional activity at most universities and at Oregon. There are some 270-odd men on the campus of which many would be glad to participate. It makes little difference whether they play Washington University or University High School just as long as they play.

"There are many smaller universities with male enrollments that still manage to field teams. This may be the last chance for many to participate at Oregon or for

ABOVE: JAKE LEICHT WAS AN ALL-AMERICA HALFBACK FOR OREGON IN 1945.

Oliver, Football Returns

The victorious veterans, Coach Oliver and varsity football returned to Oregon shortly after V-J Day. Oliver was the only prewar PCC coach to enter the military. He had set up an eight-team league in Honolulu early in the war and coached the 1944 Navy All-Stars to victory over their Army counterparts in the Poi Bowl.

Oliver stayed with the single wing, though a 1945 rule change allowed passing from anywhere behind the line of scrimmage, helping to facilitate use of the exciting new "T" formation.

That first postwar season was a disjointed one. Young rookies mixed on the field with older, battle-hardened war vets in their middle-to-late 20s. Those veterans gradually returned to the practice field from the battlefield, and it was mid-season before Oliver had his entire squad on hand.

One newcomer quickly made an impact—halfback Jake Leicht. The 159-pound triple threat led the 1945 Ducks in rushing, passing and scoring. He could run 100 yards in 9.6 seconds, which also helped him shine on defense. Leicht's 10 interceptions for 202 yards in 1945 remained a school record nearly five decades later. Though a sophomore, Leicht brought bowl-game experience to the Ducks. He played for Morse's Randolph Field team in the 1944 Cotton Bowl tie with Texas.

Weak line play blunted Oregon's offense somewhat while enabling opponents to roll up 124 points and two shutouts. Washington dumped the Ducks 20-6 in the opener, but the Ducks quickly recovered to rout Idaho 33-7 in their first postwar Hayward Field appearance.

In the first of two Civil War encounters, OSC prevailed 19-6. The following week against WSC, Leicht had his first of two three-interception games for the season, and the Ducks beat the Cougars 26-13. UCLA took a 12-0 triumph at the Coliseum, and Washington made it two for Oregon on the year with a 7-0 victory at Portland. WSC evened the score in a rematch at Pullman 20-13.

Against California, Leicht again came up with three picks to help Oregon upset the Golden Bears 20-13 on their home turf. OSC took round two of the Civil War series with a 13-12 victory at Eugene, leaving the Ducks

that matter to participate at all."

Despite the *Emerald's* urging, military football remained the order of the day in the fall of 1944. The Armyducks improved to 2-2 with victories over the 104th Cavalry and losses to the Navycats and the airmen from Salt Lake.

Three Ducks played in wartime all-star games. Tackle Dick Ashcom and guards Floyd Rhea and Bill Mayther went to San Francisco for the 1944 Shrine game. Mayther also played at center in the 1944 and 1945 College All-Star contests.

Warren, having served his interim coaching stint, soon became known as the Ducks' "utility coach," stepping in at one time or other as head varsity coach for each major sport at the University. He retired from active coaching in 1951 after three seasons as UO head basketball coach, then became the owner of a hardware and sporting-goods store in Eugene.

3-6 for the season and seventh in the PCC.

Leicht won several rare honors for a first-year player: All-PCC, New York Sun All-American, and Shrine team. His return in 1946, along with other experienced teammates, caused observers to expect an improved record.

Oliver's Final Season Fizzles

Newcomers from the GI ranks continued to emerge at Hayward Field, where Oliver greeted 14 transfers when 1946 practice sessions began. End Larry Stoeven had played for USC in the 1944 Rose Bowl while enrolled in the school's Navy V-12 officer-training program.

Oliver also welcomed back such prewar standouts as Duke Iverson, who was a Service All-Star at the Jacksonville (Fla.) Naval Air Station. Iverson was joined by fellow Jacksonville all-star center Brad Ecklund, one of many war veterans to make a major mark on Duck football in the postwar years.

College of the Pacific, led by 84-year-old football pioneer Amos Alonzo Stagg, came to Eugene for the season opener. It was the first meeting between the Ducks and the Tigers from Stockton, California, and Oregon claimed a narrow 7-6 triumph. The optimistic Ducks returned to Berkeley and came home with a 14-13 upset under their belts.

The following Saturday, Montana got a 34-0 Homecoming beating at Hayward Field. The WSC encounter, also in Eugene, proved to be the archetypical scoreless tie on a muddy field. The only scoring threat was a futile Duck field-goal attempt in the first quarter. Next, a mighty ground game led by Reynolds, Newquist and Leicht yielded a 26-13 victory over Idaho.

At mid-season the Ducks stood 4-0-1, undefeated in conference play. That was as good as it would get, as they absorbed four losses to conclude the season. USC mauled its visitors 43-0, and its crosstown rival UCLA scored twice in the second half to earn a 14-0 victory at Portland. Washington beat the Ducks 16-0, and 22,000 fans watched Oregon State win its ninth Civil War in 10 attempts, 13-0.

According to the 1947 Oregana, Oliver had expressed dissatisfaction during the season with University athletic officials. On the other hand, football fans were expressing growing dissatisfaction with him.

Changes were in order on the Oregon campus in the postwar atmosphere of 1947. Those changes would come quickly, in great number, and with long-lasting effects, as Oliver and the University's governing athletic board made way for a couple of men named Aiken and Harris.

Oregon Hires a Real AD

Jim Aiken was a product of an American football hotbed—the Allegheny Mountain region of Ohio and western Pennsylvania. He was a Washington & Jefferson University graduate and member of the president's 1922 Rose Bowl team, which held California to a scoreless tie.

The W&J first string stayed in that entire game, though, and Aiken didn't get to play. It was a strange omen for a man who 26 years later would be denied a Rose Bowl opportunity as Oregon's coach due to circumstances involving the Golden Bears.

In the early 1930s, Jim Aiken coached McKinley High School of Canton, Ohio, to victory in three of four games against future NFL legend Paul Brown's squad from nearby Massillon, in a rivalry older than the Rose Bowl.

Later, he moved up to the collegiate ranks, coaching winning teams at Akron and the University of Nevada. It was in Reno that Aiken attracted the attention of Leo Harris, new Oregon athletic director, and the two joined forces to change Duck athletic fortunes in a rapidly changing postwar era.

Harris had come to Eugene from Carmel, California, where he was superintendent of schools. He brought a strong athletic background to Oregon, having played tackle at Stanford, championship football and basketbal at Fresno High School, and on two Far West Conference title teams at Fresno State College in the mid-1930s.

The hiring of Leo Harris as athletic director was a major shift of direction in UO athletics. The decision was made by Harry K. Newburn, president of the University from 1945 to 1953. For the first time a real athletic director would be in charge of athletics; he would report to the president; and he would have the authority over all aspects of athletics.

The athletic council was killed as Newburn felt that such committees only interfered in the business of the University, and athletics was a business of the University. Student influence and the paying of coaches with student money came to an end. Fund raising and gate receipts would pay the bills, and to do this, success in athletics was mandatory. Harris, who had a big job ahead of him, would preside over an unprecedented 20 years of growth and innovation.

Harris got his tenure off to an unusual and historic start: With a handshake, he secured from Walt Disney the use of Donald Duck as the University mascot.

Previous UO-related "duck" logos had featured many generic varieties of the picturesque waterfowl. A live duck, "Puddles," began appearing with the rally squad at athletic events in the 1930s, according to University archivist Keith Richard. "I think we went from 'Puddles I' to 'Puddles V' before the Humane Society complained," Richard said.

In 1940, a Donald-like rendering appeared in the football "Duck Dope" press guide. Three years later, Disney allowed use of Donald's likeness for a one-time appearance in the *Oregana*. But the 1947 Disney-Harris pact ensured a more permanent relationship—nay, love affair—between the feisty Donald and the world of Mighty Oregon.

Aiken made two revolutionary changes of his own. The first was to bring in a new "T" formation offense to replace the single wing of the Oliver years. The second was to bring up a bench-warmer from Oliver's last year to run that offense.

In 1946, Norm Van Brocklin played just 11 minutes as third-string tailback and didn't win a letter. Tex Oliver's evaluation of Van Brocklin certainly fit a single wing mind set as Oliver said, "He's only a fair runner and he can't block." In 1947, he led the Ducks in passing with 939 yards and nine touchdowns, and he only ran twice, both times to escape being trapped behind the line.

That miraculous turnaround was the result of the changes in coaching and offense, and it began in the spring of 1947, shortly after Aiken arrived in Eugene.

Van Brocklin had come to Oregon with Acalanes High School teammates Robert Oas and George Bell. He told the *Emerald* he'd come to Eugene because Bell was "happier than a dead pig in the sun up here." When asked why no California school recruited him, Van Brocklin stated: "I guess they figured I was a better baseball bet, as a pitcher, than a football prospect." That pitcher quality to hit the catcher's mit surely was in the mind of Aiken when he commented that "here was a kid who could hit an end in the ear, cutting crosswise, at 50 yards. He threw the ball high and hard—very tough to intercept."

Aiken was happy to have them all. He made no secret of Van Brocklin, the wealth of returning talent elsewhere in the lineup or his Rose Bowl ambitions for the Ducks.

Duck fans first saw the new "T" offense and Van Brocklin in the home opener against Montana State. "Van" threw his first touchdown pass to end Dan Garza on the fifth play of the game, in which the Ducks defeated the Bobcats 27-13.

Then they got their three losses out of the way in as many weeks, dropping a 38-13 decision to Texas at Portland and falling to Aiken's old Nevada squad 13-6. Eventual Rose Bowl champion UCLA handed the Ducks their only PCC loss of the year 24-7.

Next Van Brocklin, senior Leicht, Garza, Ecklund and tackle Don Stanton paced the Ducks through six straight victories. Washington was the first to fall in a 6-0 Multnomah Stadium contest. Offense ruled the day when Oregon hosted favored San Francisco and dethroned the Dons 34-7.

Then, on a typical November trip to the Palouse country—bitterly cold, snowy and foggy—Garza blocked a punt for Oregon's first touchdown in the 12-6 victory over

the game on a chartered "Oregon Webfoot Special." The PCC gave permission for UO to pay the expenses of the wives of the players and coaches as well as those of University administrators and state officials. At Love Field, a crowd of Texas greeters waited, bearing ceremonial gifts including 10-gallon hats for players and coaches.

The sports information director at the University of Washington challenged the playing of the game. As he defined the Rose Bowl pact with the Big Nine, such games were barred. The PCC stated that the game would proceed.

In December, soon after the game was set, the UO offered to share with the PCC its take from the Cotton Bowl game. No rule required the share although California was obligated to share its take from the Rose Bowl with the rest of the PCC. The PCC officials took several days to make a decision on the UO offer and finally accepted it.

Aiken ran vigorous workouts in preparation for the game, Oregon's first against SMU, which boasted Heisman Trophy and Maxwell Award-winning quarterback Doak Walker and All-American back Kyle Rote on a 9-1 team.

The Ducks were ranked ninth in AP's final poll. *The Oregonian* and *United Press* both picked Oregon to win the game, citing the Ducks' strong backfield and passing attacks. But after December 29 scrimmages, gloomy coaches Aiken and SMU's Matty Bell each predicted his own team would lose. Bell said the Mustangs would fall by two or more touchdowns, saying they had never faced a "T" formation with a quarterback like Van Brocklin. Missouri had used a split-"T" to hand SMU its only regular-season loss. Aiken countered that the Ducks wouldn't be able to stop Walker with the defense displayed in their scrimmage.

Old Aiken friend and coaching rival Paul Brown, at the time the head coach of the Cleveland Browns, loaned five members of the pro outfit to teach the Ducks their squad's defensive scheme—adopted by Aiken specifically for the Cotton Bowl. Aiken had used the Browns' offensive plays for two years with Van Brocklin at the controls.

New Year's Day 1949 at last arrived, and 69,000 fans packed the Cotton Bowl for the long-awaited showdown.

Since the UO band did not accompany the team to Texas the Kilgore Rangerettes represented the UO at half time. They had arranged a 1,600-card stunt section that, in one of its displays, revealed a Duck in lemon yellow and green looking content. But the cards were slowly reversed to show the backside, and the Duck had a hoof print on his

bottom, left by an SMU Mustang.

SMU took a 7-0 lead on a 1-yard run by Walker before intermission. Rote's 36-yard run and Walker's PAT upped the Mustang lead to 14-0 early in the second half, but Oregon rallied for its first score with 12:23 left in the game, on a 24-yard toss from Van Brocklin to Wilkins.

Down 21-6, Oregon mounted a strong fourth-period comeback drive beginning with a 41-yard Van Brocklin pass to Darrell Robinson and culminating with Sanders' plunge for the touchdown at 6:20. But the Ducks came up a touchdown short.

Statistically, the Ducks led the Mustangs offensively in every way but the 21-13 final tally. Van Brocklin outshined the award-winning Walker with 149 passing yards to Walker's 79. Wilkins was the game's leading receiver, with four catches for 57 yards. Close behind was Robinson with three for 56. Bell and SMU's Rote led rushers with 93 yards each. Sanders and Lewis each carried 12 times for 63 yards.

The close loss was a tough one for the Ducks to absorb. Guard Jim Berwick noted that both Doak Walker and UO President Harry Newburn had January 1 birthdays. "We gave a present to the wrong guy," Berwick bitterly told reporters.

Longtime *Register-Guard* sports editor Dick Strite

The 1948 Duck football team was loaded with talent, but the players will tell you it was their combined efforts that turned what could have been just another average season into one of the greatest in Oregon football history.

"Teamwork was the key to our success," Fullback Bob Sanders recalled years later. "We had our stars, but it took the entire

Fullback #45, Bob Sanders

unit to get the job done."

They were a diverse group of men— many of them World War II veterans— who used their special talents and a tremendous will-to-win to produce a 9-1 regular season record, a tie for the PCC title and a New Year's trip to the Cotton Bowl in Dallas.

With prolific All-America quarterback Norm Van Brocklin as its leader, it was no surprise the offense boasted a strong passing game. But the Webfoot backfield, made up of Sanders and halfbacks George Bell, Woodley Lewis and John McKay, was rated as one of the best in the nation as well.

Van Brocklin's pinpoint passes, McKay's speedy, slashing elusiveness, and the powerful inside runs and line bucks of Bell, Lewis and Sanders were simply too much for Oregon's opponents to handle.

The offensive line, one of the best ever to play at Oregon, deserves much of the credit. In fact, it was the line's versatility that enabled the Duck offense to make full use of its formidable ground-gaining and aerial attacks.

Tackles Steve Dotur and Don Stanton, guards Ed Chrobot and Ted Meland and center Brad Ecklund were as quick and fierce with downfield blocks on pass plays or long runs as they were tough and tenacious at the line of scrimmage. In a crucial 8-7 victory over USC in Portland, they opened holes that led to a stellar 181-yard rushing performance. All told, the 1948 Ducks outscored their opponents by a 207-103 margin. Naturally, the defense had something to do with it as well. Particularly effective were end Wayne Bartholemy and back DeWayne "Swede" Johnson, both of whom helped stymie opponents' drives by coming up with interceptions at key moments.

Bartholemy returned an interception 43 yards for a touchdown to seal a 20-12 victory at Stanford in the second game of the season, and Johnson halted an SMU drive at Oregon's 7-yard-line to help hold the powerful Mustang offense to one touchdown before halftime in the Cotton Bowl.

Johnson, an avid student of the game, was also known for making astute on-the-field analysis—a key element in the Ducks' come-from-behind victories over Stanford and St. Mary's.

Indeed, these Ducks, like their 1994 counterparts, were known for coming up with creative ways to win. Oregon's '48 squad also fought off stiff challenges in the late going from USC and Washington.

Their only regular-season loss came at the hands of national champion Michigan, and they made SMU fight for its life in a 21-13 Cotton Bowl triumph, prevailing in every statistical category except points.

ABOVE: DUCK LOGO, 1948 OREGANA.

PLAYING FOOTBALL FOR THE DUCKS MERELY WHETTED BOB SANDERS' APPETITE FOR SUCCESS. HE NOW OWNS EIGHT LUMBER MILLS IN OREGON AND WASHINGTON. KEY COMPETITIVE STRATEGIES, SUCH AS INNOVATION AND KEEPING A WATCHFUL EYE ON THE COMPETITION, HAVE GIVEN BOB AN EDGE IN THE LUMBER MANUFACTURING BUSINESS.

THROUGH HIS STRING OF ACCOMPLISHMENTS, THIS ENTREPRENEUR FROM A SMALL TOWN NEAR COOS BAY REMAINS A MODEST MAN WHO MUST BE PRODDED TO TALK ABOUT HIMSELF.

WHEN ASKED TO RECALL HIS GREATEST OREGON FOOTBALL MOMENT, HE RESPONDED BY TALKING ABOUT THE EXPLOITS OF HIS TEAMMATES.

EVER LOYAL TO HIS ALMA MATER, BOB IS A MAJOR CONTRIBUTOR TO THE DUCK ATHLETIC FUND. OVER THE YEARS, HIS GENEROSITY HAS HELPED MAKE SUCCESS POSSIBLE FOR DOZENS OF UNIVERSITY OF OREGON ATHLETES.

Bob Sanders

called them the finest group of athletes ever assembled on a football team in the state of Oregon.

"Most of us were combat veterans in our mid- or late-20s, a focused and determined bunch of men," Garza said. "We didn't ever get really psyched up for any game and certainly not the Cotton Bowl—especially after wanting to go to Pasadena. We just went into each battle, each game, without a lot of fuss and rah-rah, and got the job done."

The 1948 Ducks played just four of their 10 regular-season games at home, one of those in Portland. They came from behind to win six of those games, scared the national champions, and made their Cotton Bowl foe fight to preserve its victory.

Their efforts helped catapult Oregon into the modern era of big-time football, and the Cotton Bowl berth yielded other far-reaching results. Garza credits Harris with having the foresight to purchase, with bowl monies, a tract of land on the north bank of the Willamette River across from the campus. Upon that tract today sits Autzen Stadium.

The 13th Cotton Bowl was the most profitable up to that time. The Ducks earned $108,912.47, while California's take on the Rose Bowl was $80,000. Oregon gave the PCC the difference—$28,912.47. In addition the UO got a $10,000 share of the Rose Bowl earnings, the same as all PCC members received. Thus the Ducks enjoyed a $90,000 payday and Leo Harris made a deposit on the future with the winnings.

Aiken earned national attention amid rumors that he and longtime Oregon State mentor Lon Stiner were contenders for the head-coaching vacancy at Nebraska. At that time, Aiken had no UO contract; he had been hired on a year-by-year basis.

After a week of speculation, Aiken canceled a planned trip to Lincoln and announced that he was not a candidate for the Cornhusker vacancy. He got a contract with the University of Oregon to replace his original 1947 contract. His pay was increased from $7,500 per year to $9,000.

More postseason competition loomed for selected Ducks. Wilkins, Berwick and DeCourcey were tapped for the first Hula Bowl classic at Honolulu. Tackle Steve Dotur went to the Shrine team and Van Brocklin was named starting quarterback for the College All-Stars in Chicago.

The professional ranks beckoned many as well. All 11 Cotton Bowl starters, and several reserves, were offered pro contracts. As a junior, Garza himself was drafted by the New York Giants and after graduation spent three seasons with the former NFL New York Yanks.

Van Brocklin completed a four-year course of study in three years, graduating with the class of '49. Speculation that the "great Dutchman" would return to Eugene for his senior year of eligibility ended when he received his diploma and a contract with the Los Angeles Rams, which drafted him fourth. He finished his UO career as the first Duck to achieve a 1,000-yard season (1948) and finished with 1,949 passing yards and 18 touchdowns. He completed 144 of 316 pass attempts for a .455 percentage.

The "Dutchman" passed for a record 554 yards in a game against the Yanks in 1951, taking the Rams to the NFL title and then repeated the title role at Philadelphia in 1960, bringing the Eagles up from a cellar-dwelling Eastern Division finish the previous season.

Van Brocklin retired as a player after the 1960 championship and became head coach of the expansion Minnesota Vikings. He resigned early in 1967 and spent a year as a TV broadcaster for the New Orleans Saints before moving to the head coaching spot at Atlanta in 1968.

He was the first Oregon letterman inducted into the National Football Foundation Hall of Fame. Other latter-day honors included the 1968 Leo Harris Trophy as alumni "Man of the Year," based on service to the University and the community. In 1992, a veteran panel of sportswriters, University staff and fans named Van Brocklin to *The Register-Guard* all-time Oregon All-Star team, and the UO Athletic Hall of Fame.

Van Brocklin died in 1983.

Title Defense Fizzles

Big things were expected from the defending PCC co-champions in 1949, despite losing a number of key players to graduation. Returnees would be counted upon to keep the Ducks competitive in a tight conference race.

Cotton Bowl backs McKay, Lewis, Sanders and Bell returned to the lineup. Sanders would become the PCC's

leading rusher at season's end. The 1949 Ducks would be the highest-scoring team in school history to that date, with an average of 25 points a game.

Competition was fierce in the quest to succeed Van Brocklin, but Earl Stelle emerged as the top signal-caller after late-summer drills. He led the Ducks in their season opener against St. Mary's—the first night game ever played at San Francisco's Kezar Stadium. The Ducks scored all their points before St. Mary's could get on the scoreboard, and the 24-7 victory was Oregon's second in a row over the Gaels.

The Ducks then ripped Idaho 41-0 for their ninth straight regular-season victory.

The streak was broken a week later, as UCLA won a 35-27 shootout in the Coliseum—the first conference loss for Oregon in nearly two years. Stelle put on an air show of record-setting proportions, completing 10 of 12. It was the Oregon individual, single-game record for the first 100 years.

The defense rebounded a week later, however, shutting out Washington State in a 21-0 victory at Pullman with Sanders scoring two touchdowns.

The Ducks returned to Hayward Field for a break from conference play for their first meeting with Colorado, and won 42-14. It was Oregon's last victory of the season, and the Ducks would taste victory just once again in the remaining season-and-a-half of Aiken's tenure.

The Hayward Field attendance record of 23,500 was set in 1949 for the Civil War, won by OSC 20-10. With the Beavers leading 20-3 in the fourth quarter, Lewis again thrilled Duck fans by fielding a punt and returning it a school-record 92 yards for Oregon's only touchdown.

He finished the season with a 43-yard kickoff-return average on nine returns for 389 yards—and those skills stood him in good stead during a long pro career with the Rams and expansion-era Dallas Cowboys.

Sanders was the team's scoring and rushing leader, with 10 touchdowns and 726 net yards. McKay's school-record average of six yards per carry in two Duck seasons was an individual career record as the Ducks entered their 100th year of football. It was one of many notable achievements in a long football career as a player and coach. McKay remained in Eugene for nine seasons as a UO assistant coach and went to USC as an assistant in 1959.

A year later, McKay began a 15-year run as one of college football's winningest coaches with three national titles and eight Rose Bowl appearances. McKay left USC in 1976 to coach the NFL's new Tampa Bay Buccaneers.

Commencement took a heavy toll on the 1949 Oregon program, as the last of the WWII veterans departed. The 1950 team's average age of 20 was down four years from the 1948 average. At the same time, the new conflict in Korea meant that draft calls would again impact college-football ranks.

1950

Aiken's Last Season

The 1950 season began as a "building year," with new uniforms and many new players to fill them, though Stelle returned as quarterback and a number of promising sophomores appeared.

New backfield coach McKay was greeted by 24 candidates for four openings, and the season was marked by frequent changes in backfield personnel. Aiken remained optimistic, telling an Oregon Club luncheon that his 1950 squad was "the most hustling one" he'd ever had. "No one is going to push us around," he said. But strong performances by the newcomers and All-Coast honoree Stelle fell short, and 1950 went down in the books as the Ducks' only modern-day, one-victory season.

After the Beavers defeated the Ducks 14-2 in the Civil War, the State Board of Higher Education's Building committee approved building plans for a new Duck stadium to be built just east of Hayward Field after the Korean War ended, and government restrictions on new construction were lifted.

Harris had recognized the need for a new football venue upon his arrival three years earlier, and immediately began planning. A 1949-50 architects' study yielded overall plans for a 52,000-seat facility, whose first phase would consist of two covered grandstands seating 27,200 spectators.

New bleachers seating 4,600 already had been purchased to replace Hayward Field's old south bleachers and the crumbling north-end "horseshoe" grandstand, which had been demolished after the 1949 season. Those bleachers would be used at the new plant until permanent stands brought the structure to its full planned capacity.

However, potential traffic problems and the need to use the land for other University buildings caused officials to scrap the idea of a stadium east of Agate Street. That's where the "Cotton Bowl land" across the river would come into the picture, but not for several years.

Aiken's days as Duck mentor were numbered. There had been rumors of improprieties in his program, especially with regard to recruiting practices and illegal team workouts. Aiken resigned in June 1951.

LEFT:
CHET DANIELS LED THE NATION IN FIELD GOALS IN 1948 AND PLAYED IN THE 1949 COTTON BOWL.

HEAD COACH
LEN CASANOVA
(left), ASSISTANT
JOHN MCKAY AND
QUARTERBACK
JACK CRABTREE
CONFER ON THE
SIDELINE DURING
THE 1958 ROSE
BOWL AGAINST
OHIO STATE.

THE LEN CASANOVA ERA

Oregon football was at its lowest ebb when the Ducks placed their gridiron fortunes in the hands of Leonard J. Casanova. It might have been the most significant athletic hiring ever made by the University.

"Cas," as he has been called by Oregon followers over the past half century, is a beloved father figure who took the Ducks to some of their greatest football successes. He did it in a manner that led him to become the most respected and admired person in Duck athletic history.

He would eventually lead the Ducks to three bowl games—including Oregon's only Rose Bowl appearance in a span of 75 years—and coach some of the greatest players the Ducks would ever send on a field. But it was hard to envision that kind of result when he took over the floundering program.

Oregon had lost 14 of its previous 15 games before Casanova took over, which is why Leo Harris was in the market for a new coach. Anxious as Casanova was to leave his current job at Pittsburgh, he wasn't sure Oregon offered the best out.

"They showed me the film of the spring football game. There wasn't much there," Casanova said, but UO officials "told me they had a tremendous group of freshmen coming in, so I took the job."

Casanova had made a name for himself at Santa Clara, culminating in the underdog Broncos defeating Kentucky in the 1950 Orange Bowl. Pittsburgh had lured Casanova away from Santa Clara, but one season in the East convinced him he wanted to move back to the Pacific Coast.

"Pittsburgh's facilities were terrible, and part of my contract was that they would be improved," Casanova said. "The school changed chancellors and it didn't happen."

With Jim Aiken's resignation, the Ducks were in a bind for a coach. A member of the always-important Portland Duck Club started a push for his former high school coach, Casanova, which eventually led to his hiring.

John McKay was held over from Aiken's staff, and Casanova brought longtime aide Jack Roche with him from Pittsburgh. Has there ever been a trio of coaches who dealt better with players and people?

"All the stories you hear over the years are about the

way Cas felt for his players," said Phil McHugh, who played four years for Cas and was later an assistant coach for a decade. "Having played for Cas, Jack Roche and John McKay, I know there really was a camaraderie among the players and the coaches. It was very special. I had a chance to see it from both sides. Cas really did care for the guys as individuals, as students, as people."

Starting virtually from nothing, Casanova compiled a record of 82-73-8, and the team went 47-31-4 in his last eight seasons. Twenty-one of his last 31 losses were by nine points or less.

"Year in, year out, we weren't the greatest bunch of athletes in the conference, but Cas could get everybody to believe that any time you went out to play you had a chance to win, and we would buy that," McHugh said. "Whomever we played, USC or UCLA . . . we still had a chance to win and that's the way we would go play. He made you believe that that was what you were there to do—win."

The number of victories and close losses was all the more remarkable considering Casanova's Ducks played only 46 of their 163 games in Eugene, due to the meager 20,000 capacity of Hayward Field. Thirty-three of Oregon's "home" games were played in Portland. "That was just something you had to live with," said Casanova.

1951

Rebuilding with Freshmen

The first game of the 1951 season, against Stanford in Portland's Multnomah Stadium, set the tone for the Casanova Era. Oregon was rebuilding, and of the 38 Ducks who played that day, 11 were freshmen who were again eligible for varsity play because so many older players had been called to serve in the Korean War.

"There were a lot of seniors on the 1950 team, and a lot of the would-be sophomores and juniors went to Korea," recalled Barney Holland, a sophomore in 1951. "We also played some walk-ons. We were very young, inexperienced and not very good."

In retrospect, it may not have been good planning to open against Stanford, which would go on to represent the Pacific Coast Conference in the Rose Bowl that year. Were the Ducks overmatched? Yes. Overwhelmed? Hardly.

Stanford got more than it bargained for in a 27-20 victory.

Wrote Don McLeod in *The Oregonian*: "A screaming throng of 22,849 peering at the Coast Conference inaugural action through the smoke and ashes of nearby forest fires sat in pop-eyed amazement as the gallant Ducks . . . came within a whisker of beating the Indians."

The Ducks only won two games that fall, defeating Arizona and Idaho. "We had seven freshman on offense and six on defense," recalled George Shaw, one of those first-year players. "We put a lot of gray hairs on Cas' head."

There was some talent among the youth, however, the most obvious being Shaw. In each of the victories, he intercepted three passes on his way to an NCAA record of 13.

But that season also marked the most humiliating defeat of Casanova's 16 seasons, a 63-6 lacing at the hands of Washington in Multnomah Stadium. The young Ducks, many of them injured or sick with the flu, were no match for Howie Odell's Huskies, led by "Hurryin' Hugh" McElhenny.

"That was a rough season, and the Washington game was the worst beating I ever took in a football game," said Casanova, who was prompted after the game to confront a Washington assistant with whom he'd been in the Navy. Casanova vowed to return the favor "If I ever get an opportunity."

"We needed that game," responded the UW assistant.

"You didn't need it that bad," Casanova retorted.

There was no doubt among the Ducks. "We all felt they ran the score up that day," said Ron Pheister, a freshman center. The Ducks would remember that Washington game for decades to come. The loss was one more reason the rivalry would become one of the most heated in college football during the Casanova years.

Though it went down as a 2-8 season, quarterback Hal Dunham made it memorable, setting a school record for passes attempted (189) and passes completed (182). His 296 yards passing in the lopsided Washington loss was also a record.

Another Losing Season, More Records

Again, Oregon faced one of the nation's top teams in its opener—this time, UCLA in Los Angeles. Red Sanders' Bruins would come within two points of an unbeaten season,

finishing the year ranked sixth in the country with an 8-1 record.

The Ducks stymied UCLA's vaunted single-wing attack, however, limiting the Bruins to a 13-7 victory. A pair of Jefferson High School graduates who came to Oregon together, Monte Brethauer and Emery Barnes, shined in the game for the Ducks. Barnes played so well on defense, the Bruin crowd cheered for him when he left the game.

Though Oregon suffered through another losing season with a 2-7-1 record, more passing records were broken: Hal Dunham threw a school-record 84-yard touchdown pass to Ted Anderson in a 14-6 loss to College of Pacific; George Shaw set two PCC passing records with 23 completions and 50 attempts in a 41-7 loss to California in Multnomah Stadium; and Brethauer set a school record with nine pass receptions in the Homecoming game against Washington State, which Oregon lost 19-6.

In one of the Ducks' two victories, a 21-20 victory over Stanford in Palo Alto, Shaw excelled as a receiver, pulling in passes from Barney Holland. The Ducks almost made it two straight victories to end the season, leading Oregon State 12-9 before losing 22-19 in the last Civil War played in Portland.

Ducks Strut Stuff For TV

Casanova hadn't had much luck in opening games. Going into the 1953 season opener at Nebraska, his teams had dropped seven straight openers dating back to his days at Pittsburgh and Santa Clara.

But 1953 would be different, starting with a 20-12 triumph over the Cornhuskers. The game was also the first nationally televised "Game of the Week" on network television, with NBC carrying the broadcast.

Television itself became an obstacle, when most of Monday's practice was spent posing for cameras and putting together a pregame show rather than preparing for the 'Huskers. There were going to be enough problems later in the week traveling to Lincoln, Nebraska.

The Ducks departed early Thursday morning, with a midway stop planned in Cheyenne, Wyoming, for aircraft refueling and a short practice. But Oregon flew over Wyoming about the same time as a severe thunderstorm, and most of the Ducks were woozy from airsickness when the plane landed. The workout Casanova planned was reduced to 20 minutes of wind sprints, then further travel delays put the Ducks into Lincoln around midnight.

What else could go wrong? Oregon awoke Friday to see the temperature pushing into the high 90s. But neither the heat or the earlier setbacks would affect Oregon's play, as the Ducks finally turned around Casanova's trend of losing openers.

Starting with that game, in fact, Oregon would win 11 of its next 14 opening games.

Despite their auspicious start, the Ducks were shut out in their next three contests, including a 14-6 loss to Washington. George Shaw scored twice in a 26-13 victory over San Jose State—once on a run and again on a pass reception—to end the skid. The victory also set up a great upset of USC the following week, the first of many during the Casanova Era.

Southern California came to Portland on a Halloween afternoon as the nation's fourth-ranked team, boasting a 5-0-1 record, and having averaged four touchdowns in their five victories. A 13-13 tie against Washington was all that marred the Trojans' record. The Trojans took the opening kickoff and methodically drove 83 yards, but the Ducks stopped them a foot short of a first down at the Oregon 6-yard line.

Oregon scored with 45 seconds left in the first half, as second-string quarterback Barney Holland threw a 16-yard pass to George Shaw. The Trojans came back to tie the game 7-7 shortly after halftime but later botched a punt attempt. Oregon began a drive at the USC 45-yard line and capitalized two minutes into the fourth quarter, with Walt Gaffney diving over from the 2-yard line to give the Ducks a 13-7 lead.

USC got one final chance, driving to the Oregon 23 before Dick James made a leaping interception with two minutes left. "I never appreciated an interception like the one Dick James made," Casanova said in the bedlam of the

RIGHT: WALT GAFFNEY SOARS FOR EXTRA YARDAGE IN OREGON'S 13-7 VICTORY OVER USC AT PORTLAND ON HALLOWEEN IN 1953.

UO locker room. For the first time in two years, the Trojans had lost to a league opponent. "This made up for a lot of things," Casanova said afterward.

Oregon gave up only one offensive touchdown in its final three games but could post only a 26-6 victory over Idaho. A scoreless tie with California was followed by a fifth consecutive loss to the Beavers in the Civil War, this time on an interception returned for the 7-0 final margin.

No team scored more than 14 points in 1953 against the Ducks, who yielded a stingy 8.5 points per contest during the 10-game season. Those statistics weren't reflected in Oregon's 4-5-1 record, however.

George Shaw's Star Shines Bright

Oregon has had few athletes to match the greatness of George Shaw, who completed his Duck career by leading the nation in total offense in 1954. He was the first and only University of Oregon player to receive the Pop Warner Award as the outstanding player on the West Coast.

Shaw was arguably the most versatile player in Oregon history. In his four years as a Duck, he played quarterback, flanker, halfback and safety in addition to kicking field goals, kicking off, punting and running back punts. As a freshman defensive back, he set an NCAA record for interceptions. And as a senior, most felt he should have been named an All-America quarterback, having led the nation in total offense in addition to setting school records for yards passing (1,358) and total offensive yards (1,536) in a season.

When All-America honors were announced, Ralph Guglielmi of Notre Dame was named first-team quarterback. Guglielmi had benefitted both from the national attention perennially bestowed on the Irish, and from a split among Western voters between Shaw and California's Paul Larson, who led the nation in passing yards. Shaw's reward would come in the form of a pro contract with the NFL's Baltimore Colts.

One of the great games of 1954 season put Larson and Shaw head-to-head as the Ducks met the Bears in Berkeley. Larson passed Cal to an early lead, but Shaw ran for one touchdown and passed for another to rally the Ducks back to a 33-27 victory.

ABOVE: GEORGE SHAW WAS THE NUMBER ONE DRAFT CHOICE OF THE BALTIMORE COLTS IN 1955.

Indeed, it was the year of the quarterback in the Pacific Coast Conference. John Brodie—who led Stanford to an 18-13 victory over the Ducks early in the season—would later quarterback the San Francisco 49ers.

Losses to UCLA and USC left Oregon 5-3 in the PCC—again out of the race for the Rose Bowl. But while the Ducks didn't have much success against their California opponents, they were finally champions of the Northwest with a sweep of Idaho, Washington State, Washington and Oregon State to cap a 6-4 season, the first winning record for Casanova in Eugene.

But what made 1954 so special for Casanova and those seniors who had arrived as freshmen in his inaugural season were those first victories over the Huskies and Beavers. At Seattle, the Ducks mounted a comeback with running touchdowns by Dick James, Lloyd Powell and Jasper McGee, and Shaw connected with Hal Reeve in the end zone to top off the 26-7 triumph. In his final game as a Duck, Shaw threw three touchdown passes to propel Oregon past Oregon State 33-14 in Corvallis.

Talk about exorcising some demons. The Ducks had suffered five consecutive losing seasons. And they'd suffered five consecutive defeats to their archrivals from Corvallis.

On a slippery field in Parker Stadium, those fortunes were reversed in a 33-14 thrashing that left the Ducks with a 6-4 season record, their best mark since the 9-2

Halfback Lloyd Powell tackles an opponent.

Cotton Bowl campaign of 1948.

For Coach Len Casanova, in his fourth season at Oregon, the afternoon produced the first of his four Civil War victories and the first of eight winning seasons. And it would be the last Civil War for OSU Coach Kip Taylor, replaced by Tommy Prothro after his fifth straight losing season.

It was the largest Civil War winning margin since the Ducks' 27-0 victory in 1916. Wrote *Register-Guard* sports editor Dick Strite: "At long last, Oregon defeated Oregon State in football!"

Leading the way was quarterback George Shaw who, on that afternoon, compiled enough yards to win the NCAA total offense title. He also ran back a kickoff 67 yards and returned an interception for 42.

Oregon running back Dick James scored two touchdowns, giving him 66 points for the season and tying a UO record set in 1928 by the "Flying Dutchman" Johnny Kitzmiller.

The Beavers scored first, taking a 7-0 lead. "It looked like a repeat of last year, when the underdog Staters upset the favored Webfoots 7-0," Strite wrote. But the Ducks answered with 33 points before the Beavers scored again. As it turned out, the Beavers' 14 points represented a season high for OSU and their second-highest total in 18 games. It wasn't nearly enough.

A Jasper McGee run of 13 yards gave the Ducks their first touchdown, though Shaw missed the conversion kick. No matter; the Ducks scored two more touchdowns before the first half ended, each on passes by Shaw, who finished the day with three touchdown passes on only five completions in 16 attempts.

Shaw's first touchdown pass was 49 yards to Lloyd Powell; his second, giving the Ducks a 19-7 lead with 40 seconds remaining in the first half, came on a 6-yard toss to James. The Ducks had scored 19 points in a span of six minutes and 30 seconds.

In the third quarter, McGee ran 4 yards for another Oregon touchdown. And Shaw capped the Ducks' scoring early in the fourth quarter, connecting with James on a 52-yard touchdown.

Wrote Strite: "Both dressing rooms were unusually quiet—probably because Len Casanova had confidence in his boys manufacturing the victory. Kip Taylor, who is usually prone to flowery talk, was subdued—probably because he was wishfully thinking of another upset to salvage a season that has seen eight straight defeats."

IN THE STANDS, SHAW'S ATΩ HOUSE ROOMMATE, JERRY BEALL, WAS ECSTATIC ABOUT THE VICTORY. FOR THE FIRST TIME IN HIS COLLEGE CAREER, THE DUCKS HAD DEFEATED THEIR ARCHRIVALS.

BACK IN PORTLAND, THE BEALL FAMILY BUSINESS WAS MORE ACCUSTOMED TO SCORING BIG. JERRY'S INVENTIVE FATHER, JOHN, HAD JUST DEVELOPED THE FIRST SUCCESSFUL TANK-HOPPER, TWO-WAY TRUCK TRANSPORT UNIT. BECAUSE IT WAS COMPARTMENTALIZED, IT COULD HAUL MOLASSES ONE WAY AND GRAIN ON THE RETURN TRIP. THE NEW MODEL WAS HIGHLY SUCCESSFUL IN THE 1950S AND 1960S, ENABLING WESTERN TRUCKERS TO CARRY TWO PAYLOADS, RATHER THAN ONE.

FORTY YEARS HAVE PASSED SINCE THOSE GREAT MOMENTS IN DUCK FOOTBALL AND BEALL CORPORATION HISTORY. JERRY IS CALLING THE PLAYS FROM PORTLAND NOW, AND BEALL REMAINS THE UNDISPUTED LEADER IN TANK TRAILER DESIGN AND MANUFACTURING CONCEPTS.

Jerry Beall

LEFT: DUCK ILLUSTRATION, 1954 OREGANA.

LEFT: THE 1955 COLLEGE ALL-STAR TEAM INCLUDED OREGON COACH LEN CASANOVA *(back row, fourth from right)*, QUARTERBACK GEORGE SHAW *(third row, third from left)* AND LINEMAN JACK PATERA *(second row, second from right)*.

The Ducks Take to the Ground

With George Shaw gone, the 1955 Ducks traveled more on the ground than through the air. Jack Morris, who had returned from military duty, joined Dick James in the backfield along with former North Bend sensation Jim Shanley. Together they led the Ducks to a record 2,527 yards on the ground—the best in Oregon's first 100 years. Shanley led with 711 yards, James added 596 and Morris 501.

The Ducks high hopes were dampened in the second game, however, by a 42-15 loss to Southern Cal in Los Angeles. "All I can remember was hearing that song "Fight On For USC" all afternoon," said Lon Stiner Jr., a captain and two-way lineman for the Ducks whose father had been head football coach at Oregon State.

Consecutive defeats to Washington and Colorado followed, but Oregon got back on track by beating California 21-0 in Portland. Next the Ducks came up with an 46-27 upset of Arizona, which was paced by the nation's

leading rusher, Art Lupino. Oregon extended its winning streak to four by blanking Idaho 25-0 and Washington State 35-0 for a sweep of the Palouse.

The momentum came crashing down the following week, when Stanford thrashed the Ducks 44-7 in Palo Alto, prompting disgruntled UO students to hang Casanova in effigy.

Even four inches of snow falling early in the week couldn't cool the heated mood of the Oregon players as the Ducks prepared for the Civil War game against Oregon State. And Casanova answered his critics with a 28-0 victory over the Beavers to end the season 6-4. Phil McHugh led a UO defense that held Oregon State to five first downs and 77 total yards. By contrast, Shanley and Tom Crabtree each scored twice on the ground as the Ducks rushed through the quagmire for 327 yards.

"That game will always be the biggest win for our class," said McHugh, who was a junior. "We came back from the loss at Stanford, and Cas was hung in effigy. We totally stuffed them. That's the one I will remember forever."

Few Ducks before or since felt differently about victories over the Beavers.

1956

Close Losses Cause Frustration

The 1956 season began with a monumental 35-0 victory over Colorado, a team that would go on to win the Gator Bowl. But after that, a series of narrow losses and frustrating ties relegated Oregon to a 4-4-2 record.

The Ducks couldn't have been much better in the first game against the Buffaloes, piling up a 444 total yards to Colorado's 98. But a week later, Oregon had to hold on to defeat Idaho 21-14.

Then came the frustration. Against UCLA, Oregon's Jim Shanley ran the opening kickoff almost to the end zone, only to have it nullified by a clipping penalty. The Ducks proceeded to lose four fumbles—the last of them setting UCLA's only touchdown in a 6-0 loss.

Oregon couldn't hold onto the football any better the following Saturday in Seattle, fumbling five times in a 20-7 loss to the Huskies. The losing streak reached four with defeats to Stanford and Pittsburgh.

The Ducks rebounded with a convincing 28-6 victory over California, but followed it with a 7-7 tie against Washington State, in which the Cougars scored on a 79-yard pass play in the last quarter.

Then came another epic contest against Southern California. Led by Jon Arnett, the Trojans were 6-1 when they arrived in Portland to meet the Ducks at Multnomah Stadium. Charley Tourville put Oregon ahead 6-0 with a 3-yard run in the second quarter, and somehow the Ducks made it stand.

The season ended with a 14-14 tie to Oregon State in Corvallis, sending the Beavers to the Rose Bowl and leaving the Ducks wondering why they weren't going to Pasadena themselves.

"We had a good team," said Phil McHugh, the team captain. "We were in every game but the Stanford game. We could have been 8-2 or 9-1." Given the 21 fumbles the Ducks lost—many of them instrumental in the two losses by a touchdown and two deadlocks—it was easy to see how.

ABOVE: *(left to right)* LEROY PHELPS, JIM SHANLEY, CHARLEY TOURVILLE AND LEN READ WITH JACK CRABTREE *(front)* OF THE 1957 CHAMPIONSHIP TEAM.

1957

The Ducks Finally Smell Roses

All the close calls and near misses were finally balanced for the Ducks in 1957, sending them to the Rose Bowl with a 7-3 record. The three defeats by a total of 13 points were matched by three victories by three points or less.

The first of the victories came in the opener, when Idaho fell 9-6. The Vandals had the ball late, and assistant coach John McKay was fretting on the sidelines, warning the Ducks that Idaho had "this field goal kicker who had a 40-yard range."

The kicker was Jerry Kramer, later of Green Bay Packers fame, but the Ducks kept the Vandals too far from the goal line for an attempt. For the fifth straight year the Ducks began the season 1-0.

Oregon could have used a potent kicker of its own the next week in a 6-3 loss to Pittsburgh at Multnomah

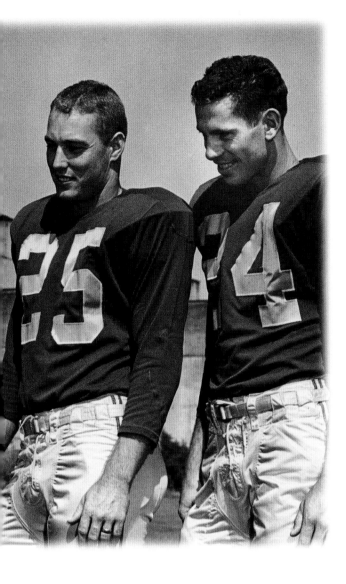

scoring a touchdown in each quarter. The outcome was finally decided with Oregon's final extra-point kick.

Oregon was 5-0 in the Pacific Coast Conference, two games ahead of Washington State, UCLA and Oregon State. The Beavers couldn't go back to the Rose Bowl under the league's "no-repeat rule," and the Bruins were ineligible because of conference sanctions. The Ducks had already beaten the Cougars. That meant Oregon only needed one victory to reach the Rose Bowl. The final three games were against two teams with a combined two triumphs—USC and Washington—and another team the Ducks hadn't lost to in four years, Oregon State.

It should have been easy. It was almost impossible.

First came the Huskies, playing for a new coach named Jim Owens. Washington had won only one of its first seven games, and the previous week had given USC its first victory of the season.

"I hate to think about Washington," Shanley recalled. "I try to forget them because Washington was the only team our senior class didn't beat. They played tough."

That day at Multnomah Stadium, the Huskies repeatedly stopped Oregon threats—when the Ducks didn't stop themselves—in a 13-6 loss. The Ducks still needed a victory, and now only two games remained.

Thankfully, Oregon avoided taking it down to the Civil War with a 16-7 triumph over Southern California in Los Angeles as Jack Morris rushed for a school-record 212 yards. The Ducks' balding fullback put Oregon up 3-0 with a 30-yard field goal in the opening minutes, then rambled 63 yards into the end zone two minutes later to give the Ducks a 10-0 lead on his ensuing extra point. Shanley scored behind a Morris block before halftime, giving the Ducks a 16-0 lead they protected until the gun sounded.

Oregon was going back to the Rose Bowl for the first time since the 1919 season.

The celebration was notably restrained. "We didn't play a bad ball game," Casanova said, "but I don't know what happened to us in the second half."

Jack Roche, his longtime assistant, tried to explain. "We were just too tense," Roche said, "and it isn't hard to understand. We were only a couple of quarters away from something nobody thought these kids could even win."

Picked to finish seventh in the Pacific Coast Conference by preseason prognosticators, the Ducks were headed for Pasadena and a meeting with Big Ten champion Ohio State. All that remained was Oregon State—and

Stadium. The drive to the Rose Bowl shifted into high gear with a 21-0 blanking of UCLA the following week in Portland.

"I still laugh about that game," said Jim Shanley, who led the Ducks with 693 rushing yards in 1957, becoming Oregon's career leader with 1,887. "It was raining, and the UCLA guys were standing around with the rain going down their necks and shivering. We were all in our element—true Ducks."

"As soon as it started raining, we started passing and the game was over," said Jerry Frei, an Oregon assistant coach and future head coach.

The winning continued with a 26-0 defeat of San Jose State. Next came a 14-13 victory over Washington State when a late Cougar extra-point attempt that would have tied the game hit the upright and bounced harmlessly away.

Maybe destiny really was wearing green and yellow?

The Ducks beat California and Joe Kapp 24-6 in Eugene, then downed Stanford 27-26 in Palo Alto for a sweep of the Bay Area schools. The triumph over the Indians was one of the season's most exciting games, with each team nobody tried to pretend it didn't matter.

"We've got to beat Oregon State to win the conference championship," Casanova said, "and really earn the trip to Pasadena."

It was a good thing the Ducks didn't need another victory. As a Hayward Field record crowd of 23,150 watched in agony, the Beavers held on for a 10-7 triumph, leaving the Civil War rivals tied for the PCC title with 5-2 records.

"My toughest loss," Casanova said of the defeat to Oregon State. Maybe the only loss that would compare to it was another defeat to the Beavers seven years later that did decide the Rose Bowl berth.

Oregon State Coach Tommy Prothro called the contest "one of the most bitterly fought games I've ever seen," and it was the rivalry at its best. The Beavers finished the season with an 8-2 record, becoming Prothro's "best team" in his words. But the Ducks, at 7-3, were in the Rose Bowl.

The outcome of the Civil War came down to Oregon's fourth-down play inside the Oregon State 1-yard line in the final quarter. Shanley, who had scored earlier on a pass from Jack Crabtree, was running into the end zone over prone Oregon State defender Nub Beamer, who alertly reached up and pulled the football out of Shanley's grasp.

"I thought I had crossed the goal line," Shanley said. "I had sidestepped Nub Beamer, but he swiped at the ball as I went down. It was a pretty serious mistake near the end of the game."

Casanova, as usual, was forgiving. Decades later he pointed out that Shanley was across the goal line, but in 1957 rules that wasn't enough. "We didn't have a break-the-plane rule, you had to get the ball in [the end zone and down it]," Casanova explained.

No matter, the Ducks were Rose Bowl bound—even if it was as three-touchdown underdogs to the unbeaten Buckeyes, who were ranked No. 1 in the nation. For the better part of a month leading up to the game, all the Ducks read and heard were derisive comments about their chances and how they had backed into the berth.

"We all remember all of the negative press we got," Shanley said. "It was degrading to think we had accomplished something while the media was saying we didn't deserve it. It was a real motivating thing for us. Our coaches did a tremendous job capitalizing on it."

To avoid potential traffic problems, Casanova had the Ducks make an early departure for the Rose Bowl on the morning of the game, and the caravan breezed to an early arrival. Now worried that the team would become overly nervous with a long wait before warmups, Casanova told each position coach to gather his players and "B.S. with the guys."

"Everybody just sat around and bulled," Casanova said. "We got 'em relaxed."

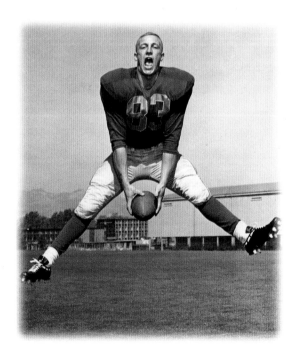

Casanova's pregame speech was almost as simple. "I just told 'em, 'You've been maligned down here. All I want to do is be proud of you.' At the end of the game, I think we even had some Ohio State people cheering for us."

Shanley scored the Oregon touchdown in the legendary 10-7 loss, and Crabtree was named the game's outstanding player for nearly engineering the upset. Ron Stover caught a record 10 passes in the game, and the Ducks outgained the Buckeyes in total offensive yardage 351 to 304. The Ducks were losers only on the scoreboard.

"There is no way anyone who was connected with it can forget the Rose Bowl game," said Jerry Frei, the assistant coach. "It was out of this world and unbelievable how we played."

When the game was over, Casanova had a message for the Los Angeles press, which had been unmerciful in ridiculing the Ducks and predicting the biggest mismatch in Rose Bowl history. "Hey, we've got a few good football players up here," he said. "When someone says that you're absolutely no good, you get a little irritated. I know I did and I know the players did."

But the Ducks couldn't hold a grudge long. They returned to the Ambassador Hotel, and the postgame gathering was anything but somber. "Mel Allen came by. He had announced the game," Roche recalled years later. "He said it was the damnedest party he ever saw for a loser."

There was one more thing to be decided, and that was whether Casanova was coming back to coach the Ducks or was listening to overtures from Stanford, which offered him a chance to return to his native Bay Area. Cas stayed at Oregon, and the legend lived on.

1958

Amazing Defense, Blundering Offense

Oregon couldn't repeat its magic of 1957, but the Ducks might have been the most amazing 4-6 team ever. They gave up only 50 points in 10 games and half of those came in one afternoon, a 23-6 loss to Rose Bowl-bound California. Not only were all four of their victories by shutout, but they allowed only one touchdown in three of their losses—all by 6-0 scores. They even lost a game in which they didn't allow the opponent an offensive point, a 2-0 defeat to Miami in the season finale in Florida.

"That was the most frustrating season I ever had," Len Casanova said. "Every time we would get into scoring position, we would do something. We would fumble or get a penalty or an interception. We'd find some way of fouling it up."

What kept the Ducks so close was defense, under the

coaching of Casanova's longtime assistant and close friend, Jack Roche. "More often than not, our defensive game plans were Jack's," said Phil McHugh, an Oregon player who became an assistant coach. "He sorted out all the B.S. and got down to the few things that counted.

"Jack recognized that he had a bunch of guys without the greatest physical tools. He would gamble. He would get innovative. He would figure out the other team's weaknesses and go after them. We played the Arkansas defense before Arkansas even figured out what it was. We went in a wide six, shifted and slanted and got away with some things no one else was doing at that time."

Roche especially liked devising special plans for certain teams. "When Red Sanders had UCLA come out of its huddle and serpentine to the line of scrimmage, Jack had our defense huddle and wait and serpentine right out with them," McHugh said. "We were the first team to do that."

After a 27-0 victory over Idaho in the season opener, in which the Vandals were held to 30 rushing yards, it was off to Norman, Oklahoma, to meet Bud Wilkinson's Sooners, the top-ranked team in the nation. This would be an exceptional test for Roche's defense and the rest of the Ducks.

"That was a big game for a guy from Coos Bay," said Bob Peterson, junior center on the team. "From the airport to the motel, we got a police escort. All the traffic had to move over."

The Ducks, however, stood their ground, holding the vaunted Sooners to a single touchdown in Oklahoma's 6-0 victory, and it took an Oregon fumble to set up the only score. The Ducks penetrated the Sooner 30 four times but couldn't capitalize, and Oregon's yardage advantage of 259-156 wasn't worth anything on the scoreboard.

The offense seemed to come alive in a 25-0 triumph over USC in Portland, ignited by Willie West's 66-yard sprint for a touchdown on the third play of the game. But Oregon lost its next three games, scoring just one touchdown in losses to Washington State (6-0), California (23-6) and Washington (6-0).

That ended any thoughts of returning to the Rose Bowl, but—as always—there was salvation to be had at the season with a 20-0 win over Oregon State. The Ducks dominated the Beavers as Dave Powell rushed for 81 yards and two touchdowns, and Oregon's tough defense limited Oregon State to 87 yards of total offense.

The Ducks had one more chance for a .500 record when they closed the season in the Orange Bowl against Miami, but it became another example of the frustrating season as the Hurricanes won 2-0 on a third-quarter safety, and six Oregon turnovers negated any chance at an offensive score for the Ducks.

Still, the defense of that 1958 team remains legendary.

Demise of the Pacific Coast Conference

Nineteen-hundred-and-fifty-nine was a season of change for Oregon, which suddenly found itself lacking membership in an athletic conference. The Pacific Coast Conference had broken up after the 1958 season, partly because of schools arguing about academic requirements but mostly over feuds resulting from NCAA and conference rules violations.

The California schools—USC, UCLA, Stanford and California—invited Washington to join them as a five-member league, the Athletic Association of Western Universities. That left the Ducks out, along with Oregon State and Washington State.

There would also be a notable change in Len Casanova's coaching staff as John McKay left to take an assistant's position at Southern California. A halfback on the Cotton Bowl team of 1948, McKay had remained at the school as the one carryover assistant from the previous coaching staff when Casanova was hired in 1951.

McKay might not have left except that USC made it clear he would spend only one season as an assistant with the Trojans before taking over the head coaching position.

Few others left Casanova's staff. He employed only 13 different assistants in 16 years; impressive, considering Cas never had more than five assistants. The quintet of Jack Roche, Jerry Frei, Phil McHugh, Max Coley and John Robinson were with him his last seven seasons.

Frei joined Cas' staff in 1955 and was with him for 12 years, succeeding him as head coach in 1967. "There were only five of us," said Frei, "and that was for the varsity and freshman teams."

The Ducks made it work, Frei said, because "the biggest thing about Cas was that he was such a detail guy. The other thing about him was that he would certainly let you coach. Cas would say, 'This is what I want,' and then he would expect you to do it."

Most of all, Frei said, "Cas taught us all how to treat people. I really believe that is the biggest single thing about him—his concern for his people. We learned a lot from him."

It showed in that 1959 season as the Ducks went 8-2, the only losses being 13-12 to Washington in Multnomah Stadium and 15-7 to Oregon State at Hayward Field. It was the biggest margin of loss by a Casanova team in a Civil War game.

Many of Oregon's eight victories were noteworthy. Air Force had a 15-game winning streak snapped by the Ducks in a 21-3 loss, and the Ducks piled up a school record 498 yards of total offense in a 45-7 rout of Idaho. Two of the victories also came against Washington State. The unusual scheduling had been forced on the two teams by the Los Angeles schools refusing to play either one after the conference broke up.

The Ducks might not have won the second of the two contests, a 7-6 victory in mid-November in Pullman, except for what they had learned watching their freshman team play the previous day in the Palouse.

"It was so cold, the field was frozen," said Dave Grosz, the quarterback, "so Cas went out and bought tennis shoes for us to play in."

The trips to the Palouse were always interesting. Earlier in the season, the Ducks traveled by train to play Idaho in Moscow. "We had the porter smuggle some beer into our car on the way back," said John Wilcox, a tackle. "I don't know if Cas knew or not."

Either way, it "was one of the most fun teams I ever played on," Wilcox said. "We weren't supposed to be that good." Instead, Oregon wasn't far from being unbeaten.

The Ducks nearly pulled out a victory against the Huskies in a game watched by 37,263, the largest crowd to ever see a football game in Portland.

"We ran an off-tackle play all game that Washington couldn't stop," said Dave Grosz, the Oregon quarterback. "I made a play up in the huddle. I told the guys, 'I'm going to fake to Dave Powell off tackle and throw the damn post pattern to Willie West or Dave Grayson.' I aimed the ball instead of throwing it, and they intercepted it. It killed us."

The other loss came against the Beavers. Oregon scored first on a 5-yard pass from Cleveland Jones to Willie West, but the Beavers rallied to win as each team compiled 143 total yards of offense. The Beavers didn't complete a pass. But the Ducks were not invited to a postseason bowl game, despite one of the best records in school history.

1960

The Liberty Bowl Beckons

How could the Ducks top the 8-2 season of 1959? They very nearly did in 1960, going 7-2-1 en route to a Liberty Bowl loss to Penn State. Only a 21-0 loss at Michigan in the second game could be described as a game the Ducks didn't have a chance to win. But they certainly felt they should have scored on the Wolverines.

On the first play, in fact, quarterback Dave Grosz surprised Michigan with a tackle-eligible play, and Riley Mattson snuck behind the secondary. "He was wide open and I threw the ball over his head," Grosz lamented. "If we had scored that, maybe it might have been a different story."

There was no bigger "maybe" that season than the 7-6 loss to Washington in Seattle. What a rivalry the Oregon-Washington game had become. Starting in 1957, the teams played 10 straight games with the outcome decided by seven points or less, and this was one of four decided by a single point. Another game ended in a tie.

The Ducks came back to beat Stanford and West Virginia in a pair of Portland games, then tied the Beavers 14-14. But this time the Civil War didn't end the season, as the Ducks were invited to play Penn State in the Liberty Bowl.

Oregon flew to Philadelphia four days before the December 17 game and found the city digging out of a 15-inch snowfall. No more snow fell during the days preceding the game, but the Ducks awoke on the morning of the game to freezing temperatures and 20 mph winds.

"We weren't prepared at all for it," said Snidow, one of the tackles. "We had no cold-weather gear . . . we'd never played in conditions anything like that. I remember the first play of the game, one of our guys crashed into [a Penn State player] and his face mask just shattered. It was one of those plastic ones that wasn't made to be worn in cold weather."

The Ducks' chances were hampered at the outset, when leading receiver Cleveland Jones was injured on the first play of the game and couldn't return. Having made a 12-yard reception with one knee on the ground, he assumed the play was over. That's when a Penn State defender crashed into his back.

"I don't think it was intentional," Jones said. "He was just carrying out an assignment."

ABOVE: STEVE BARNETT WAS A TWO-TIME ALL-AMERICA TACKLE IN 1961-62.

in Multnomah Stadium, a precise reversal of the previous year's score in Seattle. But it almost became a Washington repeat, with the Huskies driving for a potential winning score late in the game.

"They had fourth down on our 3 and decided not to kick a field goal," said Mike Gaechter, one of the UO defensive backs. "The quarterback rolled out to the right and doubled back to his left. The field was wide open, and he headed for the corner. I was fortunate enough to tackle him on the 6-inch line. It was a nail biter, the climax of our whole season."

After a victory over Stanford, the Ducks lost their final three games, including a 22-12 loss at Ohio State. "[Going into Ohio State's stadium] was like entering into a wall of noise," said Steve Barnett, a UO tackle. "There were 80,000 people there. None of us had ever seen anything like it."

"I remember that Ohio State dressed 119 scholarship players," Gaechter added. "Oregon didn't have 119 scholarships among all its sports."

The Ducks did have some athletes, though. Gaechter and Renfro, each of whom went on to professional careers with the Dallas Cowboys, also ran track. With Harry Jerome and Jerry Tarr, they comprised the UO 440-yard relay team that set a world record.

About all the 1961 Ducks lacked was a great quarterback, and on his way to the varsity was just the guy: Bob Berry.

Casanova made no excuses. "We played a poor game in the Liberty Bowl," he said. "It was cold and snowy, but we just didn't play well."

Renfro Makes His Debut

After compiling 15 victories over the previous two seasons, the Ducks opened the promising 1961 season with a 51-0 triumph over Idaho at Hayward Field. It was the highest-scoring Oregon game of the Casanova era, and Oregon's 544 yards in total offense established a school record. Moreover, the debut of sophomore sensation Mel Renfro seemed to bode well for yet another successful campaign.

But the opener was followed by three consecutive losses, all by eight points or less—at Utah (14-6), Minnesota (14-7) and to Arizona (15-6) in Portland.

After a routine victory over San Jose State, the highlight of the 4-6 season came in a 7-6 win over Washington

Cas' "Best Team" Stays Home

"It was probably my best team," Casanova said of the 1962 Ducks, and it was hard to argue. Mel Renfro, the junior halfback, was on his way to becoming an All-American. The line included tackles Ron Snidow and Steve Barnett, both of whom went on to long professional careers, and Mickey Ording, an All-Coast guard. Dave Wilcox, a future All-Pro, was in his first season as a defensive end, and Bob Berry had taken over at quarterback.

The Ducks went 6-3-1 in 1962, with road losses at Ohio State, Texas and Oregon State. They lead the latter two bowl-bound teams at halftime, and came within a play of going to the Bluebonnet Bowl.

In the opener, the Ducks very nearly preempted an unbeaten season for Texas before it started. "I made a mistake in our opener at Texas," said Casanova of the 25-13 defeat. "It was as humid as could be. We were leading [6-3] at halftime. At the time, we were playing two units. The first team, which had finished the first half, said it was ready to start the second half. They didn't realize how much the humidity had taken out of them. That was when Texas took it to us."

Renfro agreed. "We ran Texas ragged for two and a half quarters, and then that 90-degree heat got us," Renfro said.

After victories at home over Utah and San Jose State, it was back to the Lone Star State for the Ducks and a game against Rice in Houston. It would be a special night for Renfro.

"It was kind of a homecoming for me because I was born in Houston," Renfro said. "It was the first time as a young adult that I was able to see my grandfather. It was really a very touching moment."

It almost didn't come off. This was still the era of segregation, and African-Americans weren't allowed into the Houston stadium. "They made an exception because of me, and they cordoned off an area around the 30-yard line where they let 20 of my relatives attend the game," Renfro said. "They were the only black spectators in the place."

Renfro responded with one of the finest games of his superlative career. He rushed 13 times for 141 yards, caught two passes for 27 yards and returned an intercepted pass 65 yards in Oregon's 31-12 victory.

"God blessed me to have a good game," Renfro said. "It made an impression on Rice University, it made an impression on the fans and it definitely made an impression on my kin folks. They talked for years 'about the day little Melvin came down to Houston and did all these things and got us in the game.'"

Renfro's junior year was his best at Oregon. He rushed for a school-record 753 yards, completed five of 12 passes for 114 yards and two touchdowns, caught 16 passes for 298 yards, intercepted two passes for 67 return yards, returned six punts for 42 yards and returned 10 kick-offs for 244 yards.

His 13 touchdowns set another Oregon record, and in those days of one-platoon football, he was also one of the country's best defensive backs. His, and Oregon's, only disappointment was not being able to beat either of the Ducks' two fiercest rivals, Washington and Oregon State.

In Seattle, the Ducks and Huskies fought to a 21-21 tie. Even after a 26-7 loss at Ohio State, the Ducks were 6-2-1, and had been contacted by Bluebonnet Bowl officials about a bid for the postseason game in Texas. It would be offered, however, only if the Ducks defeated the Beavers in the Civil War game.

"I decided not to tell them before the game," Casanova said, "because I wasn't sure how they'd react. They were emotional enough about playing the Beavers."

Berry ran for a touchdown, then—later—found Renfro breaking past Beaver defenders Rich Brooks and Fred Jones, and lofted a 50-yard touchdown pass to his swift halfback. The Ducks led 17-6 at halftime, and Casanova wanted to make sure there wasn't a letdown.

"I told them about the bowl bid, and there was just no reaction," Casanova said. "They were a funny team that way."

BELOW:
DAVE WILCOX
WAS AN
DEFENSIVE
TERROR FOR
THE DUCKS.

Three times during this game at Multnomah Stadium in Portland, junior quarterback Bob Berry brought the Ducks back from a deficit.

The last time came with only 11 seconds left, when Berry's 29-yard touchdown pass to H.D. Murphy capped a 75-yard drive that began with 1:09 remaining. "That Berry, man, he's phenomenal," Murphy said.

On that day, perhaps more phenomenal than ever.

The Ducks, seeking to defeat a Big Ten

#15 quarterback, Bob Berry

opponent for the first time in school history, were a wounded team. Berry had an ailing knee; running back Mel Renfro, who would account for 236 all-purpose yards that day, was still recovering from bruised ribs; receiver Larry Hill was playing with his right arm strapped to his side from the elbow to the shoulder.

In the second quarter, the Ducks already trailed 13-0. Berry's second-quarter touchdown pass and Renfro's 4-yard run made it 14-13 Oregon in the third quarter.

The Hoosiers pulled ahead, 19-14, and once more Berry brought the Ducks back, 21-19, on a 37-yard, fourth-quarter touchdown pass to Hill.

The Hoosiers marched back to the Oregon 4 before a key tackle by Murphy forced them to settle for a 26-yard field goal and a 22-21 lead with 1:37 left.

Only 1:09 remained after Murphy returned the ensuing kickoff to the Oregon 25. Afterward, Berry recalled he wasn't

worried, "just a little skeptical that it could be done."

The *Register-Guard* wrote, "Berry refused to let the Webfoots die." He passed to Murphy for 7 yards. Only 59 seconds remained. Then Berry threw for Renfro; the ball was nearly intercepted by a Hoosier, but Renfro caught the deflection for a 30-yard gain. First down at the IU 38 with 48 seconds remaining. Another pass to Renfro gained 4, followed by an incomplete pass, then an off-sides penalty against IU. The Ducks had reached the IU 29 with 17 seconds remaining.

According to the *Register-Guard*, Berry slipped and almost fell as he dropped back to pass, but he kept his balance and fired long down the middle to Murphy, who was sprinting into the end zone behind the IU defense.

"I thought it might be out of the end zone," said Oregon Coach Len Casanova.

The pass covered 40 yards in the air, and Murphy made the catch just inside the end zone, a step to the side of the left goal post. "One step longer and farther to the right and there's no telling who would have won," the *Register-Guard* reported.

Murphy was mobbed by happy fans. "I didn't think I'd caught it until everybody started grabbing me," he said.

Afterward, Hill admitted he thought the game was lost when the Hoosiers got that field goal. "But as long as you've got Berry in there passing, it's never over," he said. On that day, it wasn't.

LEFT: 1963 DUCK ILLUSTRATION

J. Peter Moore

The Beavers, with Terry Baker on his way to winning the Heisman Trophy, were far from done. Baker marched the Beavers to a touchdown on their first possession of the second half. Later, he had them threatening again at the Oregon 18 before Wilcox threw Baker for losses on consecutive plays.

On fourth down at the 34-yard line, the Beavers brought Rich Brooks in for a "pooch" punt. The future Oregon coach worked it perfectly, lofting a soft kick that landed inside the 15-yard line, where the football took a weird bounce and hit Renfro's leg. The Beavers recovered at the 13, and on fourth down Baker passed for the winning score and added a two-point conversion.

"The blame for the Oregon State loss was squarely on my shoulders," Renfro said. "That was very disappointing. That stayed with me."

There was no bowl bid, but there were records for the Ducks. They gained 3,530 yards of total offense, the most ever for an Oregon team, and Renfro set school records for season rushing yardage (783), touchdowns (13) and points (78). The Ducks had done just about everything—except beat the Beavers when it counted most.

"We let them off the hook a few times," Casanova said. "We did so damn many things wrong out there it wasn't funny."

Losing to Oregon State never is.

Firehouse Four Goes to Sun Bowl

Mel Renfro was back for his final season, and Bob Berry was still only a junior. Along with Larry Hill and Lu Bain, they formed the "Firehouse Four" backfield that led the Ducks to a 7-3 season and a Sun Bowl berth.

Speed was becoming a decisive factor in college football, and Casanova's 1963 team was loaded with it. Six times during the season, the Ducks scored four or more touchdowns in a game. And after a 17-7 loss in the opening game to Penn State, the Ducks averaged 33 points during their next four winning contests.

But then came the annual meeting with Washington, which would prove to be one of the most brutal, physical games of the storied rivalry.

The Huskies came away with a 26-19 triumph and the Ducks paid a horrible physical price in the defeat. Milt Kanehe, a lineman, suffered a broken leg, and Renfro was carried off the field after he and Washington's Charlie Browning collided at full speed on a kickoff. The sound of the hit echoed through Multnomah Stadium.

Renfro and Berry were out the following week with the injuries they suffered against the Huskies. Consequently, the Ducks were upset by San Jose State 13-7, with the Spartans scoring on a punt return and intercepted pass. At 4-3, Oregon's season was on the brink of collapse. But Berry limped back into the lineup the following week at Pullman against Washington State and led the Ducks to a 21-7 victory with a pair of touchdown passes.

The next week the Ducks met Indiana with their backfield intact, but not healthy. Berry, his knee still hurting, was under instructions not to run; Renfro wore a flak jacket to protect a cracked rib; and Hill had a special harness that wouldn't allow him to lift his right arm above the shoulder he had separated two weeks earlier. You wouldn't know it by their performances, however.

Renfro gained 236 all-purpose yards rushing, receiving and returning kicks. Berry threw three touchdown passes, one of them to Hill, who shook off a tackler with his good arm and went 30 yards for the go-ahead touchdown.

Indiana took a 22-21 lead on a field goal with 1:37 left, but the Ducks had plenty of time. "As long as you've got Berry in there, it's never over," Hill said. Berry was no less confident, telling his teammates in the huddle, "Block, so I have time to throw it."

He connected with reserve halfback H.D. Murphy, who split a pair of Indiana defenders in the back of the end zone with 11 seconds remaining and the Ducks won 28-22.

The regular season was scheduled to conclude the following week against Oregon State, but the assassination of President John F. Kennedy delayed the Civil War for seven days. The night before the game was to have been played, Renfro suffered a badly cut right wrist. The damage to a nerve ended his college career.

"It was frustration over the assassination of the president; it was frustration over a problem in my marriage," Renfro said. "We sat around drinking more beer than we should have. I smashed a mirror in the bathroom with my fist.

"I almost died that night," he said. "I'm sitting there bleeding to death. Oliver McKinney finally said, 'Man, you need to go to the hospital and get that checked.' They took me to the hospital and I had surgery."

As unbelievable as it might have seemed to the Duck faithful going into the postponed Civil War, Renfro was hardly missed. Berry passed for a school-record 249 yards, including two scoring passes, giving him 16 for the season. He added 23 rushing yards for a single-season total offense record of 1,733 yards.

"Berry cut the Beavers to ribbons," said Dave Wilcox, the future All-Pro. "They had a special defense for us, and Bob would audible a lot. It was a pretty good day for Oregon." The Ducks led 31-0 after three quarters on its way to a 31-14 victory, and another postseason game: the Sun Bowl in El Paso, Texas.

Oregon would have to play in the Sun Bowl without Renfro, but their opponent was 4-6 Southern Methodist. Once again, the Ducks hardly seemed to miss their star halfback and won 21-14 to claim their first bowl victory since the 1917 Rose Bowl.

With their fortunes improving, UO fans wondered if there would be another Rose Bowl berth in Oregon's future. There would be—but not for another three decades.

Beavers Block Path to Rose Bowl

After five seasons as an independent, Oregon returned to what would soon be known as the Pacific-8 Conference, essentially the old Pacific Coast Conference minus Idaho.

Missing from the 1964 team were great players like Mel Renfro and Dave Wilcox, and spirited leaders like Larry Hill. There wasn't much left of the offensive powerhouse of the previous two seasons except for quarterback Bob Berry.

But Berry was enough. Oregon went 7-2-1, three points from an unbeaten season, after a two-point loss to Stanford and a one-point defeat to Oregon State—the result of a blocked extra point. The tie came against Washington State.

Even after the season opened with a 20-13 victory over Brigham Young in Eugene, few thought the Ducks would have a great year. "I remember calling my father after the game and telling him, 'Pop, it's going to be a long season,'" Berry said. "We were a young team. We were a bunch of overachievers. Good spirit, good coaching."

But somehow the Ducks kept winning, first 22-13 over Pittsburgh then 22-14 against Penn State. Next they defeated Idaho 14-8 and Arizona 21-0. Oregon was 5-0 and headed for Seattle to meet Washington.

Always resourceful, Berry threw a tackle-eligible pass to Lowell Dean for a touchdown and Oregon's defense held on for the 7-0 victory. Suddenly, Oregon was 6-0 and ranked seventh in the Associated Press poll. But hopes for an unbeaten season ended with a crushing last-minute 10-8 loss to Stanford in Portland.

"In all my years of coaching, I think I was robbed by officials only once," Casanova said of the loss to the Indians. "It was near the end of the game, and Doug Post was punting. He was flattened. It was flagrant roughing of the kicker. Jim Cain [the referee] reached in his back pocket and then changed his mind. After the game, even the Stanford coaches said it was a terrible non-call."

Because of an injury, Berry was unable to play the next week against Washington State, and the game ended in a 21-21 tie.

Berry returned for the Indiana game, or most of it. He stuck around long enough to toss three touchdown passes and lead Oregon back from a 21-7 halftime deficit before being ejected from the game in the fourth quarter, and still managed to throw for a school-record 273 yards in the 29-21 triumph.

"Indiana had been doing a job on my knees in the pileups, and I just kicked back," Berry said of his ejection. "The guy who retaliates always gets caught."

Only the Civil War remained for Oregon, and the stakes were higher than ever: The winner would likely go to the Rose Bowl. Nothing was certain, however, as neither the Ducks or Beavers had played Southern California, which also was in contention. A vote of the conference schools would decide the league representative in Pasadena.

First things first, and that meant beating the Beavers. Oregon drove 95 yards for a second-quarter touchdown. An Oregon State defender broke through the line to block Herm Meister's extra-point attempt, however, and it would prove to be the difference.

The Beavers were headed for the Rose Bowl, while Oregon's season was finished—as was the magnificent

collegiate career of Bob Berry, who would go on to play for the Atlanta Falcons.

"Nothing came easy for us that year," Berry said. "It was a young team, and we battled for everything we got. We were three points from being unbeaten, but six of our wins were by a touchdown or less. We could have been 5-5."

Berry left Oregon owning records for career passing yards (4,148) and total offense (4,376), both of which formerly belonged to George Shaw. Berry was arguably the most successful quarterback in Oregon history, guiding the Ducks to a 21-8-2 record in his three seasons. Five of the losses were by a touchdown or less. He also played in a bowl game and twice came within a victory over Oregon State of going to postseason play.

"The kids believed in him, that was the big thing," Casanova said of Berry. "He'd get in the huddle and say, 'Let's get 'em.' "Oh, he was a tough kid, tougher than the dickens. His passes wobbled sometimes, but they got there."

False Hopes Dashed

Three straight Victories to open the 1965 season sent an unlikely Oregon team up to 10th in the United Press International poll of college coaches, and the Ducks were believing in themselves.

Tom Trovato looked like he might be able to replace Bob Berry at quarterback, setting a school record for passing yardage (252) in the second game as Oregon flattened Utah 31-14 in Salt Lake City.

"That was my big game," said Steve Bunker, who caught a 71-yard touchdown against the Utes. It was the first of his nine scoring passes that season en route to a school record 51 receptions.

But after beating Brigham Young 27-14 to improve their record to 3-0, the Ducks went to Stanford for a game that "turned the season around," as All-Coast center Dave Tobey remembered it. For the second year in a row against the Indians, Oregon was sure it had been victimized by the officials. This time a Stanford receiver went out of bounds and came back on the field to make an illegal catch for the winning touchdown.

The Ducks had to rally to tie Air Force 18-18 in Portland, then returned to Multnomah Stadium the following week and gave up 17 fourth-quarter points in a 24-20 loss to Washington.

"We just never recovered from that Stanford loss," said Tim Casey, a linebacker for the Ducks. "That just took so much out of us, and we were never confident again like we had been early in the season."

A 17-14 triumph over Idaho turned out to be the last victory of the season for the Ducks. It was also Oregon's last triumph at Hayward Field, as the Ducks would go winless at home in 1966, then move to Autzen Stadium in 1967.

Losses to Washington State and California sent the Ducks into the Civil War with a 4-4-1 record with at least some hope of pulling out a winning season. But OSU jumped to a 19-0 first-half lead and the Ducks' comeback fell short at 19-14.

The Casanova Era Comes to a Close

The final season of Len Casanova's illustrious coaching career went into the books with a 3-7 record and two of the longest scoring plays in Oregon history: Ken Klein's 99-yard interception return against Air Force and Jim Smith's 99-yard scoring run with a fumble against Oregon State.

First, however, came three losses to open the season, two of them on consecutive weekends at Hayward Field to Utah and San Jose State.

There was some solace when the losing streak was broken by a 7-3 victory over Stanford—the team that had done such damage to the previous two Oregon seasons—in Portland. The Ducks made it two straight when Klein's runback fired up the Ducks for a 17-6 triumph at Air Force.

After all the remarkable victories of past seasons, this fall offered one of the most embarrassing losses in Casanova's reign, a 14-13 loss to Washington State in the

RIGHT:
QUARTERBACK
MIKE BRUNDAGE
RUNS FOR DAY-
LIGHT IN A 1965
GAME AT HAYWARD
FIELD.

last game played at Hayward Field. The Ducks stopped themselves when confusion over downs erupted during the final seconds.

After reaching the 2-yard line, a touchdown seemed almost certain. But what down was it? Casanova admitted after the game he thought Jones had made a first down. It turned out to be a crucial misunderstanding.

On second down, Barnes threw incomplete, but the clock stopped with 28 seconds left. That brought up third down. Barnes kept the ball on an option play but was stopped short of the goal line. Casanova tried to rush the field goal kicker into the huddle.

"The quarterback waved him off," Casanova said.

Barnes said he looked at the down marker on the side-line and saw third down, so he wanted to throw an incomplete pass and stop the clock, allowing time for the field goal attempt. Casanova said officials changed the down to fourth after Barnes had looked to that side of the field.

"In my mind, I thought it was third down," Barnes said. "We were all thinking about killing the ball . . . that's all we threw it for."

What could Casanova say?

"We blew it," he began with reporters. "I'm not

blaming Barnes, I'm taking the blame myself on that thing. I'll take half of it and give the officials the other half."

Irate fans and Oregon followers weren't so easily appeased, and there was unrest among the faithful when a 3-7 season ended with road losses at Arizona State and Oregon State.

Two months later, Casanova was named athletic director, and in his first action named Jerry Frei as the new head football coach.

Casanova's impact on the Oregon program was immeasurable. His long-lasting infulence was evidenced by the number of former players and assistant coaches who went on to successful head coaching careers themselves, including John McKay (Southern Cal and Tampa Bay), John Robinson (Southern Cal and Los Angeles Rams), George Seifert (San Francisco 49ers) and Jack Patera (Seattle Seahawks).

In 1977, when Casanova was voted into the National Football Foundation Hall of Fame, his successor, Jerry Frei, spoke for the many who had come to know "Cas" over the decades. "Cas will always be a symbol," Frei said. "He goes down in everyone's book as a gentleman, a gentleman with dignity."

ASSISTANT COACH
MAX COLEY, HEAD
COACH JERRY FREI
AND HALFBACK
CLAXTON WELCH
ON THE SIDELINE
DURING OREGON'S
FIRST GAME AT
AUTZEN STADIUM
IN 1967.

DAWN OF THE AUTZEN AGE

1967

In Italian, Casanova means "new house," and as it turned out, Cas' first year as athletic director—1967—was also the year Oregon opened its new football house, Autzen Stadium. Most of the credit for planning and building the new stadium, however, belongs to Casanova's predecessor, Leo Harris

Harris recognized early on in the Casanova era that Hayward Field, which at that time had a seating capacity of only 20,000, was inadequate for modern college football. In fact, by 1966, most of Oregon's home games were played in Portland's larger Multnomah Stadium, which since has been remodeled and renamed Civic Stadium.

As former UO coach Jerry Frei said, remembering Casanova's recruiting pitch in the pre-Autzen days, "He'd bring somebody in, and they would want to see the stadium. Well, it was pretty difficult to take them down and show them Hayward Field. Cas would say, 'Yeah, well we play our big games in Portland,' and the kid would never get to see that."

The push to build Autzen Stadium began at the June 1960 meeting of the State Board of Higher Education, in which an agreement was made to purchase surplus land from the State Highway Department out of University of Oregon athletic funds. An irregularly shaped piece of property consisting of 88.49 acres on the north side of the Willamette River was to become a site for a football stadium.

Then-UO President O. Meredith Wilson requested the purchase, explaining that the land earmarked for a new stadium east of Hayward Field was not sufficiently stable to

ABOVE: A MUDDY JIM EVENSON CONFERS WITH JERRY FREI IN THE EARLY AUTZEN YEARS WHEN NATURAL GRASS WAS THE DUCKS' PLAYING SURFACE.

support the weight of a modern stadium. He proposed swapping 22.69 acres owned by the county for 22.53 acres owned by the University, creating regular boundaries for both parties. The switch was made with an expenditure of $85,160 on the part of the University, and planning for the new stadium commenced.

With the dictum that the cost of a new stadium be in hand prior to the start of construction, the Athletic Department administration went to work to raise the needed $2.3 million. A reserve of $1.3 million in Athletic Department coffers represented a good start. Before long, the money was raised, plans were drawn and the stadium was built.

Designed as a bowl with almost perfect sight lines for all 41,698 seats, the facility honored the Autzen family, which had made the largest single donation. The field was grass initially, but the grass would be replaced by Astroturf in 1969. The gates were finally opened on September 23, 1967, and 27,500 fans braved 85-degree heat to watch Eddie Crowder's highly favored Colorado squad slip past the Ducks 17-13.

The restrooms were only 60 percent complete, and the sportswriters quickly noticed that the hot sun made sitting in the first row of the press box almost unbearable. L.H. Gregory, *The Oregonian* columnist, worried about drunken fans falling down the outer edge of the walkways.

The new $50,000 scoreboard went out in the second quarter, although it was repaired for the second half. Because ABC-TV was on strike and veteran announcer Keith Jackson had been warned not to cross the picket lines, Casanova was in the broadcast booth offering color commentary alongside Colorado athletic director Dallas Ward. "We sweated in that press box for three hours," Cas remembered, "and I think they paid us $75."

But there was no mistaking the pride in former athletic director Leo Harris' voice when he said after the game, "This is the end of a dream. I almost didn't come to Oregon 20 years ago because of the school's inadequate athletic facilities."

Leo Harris retired in January 1967 after heading the UO Athletic Department for 20 years. Casanova took over the AD reins and handpicked his own replacement: offensive line coach, Jerry Frei, a 12-year veteran of the University of Oregon staff who considered the promotion the greatest challenge of his lifetime.

"I think Cas had total control of the situation," Frei said years later. "He immediately named me his successor, which was a little bit of a surprise. I hadn't really seen it coming. But Cas taking the athletic director job when he did surprised us, too. And after he did, most of us didn't think about what was going to happen."

Like Cas, Frei was a player's coach. During his five-year run, which produced some of the greatest athletes and much of the most thrilling football the school had ever seen, the Oregon campus went through the turmoil of Vietnam, student protests and Black Power.

Frei grew up in Wisconsin and earned three letters at the University of Wisconsin playing under Coach Harry Stuhldreher, a member of the famed "Four Horsemen." He played guard for the Badgers during the 1942, 1946 and 1947 seasons on teams that featured Pat Harder, Dave Schreiner and Elroy Hirsch.

After graduation, Frei decided to travel west. His first coaching assignment was as an assistant at Grant High School in Portland. He moved on to Lincoln High and then Willamette University where he worked under the legendary Ted Ogdahl, who had previously been the coach at Grant High and had George Shaw as his quarterback. Cas lured Frei to Eugene in 1955.

Frei was the freshman coach when the Ducks went to the Rose Bowl during the 1957 season. Casanova thought Frei did such an outstanding job coaching the linemen in the Rose Bowl game against No. 1 ranked Ohio State, he elevated Frei to varsity offensive line coach the following year.

When destiny tapped Frei on the shoulder after the '66 season, he and his wife, Marian, were living happily in south Eugene, raising five children. The next five years would be some of the happiest and the saddest of their lives.

"What I do remember of those early years, obviously, is that we lost more than we won," (22-29-2) Frei said. But to show that the program had declined rapidly in 1966, Frei recalled that, "What we were trying to do more than anything was sell what we were going to be in the future. And recruiting was a big, big thing. That and trying to put a product on the field that could show people, 'Hey, eventually this program is going to make it.'"

The Frei Years Begin

Oregon had a new coach, a new stadium, new formations and new talent. As fall camp started in 1967, Autzen Stadium was amazingly nearing completion after a January 5 start. Both fans and alumni waited anxiously to see what

the new blood could accomplish.

On the first day, Frei greeted 65 players, including 6-1, 217-pound All-Coast middle guard George Dames from Medford and All-America candidate senior defensive back Jim "Yazoo" Smith from San Diego.

The Ducks also boasted a promising sophomore quarterback, Tom Blanchard from Grants Pass, but they had no depth to speak of, and only three defensive players weighed over 200 pounds.

In Frei's first game at California in Berkeley, the Ducks kicked away a 13-7 second-quarter lead and lost 21-13. Blanchard was hurt during the first 13 minutes of the game. It was an early sign of the buzzard's luck Frei and his staff would have trying to keep key players healthy.

Frei introduced his gambling, shifting style of defense, but it didn't matter because UO mistakes set up all three Bears' scores. "We were on the wrong end of the field too much," Frei explained.

After the first two games at Autzen, Frei saw his Ducks pounded by Utah (21-0), Ohio State (30-0) and Washington (26-0).

When the hated Huskies arrived, Olson had the quarterback job for keeps; Blanchard was out with knee surgery. For the first time since 1924, the Huskies were in Eugene playing a football game. In raising the funds for the construction of Autzen, the UO promised donors that home games would no longer be played in Portland but in Eugene. No matter. The Huskies took advantage of four UO fumbles and rendered the outcome a moot point. Frei took heart in substitute fullback Andy Mauer—the "Prospect Piledriver" looked like a future star.

The next week relieved UO players carried their first-year coach off the field following a 31-6 victory over Idaho in front of 16,000 fans at Autzen. The shutout streak was over at long last. The Ducks played a courageous game the following Saturday at Southern California, losing 28-6 but giving touted tailback O.J. Simpson all he could handle. Simpson was held to 63 yards in 23 carries.

Frei started sophomore quarterback John Harrington because the UO game plan was to run, and the Trojans seemed surprised by the feisty Ducks' refusal to quit. "They knocked the hell out of us, and we stood there and took it," said USC coach John McKay, the former UO assistant.

The final victory of a 2-8 season came against Washington State, 17-13.

Frei's first experience with the Civil War game as a

head coach ended in a 14-10 heartbreak. The Ducks were unable to stop Oregon State fullback Bill "Earthquake" Enyart. Enyart gained 167 yards for the No. 8-ranked Beavers, who were led by slick option quarterback Steve Preece.

1968

Two More Wins, More Frustration

As the 1968 season began, Frei realized his team was short on talent. But rather than dwell on the shortcomings, he and his assistants decided to focus on the strengths that could help the Ducks show an improvement over the previous season.

Oregon's strengths in 1968 included a veteran offensive line; George Dames at middle guard; Omri Hildreth at monster back; Claxton Welch at running back; slotback Andy Mauer, a battering ram at 6-3, 232 pounds; and wide receivers Denny Schuler and Bob Newland.

The Ducks began the season with four quarterbacks—Tom Blanchard, John Harrington, Alan Pitcaithley and Eric Olson—but by opening day at Colorado, Blanchard had been redshirted with knee problems, and Pitcaithley won the job.

When the UO assistants walked into their tiny room in the Folsom Stadium press box in Boulder, they found a noose dangling from the rafters. It seemed to portend the final score: Colorado 28, Oregon 7.

Next, the Ducks were defeated by Stanford (28-12) and sixth-ranked Ohio State (21-6) on successive Saturdays. Stanford sophomore Jim Plunkett completed 10 of 13 passes and threw for four TDs in his first Autzen appearance. Frei said of Plunkett, "It would be a miracle if he passed like that two games in a row. At least, I'd hate to think he could."

How was he to know Plunkett would go on to be one of the greatest college quarterbacks of all time?

Lack of respect for Oregon's program was apparent in the remarks made by Ohio State assistant coach Esco Sarkkinen before the loss in Columbus. "This Saturday we will welcome you to our version of *Laugh-In*," Sarkkinen told OSU boosters. Frei's Ducks read the comments and went on to play a whale of a game despite the loss.

The Ohio State contest seemed to toughen Frei's players, who proceeded to upend Washington (3-0), Idaho (23-8) and Utah (14-6) in succession. Due to a series of injuries to the other quarterbacks, Frei elected to start John Harrington, an ex-Central Catholic High (Portland) star, against the Huskies in Seattle. Oregon placekicker Ken Woody won the game with a 38-yard field goal. Woody, who grew up in Seattle, worked summers as a part-time sportswriter with the *Seattle Post-Intelligence* during his college years. Later, he would work as a television color commentator for UO football broadcasts.

The Oregonian's Don McLeod observed, "He [Woody] furnished some football history that his paper must have published with understandable anguish."

The highlight of Oregon's 4-6 season may have been

1969

Here Comes Bobby Moore

The sophomore class of '69 included some of the biggest names in modern UO football history. Foremost among them was an exciting 6-foot-2, 208-pound slotback from Tacoma, Washington, named Bobby Moore. Moore, who would later change his name to Ahmad Rashad, was joined by Tom Graham, Tom Drougas, John McKean, Bill Drake, Leland Glass and Greg Specht.

"The big schools wanted Moore," Frei recalled. "We sneaked Tom Graham in at midyear, before anybody knew about him. I think what led Bobby to Oregon more than anything was that he felt a little bit of kinship to our thinking. Those were tough days for a black kid with an Afro haircut. That affected people's thinking in those days, strangely enough. Length of hair was a real factor."

Moore secured his starting spot in the backfield when the Ducks clobbered Utah 28-17 in the opener. Moore was nervous all week and didn't sleep the night before. Then he dropped his first pass. "Some guys on the Utah side shouted that I was no good, that I wouldn't catch anything," Moore said. "That burned me up."

Not to worry. Blanchard, who had returned from injury to reclaim his quarterback position, later connected with Moore for three touchdowns—a new single-game Oregon record, and the first of 14 school records Moore would establish as a Duck.

His first catch, a sensational mid-air display of soft hands and incredible leaping ability in the end zone, took everyone's breath away. Moore was going to be special.

"You could ask him to do anything," Frei said. "Whether you handed him the football or threw him the football, some of the acrobatic, athletic things he showed you on the field were absolutely astounding."

It was more of the same the following week at Stanford, despite a 28-0 setback. "We had three men on him (Moore)," said Stanford coach John Ralston, "and he still scared us to death. I drooled just watching him in warmups."

It would be a season marked by many ups and downs, spectacular individual plays and a score of what-ifs. After a 36-34 upset loss to San Jose State in week four, Frei said he had just experienced his most disappointing loss. Not so.

LEFT: OMRI HILDRETH PLAYED MONSTER BACK FOR THREE SEASONS AND WAS NAMED ALL-CONFERENCE HIS SENIOR YEAR IN 1968.

a 20-13 loss to No. 1-ranked USC in Eugene. The talent-loaded Trojans featured Steve Sogge at quarterback, O.J. Simpson at tailback and Bob Klein at tight end. The Ducks outrushed USC 152-87, holding Simpson to 67 yards in 25 carries—one of the worst games of his career at Southern California.

A relieved O.J. Simpson said: "I think I'll stay away from Oregon from now on. Nothing good has happened for two years now. Oregon just doesn't like me."

A 27-13 triumph over 1-5-1 Washington State on the strength of Olson's three touchdown passes left the Ducks fourth in the Pac-8 at 4-4 overall and 2-2 in league play.

At long last, Frei felt like he was onto something. Then the Ducks went to Cal and got blown out 36-8. "You didn't see our football team," Frei said later. "We thought our program was really progressing on schedule, and this was like a train derailment."

The Beavers, coming off a gut-wrenching 17-13 loss to Southern California that cost them a Rose Bowl berth, were in no mood to soothe the Ducks' egos. Oregon State coach Dee Andros exhorted the Beavers to 41-19 route of the Ducks in Corvallis. It was the most lopsided Civil War victory since 1942.

plexing 17-17 tie with Army at home, *The Oregonian's* Leo Davis wrote, "At last Oregon leads the league in something. Frustration."

A 13-10 loss at home to Rose Bowl contender UCLA only added to the Ducks' frustration. John Harrington's end-zone pass to Moore from the Bruins' 15-yard line might have won the game, but it was intercepted.

At 4-4-1 overall and 2-2 in the Pac-8, the Ducks were hopeful of finally finishing with a winning record, but Oregon State was next. And Frei was once again unable to beat the Beavers' jinx. Oregon State won 10-7 in a bizarre game with a finish that left Frei wondering about the sanity of his profession. A disappointed crowd of 42,500—the first sellout with standing room only at Autzen—sat numb in the aftermath.

The Ducks finished 5-5-1, but Moore led the Pac-8 in scoring with 92 points on 15 touchdown catches, and in pass receiving with 54 receptions. In doing so, he also broke Renfro's single-season scoring record and tied the school's single-season reception record.

Lost in the fine print was perhaps the greatest single-game performance ever by an Oregon linebacker. Sophomore Tom Graham was in on 41 tackles, 24 unassisted, against the Beavers. In his last five games, he made 128 stops, a staggering total in the days when defensive statistics weren't kept as meticulously as rushing and passing records.

In three years, Frei had come close enough to believe he could get the Ducks back to where they were during the glory years under Casanova. But there were always injuries and setbacks. And, once again, the loss to Oregon State brought with it the crushing realization that Oregon's Civil War losing streak stretched back to 1964.

Seven days later, the Ducks were humiliated 60-13 at Air Force in the famous fog game.

It was the Ducks' worst defeat in 18 years, and it came on a day when no one in the stands or up in the press box could see what was happening on the field during the second half. Oregon fumbled seven times, and a distraught Frei—angered by some media jabs and rumors of dissension within the team—said that if his players couldn't rebound from the experience in Colorado Springs then maybe it was time for him to quit.

The Ducks pulled together for their principled coach who put his head on the block so his players would be spared the media knife. Oregon beat Washington 22-7 then pummeled Idaho 58-14. Moore caught three touchdown passes in the rout over the Vandals. He was already approaching Mel Renfro's single-season school scoring record. But while Moore's outstanding performances were becoming predictable, the team was anything but that. After a per-

Who's This Kid Named Dan Fouts?

In September 1970, Leonard J. Casanova retired after four years as Oregon's athletic director. Norval Ritchie, a longtime athletic department administrator, was named as his successor. Before Christmas, events would dictate still more change.

For the first time in years, the Ducks opened preseason practice amidst high expectations. In *The Oregonian,*

football beat writer Don McLeod stated flatly that the Ducks would contend for the Pac-8 title and the Rose Bowl. And Frei didn't stamp out the fires of hope. Indeed, he told the media in August: "We have the talent to go all the way, but we have to keep our fingers crossed."

Veteran quarterback Tom Blanchard was back, bad knees and all, and Oregon also had a wondrous 6-3, 180-pound sophomore from the Bay Area named Dan Fouts. "He was looking for a passing school, and we convinced him we were going to throw the ball," Frei said. "If you talked to Dan today, he would probably tell you he wanted to go to Stanford, but Stanford wouldn't give him a scholarship."

The UO roster looked impressive in 1970 with Bobby Moore, Bob Newland, Greg Specht and Leland Glass on offense. Lionel Coleman, Bill Drake, Fred Manuel, Bill Brauner and Steve Rennie led a respected defense. The Ducks were likely contenders, but once again there was no depth. The program couldn't afford major injuries, and the injuries came early.

In the season-opening 31-24 victory over Cal at Portland's Civic Stadium, All-Conference linebacker Tom Graham was carried off the field with a knee strain. Newland suffered a mild concussion, and Blanchard, in a scene typical of his entire career, re-injured his troublesome knee tripping over a loose piece of artificial turf on the Civic Stadium infield.

Oregon lost five fumbles, had four passes picked off, but still managed to take care of the Bears. Fouts made a George Gipp-type entrance into Oregon football, engineering two second-half touchdown drives, including a 32-yarder to Thurman Anderson with 1:44 left to win the game.

The Sunday papers described the young quarterback as "a skinny-legged soph who grew up in the shadow of Sproul Hall [on the Cal campus]." Neil Cawood, who covered the Ducks for the *Eugene Register-Guard*, took one look at Fouts' slender frame and christened him the "Splendid Splinter," swiping the nickname of baseball's Ted Williams. "God, I hated

that nickname," Fouts would later say.

But Fouts, who was destined to be inducted into the National Football League Hall of Fame as one of the greatest pro quarterbacks ever, proved to be a lot tougher than he looked.

The following week, Illinois stopped Moore—who didn't start and played sparingly because of a dislocated toe—on the 1-yard line in the last two minutes to edge the Ducks 20-16 in Champagne. Blanchard and Newland teamed up on a 95-yard pass play, the longest in school history. Graham was still out with a bad knee, and once again Fouts had to replace Blanchard late in the game.

Fouts' made his first start for the Ducks on September 26, 1970. The opponent was Jim Plunkett's Stanford, a team barreling toward the Pac-8 championship and a Rose Bowl berth. Plunkett completed 18 of 38 passes for 250 yards and three scores in the Indians' 33-10 victory over Oregon. But Fouts' numbers (27 of 51 for 271 yards and one touchdown),

were even more impressive. However, he also threw three interceptions.

After the first three weeks of the season, Oregon lead the nation in passing, averaging 326 yards per game. But the Ducks' running game had accounted for only 95 net yards.

"Embarrassing," Frei admitted. But he wasn't about to change his earlier decision to move the multi-talented Moore from his usual position of slotback to tailback. Complaints that Moore fumbled too much and couldn't handle the tailback position continued until week four when Oregon ran over Washington State 28-13. Moore rushed for 183 yards on 25 carries and the Ducks gained 286 yards on the ground. Frei wasn't surprised by Moore's performance. "I know that young man's pride and courage," he said.

Moore would finish the season with 924 yards, breaking Mel Renfro's school record of 753, despite missing almost two full games.

On the night of October 10, 1970, Oregon met UCLA in Los Angeles for what would be remembered as one of the greatest comebacks in college football history.

With 4:28 remaining, Oregon trailed UCLA 40-21. Sophomore Dan Fouts had quarterbacked the Ducks throughout the game, but now Frei sent in senior Tom Blanchard, nursing a sore knee.

It took Blanchard three plays and 24 seconds to get the Ducks into the end zone, the touchdown coming on a 29-yard pass to Bobby Moore. It was 40-28 with 4:04 remaining.

Needing simply to hold onto the ball, the Bruins couldn't. Delton Lewis recovered a fumble for Oregon on the UCLA 40. Two plays later, Blanchard hit Moore down the sideline, behind the UCLA defense to make it 40-35 with 2:24 remaining. Oregon's Don Frease recovered the ensuing onside kick.

Blanchard suffered an injured shoulder on the next play and Fouts returned. With less than a minute left, he fired a 15-yard touchdown pass to tight end Greg Specht for the victory.

Afterward, Oregon Coach Jerry Frei wiped tears from his eyes. "This has got to top anything that ever happened to me," he said. "This is about as much guts as a team could show."

Oregon crushed Idaho 49-13 in the next game, bringing its record to 4-2 overall and 3-1 in the Pac-8. The Ducks were raring to get after USC the following Saturday in Eugene, and they did.

USC was stifled offensively, and Linebacker Tom Graham, incensed over the Los Angeles media calling the UO defense "Swiss cheese," told reporters afterward, "I'll bet it's cheddar now." Indeed the Trojans, who had won four consecutive Pac-8 titles, were overwhelmed by the Ducks in the driving rain.

That night the city of Eugene celebrated. Sunday's headline blared, *UO Hobbles Troy, 10-7; Roses Alive*. Days later, Oregon was ranked 16th by the Associated Press.

The roses wilted the next weekend in Seattle, however, when Sonny Sixkiller out-dueled Fouts. Oregon, leading 23-22 in the fourth quarter, seemed content to run out the clock, but Fouts had the ball knocked loose after he ran for a first down. Washington recovered with 1:30 on the clock, and the Huskies defeated the Ducks 25-23 on Steve Wiezbowski's 19-yard field goal in the final minute.

A potentially fantastic season began going the other way. A few days after the emotional loss in Seattle, Frei was forced to suspend Moore for an incident in Portland.

Oregon then played back-to-back non-conference games against teams of the armed forces. Fouts threw four touchdown passes in a 46-35 triumph over Air Force, snapping the Falcons' eight-game winning streak, and Army tied Oregon 22-22 at West Point.

The Ducks, now 6-3-1, faced 5-5 Oregon State in the season finale, knowing that a victory would assure a tie for second in the Pac-8—a remarkable achievement considering everything Frei's players had gone through. Certainly, this would be the end of Oregon State's six-game winning streak in the Civil War.

Frei didn't recognize his team. Oregon lost three fumbles, had three passes intercepted and coughed up the football four times inside its own 35-yard line. Meanwhile, Oregon State unleashed reserve fullback Mike Davenport, a 210-pound sophomore, and he scored two fourth-quarter touchdowns in a surprising 24-9 victory.

More Frustration and Frei's Exit

In Frei's day, Oregon was willing to accept suicide road games with powerhouses such as Nebraska and Oklahoma because the athletic department needed the money. Hence a 34-7 loss to No. 1-ranked Nebraska to start the 1971 season wasn't so bad from a financial standpoint. The Ducks got $100,000 for their trouble, and the Cornhuskers picked up their 19th straight victory.

The following week, Bobby Moore romped for a school-record 249 yards rushing in a 36-29 triumph over Utah at Autzen Stadium. He also caught three passes for 89 yards and tossed a 34-yard touchdown pass of his own. "I guess we made an All-American out of him tonight," said Utah coach Bill Meek. Moore would have been closer to 300 yards rushing, but a 35-yard run was wiped out by a penalty.

Anticipation ran high before the game with No. 10 Stanford. Frei called it "the most important game on our schedule." But the Ducks lost more than the game as quarterback Dan Fouts went down with strained knee ligaments

in a 38-17 defeat. Moore rushed for 150 yards, and afterward, Stanford assistant Bill Moultrie told him he was the best back he had ever seen. "Better than O.J.?" Moore asked. Moultrie nodded. "Yep," he said. "You can do it all and you're bigger."

Norval Turner and 5-foot-8 Harvey Winn alternated at quarterback during the next week's practice as Oregon prepared for another "payday game," this one at powerful Texas. Moore rushed for 110 yards—his third straight 100-yards-plus game—and the diminutive Winn threw a 44-yard touchdown pass to Leland Glass in the fourth quarter. But the Longhorns romped 35-7.

Frei called an emergency meeting of his staff under the wing of the team plane. "From now on, Harvey Winn is 6 feet tall," Frei announced, a signal to the media that Oregon would no longer change its offensive attack because of Winn's size.

Nonetheless, the Ducks weren't given much of a chance without Fouts. The junior from St. Ignatius High in San Francisco had set six single-season records and tied another as a sophomore. In just one season, he had moved

to No. 3 on Oregon's all-time passing list behind Bob Berry and George Shaw, and earned *Football News* All-America honors.

Southern Cal might have expected an easy game without Fouts, but the Trojans forgot to duck, as Winn unloaded three touchdown passes in a stunning 28-23 victory. Before Winn could be named the most unlikely football hero of the season, Southern Cal's Jimmy Jones' 77-yard touchdown pass to speedster Edesel Garrison in the final seconds had to be called back because of an illegal receiver downfield.

Breathing in the intoxicating smell of success, the Ducks rode the momentum to a stirring 23-21 victory over Washington, in which Moore broke Jim Shanley's school rushing record in front of a roaring home crowd of 44,200. But Dave Pieper's 47-yard interception return provided the spark. Pieper waved the football in the Huskies' faces as he crossed the goal line with the errant Sonny Sixkiller pass.

The Ducks then mopped up San Jose State 34-14, losing key defensive back Dave Pieper for the year in the process, but improving their record to 4-3 overall and 2-1 in the Pac-8.

Oregon clung to a slim ray of hope in the championship race after Washington State shocked Stanford, but Frei's squad lost a bitter 31-21 decision to WSU in Pullman the following week on a bitingly cold 31-degree day.

By the time the Ducks got to the '71 Civil War game, they were 5-5 and limping badly. Among the missing were junior college transfer wide receiver Larry Battle, Fouts' fastest target, and the great Bobby Moore, who watched what should have been his final collegiate game from the sidelines with a bruised left leg.

"I kept hoping for the miracle," Frei told *The Oregonian.* "I suspected [Moore] wouldn't play, but I just wouldn't believe. It wouldn't have been fair to play Bob. I did what I thought was right."

Oregon State won the battle 30-29. The Ducks competed, but for the eighth straight time, it was Oregon State celebrating at the gun.

Dissatisfaction with Frei and his staff—however unfair—was boiling over among a few prominent boosters, most of them from Portland. New Athletic Director Norv Ritchey was concerned, but he did not communicate those concerns to his head coach, who had stood by his principles and put the well-being of his players first when he told Bobby Moore to sit out.

On January 18, 1972, Frei returned from a three-week trip in which he had been at the NCAA coaches' meetings in Hollywood, Florida, screening applicants for jobs; had helped Nebraska's Bob Devaney coach in the Hula Bowl All-Star game; and had buried his father, who passed on in Wisconsin.

John Robinson, an assistant at Oregon for 12 years, left to become an assistant coach at Southern California. Defensive coordinator and right-hand man Norm Chapman resigned to go into private business. Ritchey told Frei that meetings had been held about the program without Frei's knowledge. Under pressure from Portland boosters, who also put pressure on the administration of the University who in turn put pressure on Ritchey, Ritchey suggested Frei get rid of his remaining assistants. One of them was George Seifert, who would go on to win two Super Bowls as the head coach of the San Francisco 49ers.

Frei refused, announcing his resignation on January 19. His statement read, "In the existing atmosphere of rumor and innuendos, as printed in the newspapers, it would be impossible for me to carry on in the manner in which I felt necessary to make continuing progress with our program."

Less than a month later, offensive line coach Dick Enright took over after passing muster with a 15-member screening committee that included UO players Dan Fouts and Tim Stokes. Frei, meanwhile, was almost immediately hired as an assistant coach by the Denver Broncos.

Moore, who left behind school records for the most yards rushing (2,306), most receptions (131) and most points scored (226), was taken by St. Louis as the No. 4 pick in the first round of the NFL draft. But his best days as a pro came years later at Minnesota, where he played in four Pro Bowls and helped the Vikings to the Super Bowl.

Tom Drougas was drafted in the first round as well, as the No. 22 overall pick, by Baltimore. Tom Graham went to

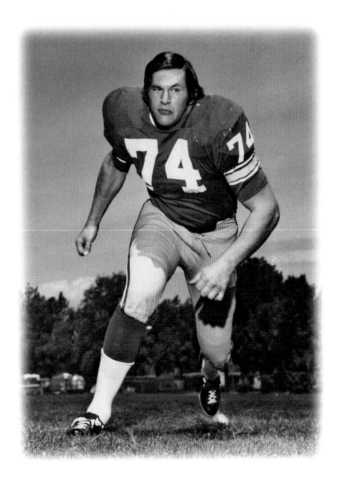

ABOVE: TOM DROUGAS WAS AN ALL-AMERICA OFFENSIVE TACKLE IN 1971.

Denver in the fourth round, no coincidence. Frei and Graham lived in Denver for many years thereafter and became close friends.

The Enright Years Begin

Over the next five years, the football program at the University of Oregon was sent to the showers. Interest waned as time passed, and the gate receipts continued to drop. Frei had compiled a 22-29 record in his five years at the school. In the following five years, Oregon went 14-40-0.

Oregon's football future looked bleak. After watching a 5-2 loss to San Jose State in 1975, new UO President William Boyd said, "I'd rather be whipped in public than watch a game like that."

Enright, a stocky, gregarious man, was 37 when Frei offered him a job as the Ducks' offensive line coach in the

spring of 1970. He had played football for Jess Hill at Southern California, then had his brief pro career with the Los Angeles Rams cut short by an automobile accident.

After the accident, Enright entered private business, only to be lured back to his to alma mater Gardena High School to coach football in 1962. He compiled a 70-11-0 prep coaching record in eight years before accepting the UO position. Three of Enright's Gardena players were on the '71 Oregon squad: fullback Greg Herd, defensive end Keith Davis and linebacker Tim Guy.

As the Ducks' newly appointed head coach, Enright told reporters before the 1972 season that he would retain assistant coach John Marshall. He also said the Ducks would employ more rollout and option plays in their offensive attack and switch to a Nebraska-type 5-2 defense.

Oregon had a classic drop-back quarterback in Fouts, who was returning for his senior year, so the option strategy was puzzling. "He's a better runner than most people realize," Enright insisted. "His knee is 100 percent, he's 10 pounds heavier, and he has legitimate 4.7 speed."

Before Fouts was through, and despite a disappointing 4-7 season, he would rank No. 7 on the NCAA's all-time passing list. He set 19 school records before the San Diego Chargers made him their No. 1 draft pick. And the Chargers weren't paying him to run the option: Fouts was the heir apparent to San Diego's aging legend, Johnny Unitas.

Even with Fouts flinging to stellar tight ends Russ Francis and George Martin, and backs Don Reynolds and Greg "Buffalo" Herd running the ball, the Ducks were badly outmanned in many of their games.

The '72 team wasn't without talent—Enright's first roster included Reggie Lewis, Eugene Brown, Tim Stokes, LeFrancis Arnold, Greg Specht and Tim Guy.

Oregon suffered a humiliating 68-3 loss at Oklahoma in week three. Don Read, who coached the quarterbacks and receivers, remembers being in the press box that day at Norman, Oklahoma, yelling down excitedly at Enright, "They're only going to rush three people! Fouts will kill 'em."

The comical postscript to the 65-point loss came later, when Kerry Jackson's ineligibility because of a doctored transcript gave Oregon a 2-0 forfeit in the official record books. Oregon sports information director, Hal Cowan, asked Oklahoma officials, "Does this mean we get the game ball back?"

The Ducks arrived somewhat worse for wear for the Civil War game. They were 3-7 and insulted by the odds makers installing the 2-8 Beavers as a slim favorite. Enright, noting Oregon State's eight-game winning streak in the series, said at midweek, "Dee [Andros] is like the guy playing Russian roulette. He knows there has to be a bullet in the chamber somewhere."

The Ducks found a bullet. Reynolds' 60-yard touchdown run on the first play set the tone, and Fouts had a fat cigar in his mouth on the sidelines after the 30-3 Oregon victory.

At San Diego, Fouts teamed with the likes of Charlie Joiner to put on some of the most exciting aerial displays in NFL history, prompting comparisons with Unitas and the other all-time greats. He earned a reputation for toughness, staying in the pocket longer than most dared, and releasing the ball with pinpoint accuracy at the last possible moment.

Upon retiring, he embarked on a successful career as a broadcaster, following in the footsteps of his father, the long-time voice of the San Francisco 49ers.

Goodbye, Dick, We Hardly Knew Ya

Dick Enright had no reason to believe his second season would be his final season. The Ducks had won their last two games in his first year and finally buried the Oregon State jinx. Moreover, Oregon returned 39 lettermen in the fall of '73, including eight starters on offense and eight on defense. Enright said Norval Turner, the heir apparent at quarterback, had a "superior football mind." This was an interesting comment in that the much-maligned Turner would one day become a highly regarded NFL head coach with the Washington Redskins.

The pieces seemed to be in place for at least a slight improvement from the 4-7 mark in 1972. But it didn't happen. Oregon went 2-9, and that was the end of the Enright era.

Enright should have seen it coming in week one, when 14-point underdog Arizona State came to Eugene and pulled off a 26-20 upset, despite Don Reynolds' considerable heroics. The little tailback had 128 yards rushing, 102 more on kickoff returns and 58 yards on pass receptions. But the Sun Devils had Danny White at quarterback and Portland's own Woody Green to run the ball.

Oregon lost 24-17 at Air Force, although the ABC-TV audience came away talking about Russ Francis' brilliant 68-yard touchdown catch and Reynolds' dazzling 46-yard run that featured at least a half-dozen changes of

direction. Singleton didn't get off the bench. An eligibility question had to be cleared up before he could compete with Turner.

The Ducks returned home only to be belted 35-17 by Utah in a game marred by seven UO turnovers. Once again Reynolds was a one-man highlight film with 179 yards rushing, but it wasn't enough to counteract the turnovers.

It was Enright's bad luck to catch Michigan in a foul mood at home. The Wolverines had just beaten Navy 14-0, but Coach Bo Schembechler was steaming. His team rolled over the Ducks 24-0.

Turner's future, meanwhile, looked bleak. "We found our quarterback today," Enright said at Michigan. And he was talking about Herb Singleton.

After a 41-10 victory over California, in which the 5-foot-8 Reynolds scored three times and ran for 178 yards, Oregon, sporting a 1-4 record, arrived in Los Angeles for a game against John McKay's Southern Cal team. The Trojans won 31-10.

Surprisingly, Oregon blew out Washington 58-0 in the next game, as Singleton threw three touchdown passes and Steve Donnelly reeled off a 78-yard punt return.

Humiliating the Huskies was the high-water mark for Enright, who would see his team lose to Washington State (21-14), UCLA (27-7), Stanford (24-7) and Oregon State (17-14) in the next four weeks. Oregon was slowed by the flu at Stanford, where Cardinal Coach Jack Christiansen said after the game, "Oregon is better than 2-8. It can beat anybody, anywhere."

The Civil War game in Corvallis, Enright's final three hours on the sidelines, seemed like a continuation of the

LEFT:
HALFBACK
DON REYNOLDS
CARRIES AGAINST
STANFORD.

Stanford game. The Ducks committed seven turnovers. Enright started Turner because the game plan called for more running. He was roundly criticized for waiting too long to bring in Simpleton .

On Friday, January 4, Enright was fired. The University bought out the remaining two years of his contract at $23,625 per year. Athletic Director Norv Ritchey told Enright he was not happy with the direction of the program. "This is one of the saddest days of my life, but it is a move I think is necessary," Ritchey said in a prepared statement, noting he hadn't slept in three weeks agonizing over the decision.

For what it was worth, Enright left as the first UO football coach since Jim Aiken (1947-49) not to have a losing record against Oregon State.

Ritchey didn't look far for a replacement. He just walked down the hall. Don Read, the Ducks' quarterback and receiver coach, was hired immediately.

Read had to tell Bud Riley, the head coach of the CFL Winnipeg Blue Bombers, that he wasn't interested in an assistant's job. Something better had come up. At the age of 40, he was considered a brilliant offensive mind. He had written two books, *The Complete Passing Game* and *The Line*

of Scrimmage.

Read joined the Oregon staff in 1972, after serving as head football coach and athletic director at Portland State. He distinguished himself by coaching Dan Fouts, who would later say that Read was much more than his position coach. "He was like a father to me," Fouts recalled.

Two assistants, Fred von Appen and Steve Sogge, said they would stay on. Read was ready for the challenge of his career. He thought he could succeed, but events conspired against him, beginning with Singleton's freak broken wrist injury later that summer.

LEFT:
QUARTERBACK
NORV TURNER
ROLLS OUT TO
PASS DURING A
1973 HOME GAME.
TWO DECADES
LATER, TURNER
WAS THE HEAD
COACH OF THE
WASHINGTON
REDSKINS.

A Rude Awakening for a Nice Man

Read closed preseason practices as Oregon worked on a veer offense designed to take advantage of running backs Don Reynolds and Rick Kane. Oregon's defense, amazingly, was ranked No. 2 overall in the Pac-8 and first against the run in 1973. Eight starters returned, including All-Coast performers Reggie Lewis, a defensive tackle, free safety Steve Donnelly, cornerback Mario Clark, and linebacker Bobby Green. For better or worse, Norval Turner was the quarterback.

After a 2-1 start, with victories over Air Force (27-23) and Utah (23-16) following a 61-7 thumping at Nebraska, Read's Ducks lost eight straight. It was the beginning of a horrible 14-game losing streak, which would last more than two years and ultimately cost yet another decent man his job. Eugene was turning into a coaching black hole.

Read lasted three seasons, but he won't soon forget year one, when most of the setbacks were of the staggering variety, such as a 66-0 defeat to Washington at Seattle.

Afterward, Read apologized to Oregon fans, who by now were a sullen, fatalistic lot. Before a 21-0 loss to UCLA, Read reluctantly kicked Reggie Lewis off the squad for disciplinary reasons.

The season ended on a sour note with the Beavers beating the Ducks 35-15.

More Buzzard's Luck for Read

Read improved Oregon's record by one game the following year. The Ducks finished 3-8 and beat Andros' Beavers 14-7, their first Civil War victory in Eugene in 12 years.

The Ducks opened with a dreadful 62-7 loss at Oklahoma. The No. 1-ranked Sooners gave Oregon $125,000 for its trouble, which tickled the athletic department but did little for Read's peace of mind.

A 5-2 loss at home to San Jose State was the season's low point. Finally in week seven, Oregon snapped its 14-game losing streak with an 18-7 victory over Utah. Happy players threw Read into the showers. He had just received a contract extension that carried through the '76 season.

Along with the Civil War game came the news that Andros was retiring at the end of the year. Chuck Wills' 15-yard interception return highlighted the Ducks' triumph over Oregon State.

Declining Attendance Sinks Read

Read began the 1976 season with a promise of a more exciting, wide-open offense led by junior quarterback Jack Henderson. Later, he said he made the comments in a deliberate attempt to boost his players' spirits after the trauma of '75. The Oregon coach wanted the pressure on his shoulders rather than on his players. "We went out on a limb," Read admitted during his final days in November.

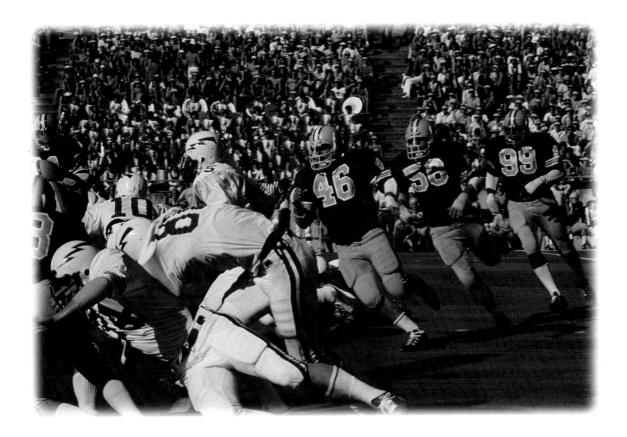

After a 3-1 start, it seemed Read's bold words weren't so far-fetched. Oregon victories over Colorado State (17-3), Utah (21-13) and Utah State (27-9) were sandwiched around a 53-0 spanking at the hands of Southern California.

In week five, Cal beat the Ducks 27-10, starting them on a six-game slide. Then came lopsided losses at Notre Dame (41-0) and UCLA (46-0), in addition to a hard-fought defeat at home to Stanford (28-17).

Civil War week finally arrived. Oregon was 3-7, Oregon State 1-9. *Basement Bowl*, read the headlines. *The Game of the Weak.*

Days before the game, rumor had it that Read was either resigning voluntarily, being forced to resign or retiring. "We were told a week before the Civil War game that we were being evaluated," Read said.

Read's finale was memorable: Henderson brought Oregon back from a two-touchdown deficit and the Ducks won 23-14, fueling speculation that the head coach had been saved in spite of a three-year run of 2-9, 3-8 and 4-7 seasons.

UO players wrote a letter to new Athletic Director John Caine, pleading the popular Read's case. Former Athletic Director Ritchie had earlier been relieved and given an administrative position in the College of Human Performance and Development. Caine and UO President William Boyd were to meet the Monday after the Civil War game.

Read said he wouldn't quit. "There will be no surprise announcements from me," he declared.

Three days later Read was fired. Caine said a successor would be found from outside of the University of Oregon. Members of the current staff need not apply. Read received $28,000 for the remainder of his contract and gracefully said his goodbyes.

Attendance in 1976 averaged just 27,180 per home game, not nearly enough to support a low-budget program such as Oregon's. Utah State brought a mere 17,300 to Auzten. In addition, the budget was now cut into more slices with women students entering intercollegiate competition.

In 10 tumultuous years, the Ducks had three football coaches, four athletic directors, three presidents and just one winning season (1970).

Oregon football couldn't go much lower. Somewhere there was a coach who could get Oregon back to the Rose Bowl. The trick was finding him.

RICH BROOKS RIDES
TRIUMPHANTLY ON HIS
PLAYERS' SHOULDERS
AFTER A VICTORY AT
AUTZEN STADIUM
EARLY IN HIS 18-YEAR
TENURE AS HEAD
COACH.

THE RICH BROOKS ERA

The University of Oregon was not exactly over-whelmed by big-name candidates when it went looking for a new head football coach following the 1976 season.

The Ducks had managed just one winning season in the previous 12, and during that span Jerry Frei had resigned under pressure, while Dick Enright and Don Read were fired. The UO facilities were regarded as the worst in the Pac-8 Conference, the athletic budget did not compare to that of many competitors, the talent level in the football program was obviously low and the morale was even worse.

The program was a mess and proven head coaches wanted no part of it. Neither did many highly regarded assistants who would later make their marks elsewhere, including Bill Walsh (then) of the San Diego Chargers and Jim Mora of Washington. But despite all that, could the Ducks bring themselves to settle for a former player and assistant coach at rival Oregon State, one who had a year earlier been rejected by the Beavers themselves?

That's what Rich Brooks wanted to know. "I had real doubts about how I would be received in Eugene," he recalled. "I remember I went straight from the airport to the Valley River Inn for a meeting with boosters and alumni, and the first thing somebody said as people were

ABOVE: BROOKS WAS NAMED OREGON'S HEAD COACH IN LATE 1976 AT AGE 35.

BELOW: DEFENSIVE TACKLE VINCE GOLDSMITH WAS A TWO-TIME ALL-CONFERENCE STAR ON THE EARLY BROOKS TEAMS.

sort of sizing me up was, 'So you're that damn Aggie.' I thought to myself, 'Here we go!' To this day, I know I wasn't their first choice. But I don't really care about that."

Brooks just wanted a chance, and he felt confident he could lead a major college football program. A safety and backup quarterback to Heisman Trophy winner Terry Baker at Oregon State, Brooks had coached under Dee Andros during the glory years at OSU in the late 1960s; then Tommy Prothro at UCLA and the Los Angeles Rams; Dick Nolan at the San Francisco 49ers; and Terry Donahue at UCLA.

He had joined Donahue's staff for the 1976 season almost reluctantly after nearly getting out of coaching. "In a span of months, I missed out on the Oregon State job that I wanted very badly, then our staff was fired by the 49ers and

then I didn't get jobs I thought I would at Green Bay and Cleveland," Brooks said. "I was prepared to go into business rather than take a step backward.

"Finally, I decided to take the UCLA thing, work my butt off and see if I could turn things around. You just can't quit, but there's no rhyme or reason to what happened. One year I missed the job I really wanted and the next year I got the job most people would have regarded as the one I would be least likely to get."

At age 35, Brooks became the UO head football coach just before Christmas 1976. The lesson he learned chasing his dream one final time by returning to UCLA—"You just can't quit!"-would time and again be a fitting epithet for the Brooks Era of Oregon football.

High Hopes and Hard Times

The enthusiasm and optimism that always kick in with a coaching change carried the Ducks early in the 1977 season. They were competitive in a 26-16 loss at Georgia in Brooks' first game as head coach, then won 29-24 the next week at Texas Christian.

They lost respectably to Wisconsin and Stanford. But then came the rude awakening as the Ducks were bombed 54-0 at Autzen Stadium by Washington.

"Coaches are people who overestimate their own ability, and ego sometimes gets involved," Brooks said. "I thought we could come (to Eugene) and turn this thing around in short order. Obviously, we found we had a lot further to go than we realized. Maybe the guys who didn't take this job were smarter than I was. We were not a very good football team."

Against Washington, the Ducks weren't even competitive. Once the snowball started rolling, Brooks didn't

feel his team did much to stop it. He did not report to practice the following Monday with morale-building on his mind.

"We usually practiced in helmets and shorts on Mondays," offensive lineman Steve Greatwood recalled. "The coaches came down for practice a little late, and word got out we were going in full gear. We scrimmaged, we went one-on-one; it was the most brutal practice I've ever seen. We lost Fred Quillan and Mel Cook for the season, so maybe it backfired a little bit. But Rich felt we'd given in to adversity, and we had. He wanted to instill in us that no matter what happens, we were going to fight and compete."

The fruits of that lesson would not be reaped in 1977, however. The Ducks continued to lose decisively each week, giving up 56 points to both Louisiana State and Washington State, and 48 to UCLA. But Oregon finished Brooks' first season on a positive note with a 28-16 upset of Oregon State, though Oregon's overall record was just 2-9. Brooks obviously wasn't going to be a miracle worker.

1978

Bittersweet Improvement

A cursory look would suggest Brooks' second season was no better than his first. Oregon was again 2-9, as the Ducks won for the first time on week No. 8 with a 31-7 thrashing of Washington State, then again finished the season with a 24-3 upset of Oregon State. But the 1978 season, marked by the addition of Arizona and Arizona State to form the Pac-10 Conference, was a bittersweet one for the Ducks, albeit a lot more bitter than sweet.

The Ducks, despite their record, were remarkably improved. Excellent young players recruited by Brooks, such as defenders Vince Goldsmith, Willie Blasher, Bryan Hinkle and Mike Nolan, plus standout running backs Vince Williams and Dwight Robertson, began to pay dividends. Some veteran holdovers from the Read regime bought into the Brooks approach and began making positive contributions. But the Ducks couldn't win for losing, dropping six games by a total of 19 points.

"When you are used to losing, it's really easy to callous yourself as a player or coach and not let yourself get emotionally involved for fear it will happen again and hurt even

worse," Greatwood said. "We didn't do that. We kept laying it on the line, and it kept hurting worse and worse."

Brooks even took to reading books about positive thinking as he searched for ways to turn around the psyche of his struggling team. "If people think they are not supposed to win and they are playing well just by reacting," explained Brooks, "when it gets to crunch time they will start thinking, 'Oh, God, we could win this thing,' and all of

ABOVE: VINCE WILLIAMS WAS OREGON'S LEADING RUSHER IN 1978.

a sudden they won't react and play like they did to get in that position."

The agony of 1978 was compounded by the fact that in five of Oregon's six close losses, the Ducks led entering the fourth quarter or at some point during the final quarter. "We made the mistakes we had to make to lose," Brooks said. "We lost a lot of tough games and it was really discouraging. But we were a vastly improved football team."

Not only Brooks thought so. *Football News* looked

past the Ducks' record and rated them the fourth most improved team in the country.

Ogburn Breakthrough

Improved or not, no one was quite ready for the way Oregon opened the 1979 season. The Ducks played at Colorado, where the Buffaloes were heavy favorites and about to usher in the Chuck Fairbanks era. The former Oklahoma coach had just landed in Boulder after leaving the New England Patriots.

It couldn't have been laid out more perfectly for the Ducks. The entire nation was watching because of Fairbanks, but instead saw an unheralded JC transfer quarterback from Oregon rush for 108 yards and pass for 168 as the Ducks registered a shocking 33-19 upset victory.

"Reggie Ogburn was the key," Brooks said. "He was a phenomenal football player. Everybody remembers the way he could run the option, but the thing is he completed nearly 60 percent of his passes and had a great arm. We had some very impressive wins for a team that didn't know how to win. We were heavy underdogs against Colorado, but Reggie Ogburn single-handedly killed them running and throwing the football."

"Ogburn was a guy who could do things that nobody had been able to do before, and it opened up everything considerably," wide receiver Greg Moser added. "He was also a really deceptive leader because he was so intense and competitive. He wasn't boisterous or rah-rah, but he wasn't afraid to get in a guy's face, and he worked his butt off all the time. He made things happen that probably shouldn't have happened."

The UO program wasn't out of the woods, though. The Ducks were dominated 41-17 by Michigan State the next week, then lost a 21-17 game to Washington on Mark Lee's 53-yard punt return in the final minutes. It was one of the most heartbreaking losses Brooks would ever endure at Oregon, and there was no relief the next week as the Ducks barely lost to Purdue.

Oregon registered an important 19-14 upset of California to end their losing streak, but finally the season came down to beating the Beavers for Oregon's first win-

ning season since 1970. Brooks was 8-0-1 in the Civil War rivalry as a coach and player at Oregon State. There was no greater stamp he put on his UO program in the early days than his determination to dominate that rivalry, which he did for a third straight time at Oregon with a 24-3 victory that gave the Ducks a 6-5 season.

"Getting over that hump was extremely significant because so many losing seasons had stacked up on top of each other since 1970," Brooks recalled. "To have a winning season, to become a factor in the conference and win some conference games, that was incredibly important from the standpoint of believing we could win."

Excitement and Chaos

There has never been a season at Oregon like 1980— so much excitement and anticipation on the field, so much chaos and controversy off it.

Following the 1979 season, the Ducks were implicated along with four other Pac-10 schools in a phony credits scandal. The scheme was uncovered as part of a separate investigation into the New Mexico basketball program. Athletes were receiving credit for classes they weren't attending at a California junior college.

At Oregon, there were ultimately other charges, including improper telephone usage by coaches and athletes, and illegal travel reimbursement for players. By the time the season started, offensive coordinator John Becker had resigned; several players were declared ineligible for all or part of the season; Brooks and five other coaches were fined a total of $9,000; and the Ducks were placed on a two-year probation, stripped of three scholarships and ineligible for postseason consideration in 1980.

Brooks turned in his resignation. "I didn't have any feeling whether they would take it or not," Brooks recalled. "I was humiliated and felt it was the right thing to do."

Then-UO President William Boyd declined to accept Brooks' resignation. "We have conducted as thorough an investigation as I know how," Boyd said in February 1980. "Basically, all the facts are in now, and I think it is significant here at the end of all that, I still find Rich Brooks an honorable coach."

Finally, attention turned to the 1980 season, one that still held much promise for the Ducks. "There wasn't anybody at Oregon who had been to a bowl game," safety Mike Nolan said. "It wasn't like we thought much about missing out on that. We'd been playing for pride from the very beginning anyway. For whatever reason, it seemed we were able to block out a lot of that and just take a lot of pride in beating people."

But the Ducks were frustrated on the field as well. "Until my final years, that was clearly the most talented team we had at Oregon, and it probably should have ended up 9-2 or 8-3 under normal circumstances," Brooks said. "But they weren't normal, and I look back with pride that the players focused and came through it as well as they did."

Without Ogburn, who was ineligible for one game, the Ducks opened the season with a 35-25 loss to John Elway and the Stanford Cardinal. Even with Ogburn back the next week, they tied with Kansas 7-7.

"It was disappointing to start out the season that way," Brooks said. "We knew we had an outstanding team." It would soon be apparent. Michigan State came to Eugene thinking the Ducks would be easy pickings, as they had been the year before, and wound up leaving on the short end of a 35-7 score. It was Oregon's first win over a Big Ten

team since 1964.

"I remember Michigan State coming off the field after their Friday walk-through," Brooks recalled, "and their players were quacking at us, saying we'd be Duck soup and making fun of us. It was very satisfying to go out the next day and totally dominate the game. It was one of the more dominating games against a pretty talented team in all my years at Oregon."

But that was nothing compared to what would happen the next week. The Ducks broke a six-game losing streak to Washington and won in Seattle for the first time since 1968, thrashing the Huskies 34-10 to hand them their only Pac-10 loss in a Rose Bowl season.

However, the Ducks soon discovered that it can be as difficult to learn how to handle success as it can be to learn how to win. Oregon players had a week off following their victory over Washington and used it primarily to congratulate themselves.

The next week the

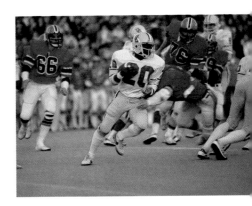

The Ducks had gotten off to a rocky start in Seattle, fumbling away their first two possessions. They were fortunate to be trailing only 10-6 at halftime, having managed two Pat English field goals.

Few words were spoken in the locker room at intermission.

"We were sitting back and trying to

Reggie Ogburn runs the options against the Huskies

figure out what Washington was doing on offense," Steve Brown said.

Later in the game, the sophomore cornerback would be instrumental in ensuring an Oregon victory.

Early in the third period, UO quarterback Reggie Ogburn hit flanker Curt Jackson on an 8-yard touchdown pass to give the Ducks a 13-10 lead.

But the turning point came later, when a near-interception by Brown and a key tackle by free safety Joe Figures stopped the Huskies four yards shy of a first down to end Washington's last serious drive of the contest.

Oregon took full advantage, marching

94 yards to score on a 3-yard keeper by Ogburn and increase its lead to 20-10.

Ten seconds later, Brown drove the final nail into the Huskies' coffin.

Washington quarterback Tom Flick—who began the game as the nation's leading passer—saw his flanker, Paul Skansi, breaking open over the middle.

He didn't see Brown.

"I was watching [Flick's] eyes, and I could see he was looking at [Skansi], Brown said. "So I left my man and went for the ball."

With 11:17 remaining, Brown stepped in front of Skansi at the Husky 36. He intercepted the ball and raced down the sideline to the end zone.

The rout was on.

Ogburn scored the Ducks' final touchdown on a 1-yard plunge with 4:13 left to give Oregon one of it's sweetest victories, 34-10.

The game also helped take the pressure of Oregon coach Rich Brooks, who called it the biggest victory of his career to that point.

"This was the first time we have beaten a ranked team," Brooks said. "We finally were able to end Washington's strangle-hold on the Northwest, and we were able to do it in a hostile stadium."

It was the first time the Ducks had beaten Washington in nine years, and Oregon's first triumph in Husky Stadium since 1968.

"This was like a bowl victory for us," said Brown, who, as Nick Bertram of *The Oregonian* pointed out, was "becoming one of the best at his position in the country."

CORNERBACK STEVE BROWN HAD SOME SPECIAL MOTIVATION FOR HIS OUTSTANDING PERFORMANCE IN OREGON'S 34-27 VICTORY OVER THE HUSKIES ON SEPTEMBER 27, 1980.

BEFORE THE GAME, STEVE HAD ADMIRED A SPECIAL OREGON DUCK LAPEL PIN WORN BY STAUNCH DUCK SUPPORTER HAROLD TAYLOR.

"YOU PICK OFF A PASS FOR ME AND YOU CAN HAVE IT," HAROLD BARGAINED.

STEVE GRINNED, THEN REPLIED THAT HE WOULD DO HIM ONE BETTER.

"I'LL SCORE A TOUCHDOWN WITH IT," HE SAID.

STEVE KEPT HIS PROMISE EARLY IN THE FOURTH QUARTER, WITH A DRAMATIC PICK AND A 36-YARD RACE TO THE END ZONE. IN THE POSTGAME CELEBRATION, HE SOUGHT OUT HAROLD.

"I TOLD YOU SO, HAROLD!" HE GUSHED.

HIS INSPIRATIONAL GESTURE WAS ONLY ONE OF MANY WAYS HAROLD HAS SHOWN HIMSELF A LOYAL FRIEND OF THE DUCKS.

STILL PROUDLY WEARING HIS SPECIAL DUCK PIN 15 YEARS LATER, STEVE VOWS, "I'LL NEVER, NEVER PART WITH IT."

HAROLD TAYLOR *(left)* WITH FORMER HEAD FOOTBALL COACH RICH BROOKS *(center)* AND FORMER ATHLETIC DIRECTOR BILL BYRNE *(right)*.

Photo by Chris Pietsch, Register-Guard

Ducks suffered an unbelievable 31-6 loss to a California team that would finish the year 3-8. "After two great wins, we just weren't ready to play Cal," Brooks admitted. "We were fatheaded and lethargic. It was an extremely tough loss."

Oregon tied USC 7-7 the next week, leaving the Ducks with a zany 2-2-2 record, certainly not the makings of a very special season. But then the Ducks ran off four straight wins, including a 40-21 thrashing of Oregon State, before falling to Arizona State 42-37 in a season finale that the Ducks billed as their "bowl game," to finish 6-3-2.

The 1980 season marked the end of a brilliant UO career for defensive tackle Vince Goldsmith, who was named first-team All-Conference for the second year in a row. He was a special player, bringing to the Oregon defense many of the same qualities Ogburn did offensively.

"People couldn't block him," Brooks added. "He was the dominant player in the conference. He was phenomenally quick and strong, and he had great instincts. He was a great athlete with a great attitude."

Goldsmith was just one of several UO seniors who were part of Brooks' first recruiting class at Oregon. Many were now part of his first class to complete its eligibility and move on.

"My first recruiting class was rated last in the Pac-10," Brooks said. "But it was pivotal in turning this program around. Scott Setterlund, Vince Goldsmith, Vince Williams, Rick Price, Mike Delegato, Greg Hogensen, Jon Brosterhous, Gary Beck, Stuart Yatsko and a few others I've probably overlooked have been the key people in rebuilding this program."

Ogburn, who came in from junior college in 1979, was certainly one of those people. If the contribution of these players was understood, the significance of their absence the following season was not.

False Rose Bowl Hopes

Following the 1980 season, Brooks signed a contract extension through 1985. His loyalty to the school, which had pretty much put the phony credits scandal behind it, was underscored when he revealed the escape route he had

been offered by another school.

"If I had been looking to move I'd be at Memphis State right now," Brooks said prior to the 1981 season. "They offered me a lot more than I'm making here, and last year there were a lot of reasons I could have wanted to jump ship."

Most believed continued improvement on the field was all but assured for the Ducks in 1981. Those subscribing to that theory were in for a rude awakening, however, and they didn't have long to wait. That included Brooks, who prior to the season had declared the Ducks contenders for the Rose Bowl.

"I'll never forget going down to Fresno State to open the 1981 season," defensive end Mike Walter said. "People were writing how the Ducks had a chance to win the conference, and it was pretty great to be thought of like that. Everybody thought we'd go in there and crush them, but we got it handed to us." The final score was 23-16, but it might as well have been 100-0.

"I remember showing up at Autzen Stadium the next day," Walter said. "It was like, 'Where do we go from here?'"

Well, nowhere offensively. While Walter was destined for a long professional career, which included two Super Bowl appearances with the San Francisco 49ers, the 1981 Ducks were in for a tough season. Oregon would score more than 16 points only twice during the year—a 34-0 win over Pacific and a 47-17 thrashing of Oregon State—in their only victories in another 2-9 season.

"A couple of things happened that season," Moser recalled. "We had a lot of guys reading their press clippings, and that can really get you removed from what it takes to reach the level we were at in 1980. Also, we missed four or five good leaders who had left the year before, and we floun-

BELOW: MIKE WALTER (54) AND STEVE BAACK (39) TRAP PACIFIC'S QUARTERBACK IN A 34-0 TRIUMPH AT AUTZEN STADIUM IN 1981.

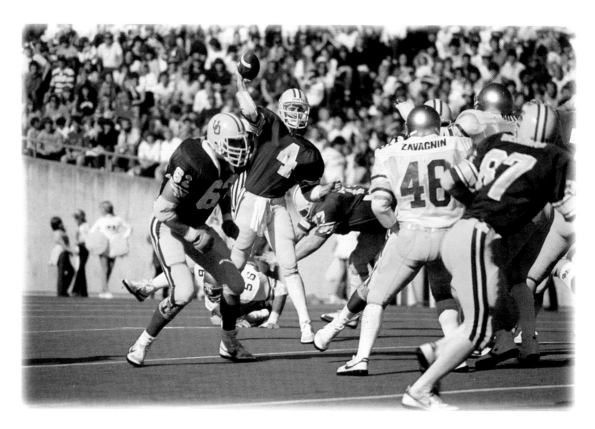

ABOVE: MIKE JORGENSON (4) FIRES AGAINST NOTRE DAME DURING A 13-13 TIE WITH THE IRISH IN 1982.

dered without them. We didn't have a leader on offense or defense. The guys who had set the example of how you play at a fever pitch were gone. Without them we were nowhere, and it snowballed into a catastrophe."

A Turn For the Worse

Things got no better in 1982, though the defense held opponents to 18 points or fewer in seven of 11 games. Oregon scored more than 13 points only once all season and was 0-6 when Notre Dame made a long-awaited appearance at Autzen Stadium on October 23.

Oregon took a 13-10 lead early in the fourth period on Terrance Jones' 1-yard touchdown run, and appeared ready to make it stand until the Irish got close enough for Mike Johnston's 35-yard field goal with 11 seconds remain-

ing. The nation considered winless Oregon's 13-13 tie with Notre Dame quite an accomplishment, even if it was a less-than-vintage Irish squad. It was just one more bitter pill for the Ducks.

"A lot of people were happy, but the players weren't," Walter said. "I remember getting a pretty good pass rush. I had hold of the quarterback's leg, but I didn't have enough leverage to pull him down. He completed the pass that set up the field goal. I was so close to really doing something."

Oregon lost to UCLA and Washington State after that, but the next week the defense intercepted five passes and the Ducks upset Arizona 13-7 for their first triumph of the season. They finished the year the next week with a victory over the Beavers, though this time it took a touchdown pass from Mike Jorgensen to Osborn Thomas late in the fourth period to produce a 7-6 outcome.

In the end, it all added up to a forgettable 2-8-1 season. "We had turned things around in 1979 and 1980," Walter recalled. "It was pretty tough to kind of watch it sink back into the depths again. But at least we didn't lose to

Oregon State. We weren't the ones to end that string."

Turning the Program Around

There were probably three seasons during his 18 years at Oregon in which Brooks' job was in serious jeopardy. The first was in 1983, when anything approaching another two-win season might have been fatal.

In each of those seasons, there was also a single, seemingly insignificant game that ultimately may have saved Brooks' program. In 1983, that game was a non-conference encounter against Houston at Autzen Stadium after the Ducks had suffered an embarrassing 21-15 loss to Pacific in their opener and then lost at Ohio State 31-6.

Oregon had a week off after the Ohio State loss, school was not yet in session and in those days there were no restrictions on practice time. Brooks ordered a return to daily doubles during the off week.

"Guys who play now have no idea," linebacker Don Pellum recalled. "Telling people what that week was like is like the stories about parents telling their kids how they had to walk five miles to get the cows and take them to the barn before school. I tell guys how tough it was and they just don't believe we could have done anything like that. But Coach Brooks said we were going to learn to hit, and we hit every day."

The play of the game, probably of the season and perhaps one of the biggest during Brooks' tenure, came on fourth-and-one at the UO 17 midway through the final quarter. Houston had the ball and a field goal would have given them an eight-point lead against an Oregon team that had struggled on offense for three years.

But the Cougars wanted the first down and a touchdown that would break Oregon's back for certain. Pellum broke through to bring down running back Donald Jordan, who gained 127 yards that day, giving the Ducks the ball and the momentum for the winning touchdown drive.

"We had a stunt called a smash," Pellum said. "I was at outside linebacker, and as soon as the ball was snapped I was supposed to go for the quarterback, with the strong safety going for the pitch back. But [strong safety] Dan Wilkin went flying by me and beat me to the quarterback. I

redirected and bounced outside, and Jordan probably could have beat me if he'd kept going outside. But he cut back and ran right into my arms."

Pellum didn't appreciate the significance of his game-saving play until much later. "Coach Brooks told me on the sidelines, 'Today you grew up as a football player.' But later he told me that game and that play might have saved Oregon football."

It proved to be no exaggeration. "I really felt had we not won that game, things would have gotten really ugly and the team would have lost incentive because of how hard I had worked them," Brooks said. "I thought that win started us on the road back to becoming a competitive program."

The future of the program rested on the shoulders of a freshman quarterback from Sheldon High School named Chris Miller. He had been a three-sport star in high school, and a major college prospect in football, basketball and baseball. But he suffered a knee injury his senior year in high school, ruining his final basketball season and scaring off the baseball and football people enough to open the door for Oregon.

At the same time, Brooks had brought in Bob Toledo, the former head coach at Pacific, to be his offensive coordinator and switch the UO emphasis from run to pass. Toledo's presence and his offensive package were also huge factors in keeping Miller in town. Miller was expected to redshirt in 1983, but an injury to Jorgensen and continued offensive frustration led Brooks to go with Miller late in the year.

Miller played during the second half of a loss to UCLA, throwing a touchdown pass, then started the next week and led Oregon to a 16-7 upset over Stanford. The season ended in a game played on frozen plastic, with the temperature below freezing throughout the contest, and the Ducks and Beavers playing to a 0-0 tie.

Despite the dismal showing, Brooks' job was safe and there was even reason for optimism for the first time in years, despite the team's 4-6-1 record.

With the close of the 1983 season, offensive guard Gary Zimmerman completed his eligibility and moved on

BELOW: ALL-AMERICAN GUARD GARY ZIMMERMAN BLOCKS AGAINST THE BEAVERS IN 1983.

to professional football. In his four years at Oregon, Zimmerman set a high standard in his ability to play against the very best. In the pros, he played in several Pro Bowl games despite not playing with a contending team.

Miller Time

The Chris Miller era took a little while to get off the ground. The young quarterback didn't even start the 1984 opener but came off the bench with Oregon trailing Long Beach State 17-7 in the second half. Miller completed 12 of 17 passes for 129 yards as the Ducks scored three touchdowns and came back to win 28-17.

It was a small victory with huge implications. "To have us get behind and not play well, and then come back and get the job done, is something that hasn't happened since I've been here," Brooks said.

Miller was finally "the man" after that game. "He was the guy we wanted to build the franchise around," Toledo said. "He was the guy who allowed us to do what we wanted to do with the offense. He was a finesse guy who relied a

lot on his athletic ability, but he had a great sixth sense; he could avoid the rush and he made a lot of big plays."

Oregon had scored 20 or more points only five times in the previous three years. Yet, the Ducks scored more than that in each of the next three weeks to beat Long Beach State, Colorado, California and Pacific, and jump to a 4-0 start. It was the first time in 20 years the Ducks had opened so successfully.

Then the Ducks lost to Arizona, USC and Washington. Washington State defeated the Ducks on the day Reuben Mayes of WSU set an NCAA rushing record of 357 yards.

Miller delivered a 20-18 upset of UCLA on the road, before Arizona State clobbered Oregon 44-10. The Ducks then routed the Beavers 31-6 to finish 6-5.

"We still didn't have the talent everybody else had," safety Anthony

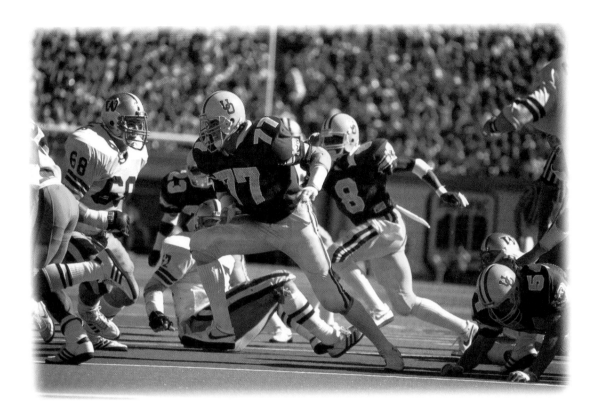

Newman recalled. "When the starters were in there, we played hard and pretty well, and we beat the middle-of-the-road teams. But we still couldn't compete with the big dogs."

But at least the Ducks were entertaining once again. Until then, only Dan Fouts had thrown for more yards than Miller's 1,712 in a single season at Oregon. Wide receiver Lew Barnes and tight end Doug Herman were both named all-Pac-10.

Great Offense, Sad 'D'

There have been few Oregon football games more entertaining than the one that opened the 1985 season. Oregon was matched against Washington State and its highly touted RPM backfield of Mark Rypien, Kerry Porter and Reuben Mayes. The Ducks matched WSU touchdown for touchdown and came away with a 42-39 victory.

But the euphoria of that victory hid a very alarming fact. As Oregon's offense was getting better, its defense was getting worse. Sadly, the Miller years would be the only ones during Brooks' tenure when the Ducks would play consis-

tently poor defense.

The Ducks were last in the Pac-10 in both rushing defense and total defense in 1985. They gave up an amazing 204.7 yards per game on the ground, which didn't do much to keep Miller's offense on the field, and surrendered a total of 437.5 yards per game.

Miller threw for 2,237 yards, second on the Oregon single-season list, leading the conference and setting a UO record with 18 touchdown passes. And he had a legitimate running threat in Tony Cherry, who rushed for 1,006 yards, second on the single-season list. Lew Barnes was a big play receiver who caught 50 passes for 789 yards, the third-highest single-season yardage total in UO history.

But Oregon still finished 5-6, despite losing each

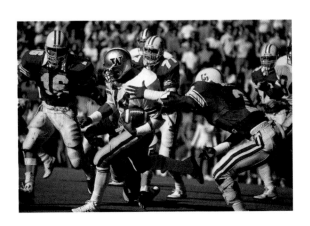

ABOVE: Derek Loville looks for running room against Arizona State in 1986.

football coach or healthy for the program. He vowed the Ducks would no longer schedule such games after a final 1986 commitment to play at Nebraska—where, ironically, he would become athletic director after leaving Oregon.

Records for Miller

The 1986 season was one of the best ever for an Oregon quarterback. Chris Miller finished his career by setting UO single-season records for passing and total offense, while eclipsing Dan Fouts' career marks for passing, total offense and touchdown passes.

But Oregon's defense continued to go from bad to worse, finishing 10th in the Pac-10 in rushing (214.2) and scoring (30.6) and ninth in total defense (412.3).

"We brought some excitement to the program, and people could go to the games and see a good offensive show," Miller said. "But we were in a lot of shoot-outs. We had to score a lot of points to win, and we had some brutal games."

After opening with a victory over San Jose State and beating Colorado on a last-second Matt MacLeod field goal, the Ducks were pulverized by one of the toughest schedules in UO history. Oregon played six nationally ranked teams over the next six weeks, and didn't come close to beating any of them. In fact, the Ducks actually felt relieved to lose only 48-14 at Nebraska.

"We went to Nebraska with the knowledge it was a money-making game versus a competitive one," linebacker Mark Kearns recalled. "I was a freshman, and I remember

game in which it did not score 30 or more points. The Ducks fell short of a winning season for a couple of reasons.

First, they lost 27-24 to California after leading 21-0 in the first period of the 100th game played at Autzen Stadium. Second, the Ducks were destroyed 63-0 at Nebraska. As in earlier years, the Ducks had programmed themselves for failure by scheduling major powers on the road to guarantee a huge payday with which to balance the athletic budget. Then-Athletic Director Bill Byrne considered that illogical economics because Oregon had little or no chance to win such games, and attendance suffered at home because fans found little to get excited about.

Also, there were fewer home games because the big-name teams wouldn't come to Oregon, which made it harder to win consistently. Byrne didn't think that was fair to his

RIGHT: OREGON'S RALLY SQUAD IS A FIXTURE ON THE AUTZEN STADIUM SIDELINES ON GAME DAY

the older guys going out and talking about getting blown out and hoping we could just get through the game. But week in and week out, we just kept getting bludgeoned."

After a 38-3 loss at Washington the Ducks were 2-6. Criticism of Brooks began to mount. The 10th-year coach had said something very prophetic back in 1981: "One thing that happens when a coach stays in one place for a long time is that people don't remain neutral," he said. "Right now a lot of people like me and a lot of people probably don't, but the biggest majority don't feel strongly one way or the other. After awhile those people will take a stand one way or the other."

Clearly, Brooks' popularity had crested, though it remained strong within the administration and with the Ducks' more influential boosters. "Well, here I am with my back to the wall again," Brooks said as he greeted the press in a hallway following the loss to Washington. But if the Houston game in 1983 bought the Ducks time to improve, so did a 27-9 triumph over Cal in Berkeley in the ninth week of 1986.

Suddenly, the Ducks weren't playing a power, and they came away with a convincing victory as Miller threw for one touchdown and ran for two more. "It was a big win," Brooks said. "But I don't think you could classify it on a par with the Houston game. The losses preceding the Cal game were tough, and people weren't very happy, but there was an understanding that we'd been through a pretty murderous schedule."

The Ducks won again the next week, defeating Washington State, then closed out the year with a resounding 49-28 victory over Oregon State to finish 5-6.

Miller concluded his career in the Civil War by completing 21 of 27 for 257 yards, leading the Ducks to 479 yards in total offense. Miller had left his mark in the record book and in the memory of his coach. "He had a great career," Brooks said. "He was a special athlete who did some amazing things."

Miller was taken by the Atlanta Falcons with the 13th pick in the 1987 NFL draft, the highest any Oregon player had been selected since Bobby Moore was chosen fourth in 1972. Though his pro career would be marred by frequent injury, Miller would experience a rebirth of sorts when Brooks once again became his mentor as the new coach of the relocated St. Louis Rams.

If 1986 marked the end of an era, it also provided a glimpse of the next. It was difficult to envision with the loss

ABOVE: BILL MUSGRAVE LED THE DUCKS TO CONSECUTIVE BOWL GAMES IN 1980-90, OREGON'S FIRST POSTSEASON APPEARANCES IN 26 YEARS.

of Miller and the current state of the defense, but brighter days lay just ahead for the Ducks.

Bill Musgrave to the Rescue

Few upsets in UO history have been more shocking than Oregon's 10-7 triumph over Colorado to open the 1987 season. The Ducks were more than two-touchdown underdogs, with a defense that had been the worst in the Pac-10 the year before and a redshirt freshman quarterback named Bill Musgrave.

It had all the makings of a disaster, but the Oregon defense limited Colorado to one touchdown, forcing five turnovers, and a cool-headed Musgrave played mistake-free.

One of the keys, and something the Buffaloes couldn't have anticipated, was the change in Oregon's defense. During fall practice, UO coaches made the switch from the 4-3 "flex" to an aggressive 3-4. It made all the difference.

"The 4-3 depended on having people equal to or superior to your opponent," safety Anthony Newman said. "The philosophy was read and react. But with the 3-4, we attacked and created problems for the offense that made them think and adjust. As players, we loved that defense."

Oregon improved to third in the Pac-10 in rush defense (145.1), fourth in total defense (340.2) and fourth in scoring defense (20.7). "I liked the philosophy of attacking, I liked the idea of giving the kids something new, and when we had success early it was a real shot in the arm mentally as well," defensive coordinator Denny Schuler said. "But the bottom line is we had some good football players. A lot of those guys went on to the NFL."

Along with Newman, the talented defensive group included nose tackle Rollin Putzier, defensive lineman Matt Brock, linebacker Scott Kozak and defensive backs Thom Kaumeyer and Chris Oldham, all future pros.

But Musgrave stole the show. After a close loss at Ohio State, the freshman from Grand Junction, Colorado, led the Ducks to a victory at San Diego State and then big upsets over Washington and Southern California at Autzen Stadium. Suddenly the Ducks vaulted to 16th in the Associated Press poll, the first time a UO team had been ranked since 1970.

Inexperience caught up with the Ducks over the next four weeks, however, as they fell to UCLA, Stanford, California and Arizona State in succession. They rebounded with a 31-17 triumph over Washington State, and once again it took a win over Oregon State, this time 44-0, to nail down a 6-5 season.

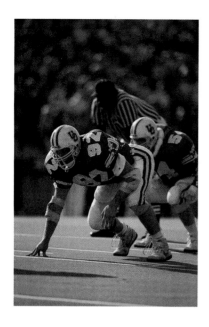

ABOVE: MATT BROCK (92) AND SCOTT WHITNEY (54) READY FOR THE SNAP DURING 1988 ACTION AT AUTZEN STADIUM.

But the Ducks were back as far as the fans were concerned. They set a single-season Autzen Stadium attendance record with a 39,199 average, and Musgrave was on his way to becoming probably the most popular UO football player of all time.

"Some people on my own staff were surprised when I went with Bill to start the season," Brooks said. "But in scrimmages, even if he didn't look pretty, he got the team down the field. He was a great leader." What Musgrave meant to the Ducks would become clear soon enough.

A Season Turned Upside-Down

Oregon emerged as a powerhouse in 1988, beating overmatched teams such as Long Beach State and Idaho State soundly, outscoring the likes of Washington State and San Diego State, and finding a way to win the close ones against Stanford and Washington.

The Ducks were 6-1, having lost only to USC, and ranked 16th in the country when Arizona State came to Autzen on October 29—a day that lives in UO football infamy. Oregon was favored to beat the Sun Devils, and was leading when Musgrave went down in the first half with a broken collarbone.

Oregon did not have a quality backup quaterback. The team and the coaches had put all of their hopes and future in Musgrave, and the injury to him spelled disaster.

Linebacker Mark Kearns was also lost in the ASU game, but it was the loss of Musgrave that resulted in Oregon losing not only to Arizona State but also to its remaining four opponents, including Oregon State for the first time since 1974. The Ducks wound up 6-6.

"Looking back, that may have been Oregon's most talented team during the years I was there," Schuler said. "On both sides of the ball, it was a darn good collection of players. There was no question it was going to be a bowl season, and it was hard to believe one injury could do that much damage."

"That team, as much as any I had until 1994, had the potential to go to the Rose Bowl," Brooks added. "It was a travesty, the toughest blow in all my years there because we were on the verge of greatness, and then just like that we

became a very average football team."

Oregon was 6-0 with Musgrave and 0-6 without him that year. For his career, the Ducks would go 25-10 in games Musgrave started and finished and 3-9 in games he didn't. There were indeed several other outstanding athletes during this period. A dozen would play in the NFL. But the Ducks could never get it done without Musgrave.

"That's the nature of the quarterback position and it happens to a lot of teams," Musgrave said. "A quarterback has so much influence on what happens, when he suddenly leaves it takes awhile for everyone to adjust."

But the Ducks never adjusted. They didn't have anyone to take up the slack. But beyond that, this was a team that relied on Musgrave both physically and mentally.

"Bill was amazing," linebacker Joe Farwell said. "Anytime he was out there, there was no question we could play with anybody. When you took Bill out of the equation, as it was proved enough times, the offense would sputter and the defense would get discouraged anytime we got behind. We were lost without Bill."

1989

Bowl Draught Ends

"I had always said it would be more fun to go to the first bowl game with Oregon than to go to the Rose Bowl with USC," Schuler recalls. "That was really the case. It was so exciting to be a part of the group that finally succeeded in getting the thing done."

The "thing" was Oregon's first postseason appearance in 26 years. It came about with an invitation to the Independence Bowl following a 7-4 season in 1989, Oregon's first seven-win regular season since 1964.

Fittingly, it wasn't easy. Ultimately, it was even controversial. Musgrave remained healthy all year for the only time in his career, but the season was a roller-coaster ride.

The Ducks were impressive with opening triumphs over California and Iowa, but then blew a 17-point lead and were upset by Stanford. They registered an important victory over Arizona,

A storybook ending for a storybook career. After his last game at Autzen Stadium, when senior quarterback Bill Musgrave rallied the Ducks from an 11-point fourth-quarter deficit, many of the 45,901 fans swarmed the field and tore down the east goal post.

The game winner came on Musgrave's last pass at Autzen—a 16-yard touchdown pass to Vince Ferry with 2:01

Fans challenge the goal posts after the Ducks beat UCLA.

remaining that gave the Ducks the lead for the first time in the game.

So much rode on that pass; it was classic Musgrave in that situation, it was thrown perfectly. "He threw his tightest spiral and had his best velocity on the most crucial play of the game," offensive coordinator Mike Bellotti said. "We talked all week about performing at crunch time, and I guess we pretty much did."

Because they did, the Ducks earned a bowl berth for the second consecutive season—the Freedom Bowl came calling before the week was out—and posted their first unbeaten season at Autzen Stadium, going 7-0.

As for Musgrave, he left the stadium with a career record of 19-1 in Eugene. "It was a good comeback win for us," Musgrave said. "Coming back in that situation is difficult because there's a lot of pressure. We knew we weren't out of the game, but there was a sense of

urgency."

The game seemed beyond reach when UCLA quarterback Tommy Maddox connected with wideout Scott Miller for a 62-yard touchdown, giving the Bruins a 24-13 lead with 9:32 remaining.

But Musgrave led the Ducks on a 72-yard drive to make it 24-21 with 6:10 remaining. Fullback Juan Shedrick scored the touchdown, and Ngalu Kelemeni got the two-point conversion. On the next series, Oregon's defense forced the Bruins to punt from their 29, and Brian Brown set up the winning drive with a 24-yard punt return to the UCLA 45 with four minutes remaining.

On second down, the Ducks went back to a play they'd used before—a screen to tailback Sean Burwell, who gained 28 yards to the UCLA 17. It was a tremendous effort by Burwell, who stayed in the backfield to slow a blitzing linebacker, then slipped out to receive the pass that Musgrave wouldn't have been able to throw without the block.

The winning pass came on third-and-9. As the play developed, it resembled the screen to Burwell, except that the Ducks had added a twist—instead of blocking, the tight end would go down the sidelines as a receiver. The Ducks had saved the play for this moment.

On this play, the tight end was Vince Ferry, a sophomore non-letterman, who'd entered the game because starter Jeff Thomason suffered a fractured ankle. Musgrave found Ferry at the goal line; it was only the fourth reception of Ferry's career. Autzen Stadium has rarely been louder.

"I just faked the block I usually make on the corner and went up the sideline," Ferry said. "It was such a perfect pass and it got there so quickly, I didn't have time to think. Bill just put it there perfectly."

Just like in the storybooks.

but suffered tough losses to Washington State and Washington.

They beat Arizona State as Derek Loville rushed for 203 yards, got past Long Beach State as expected, but then fell 45-41 at Brigham Young despite a 19-point second-half lead. Oregon came back to beat UCLA in Pasadena 38-20, and then defeated Oregon State 30-21.

Some of the enthusiasm over Oregon's accomplishment was blemished by controversy over UO Athletic Director Byrne's decision to purchase 14,000 tickets for $350,000 to secure Oregon's postseason invitation, and the fact the Ducks ultimately lost $178,000 on the game.

ABOVE: ANDY CONNER (47) SACKS TY DETMER DURING OREGON'S 32-16 VICTORY OVER FOURTH-RANKED BYU IN 1990.

Gregg McCallum's 20-yard field goal with 3:07 left produced a 27-24 triumph for Oregon, one in which the Ducks had more than 400 yards total offense for the eighth time in 12 games. The Ducks set school records that season for points (379), touchdowns (44) and field goals (24). They averaged 418 yards per game and came within 33 yards of the all-time UO record. Defensively, the Ducks were second in the Pac-10 in total defense, giving up 336.9 yards per game.

"It was a real big deal for us as players," Musgrave said. "I don't think we realized how big a deal it was for the community until we saw how many people showed up in Shreveport and braved the cold."

It didn't seem all that cold after Oregon won. "It was a game most people would have been very disappointed if we had lost because Tulsa didn't have a big name," Brooks said. "But they turned out to be a pretty good team with players who went on to play in the NFL. To win coming back like we did was very gratifying. It was the perfect ending."

But those close to the UO program viewed it as a necessary investment. "I know there was a lot of controversy over that," Brooks said. "But that was the best thing that ever happened to Oregon football. It was the breakthrough that the program needed, and it wouldn't have happened without the vision of Bill Byrne to sell that and get us over the hump."

There was no controversy for any of the estimated 5,000 fans who followed the Ducks to Shreveport, Louisianna, for the Independence Bowl game with Tulsa, despite frigid temperatures and a wind-chill factor below zero. "I'm not sure I can describe the feeling of that experience," Brooks said. "The pep rally at the convention center, when the band came in, the pride everyone felt, it was incredible."

Oregon fell behind Tulsa 24-10 in the second half, but Musgrave threw a touchdown pass to Joe Reitzug and ran in for another score to tie the game early in the fourth quarter.

1990

Back-to-Back Bowls

During the Musgrave years, the Ducks weren't winners when Bill was out of the lineup. But they were often incredible when he played, and never more so than on September 29, 1990, when fourth-ranked Brigham Young

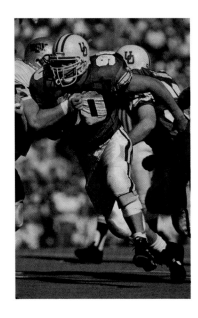

came to Eugene to meet the Ducks on national television.

"The most fun game of my entire career was the BYU game," Musgrave said. "It was the most beautiful day I can remember at Autzen, we were on national TV, and our defense intercepted Ty Detmer five times and Marcus Woods sacked him for a safety. Our defense was so good, we didn't need to score very many points."

Detmer would win the Heisman Trophy in 1990, and he passed for 442 yards against the Ducks. But Musgrave was more effective, completing 23 of 37 for 286 yards and three touchdowns. He also ran for another score as the Ducks dominated the Cougars 32-16.

The Ducks finished the regular season 8-3, their first eight-win regular season since 1959. They lost at Arizona 22-17 when Musgrave was stopped inches short of the goal-line on fourth down in the closing seconds. They were routed 38-7 by Rose Bowl-bound Washington, and they fell 28-3 at California with Musgrave on the injured list.

But the Cal game was an afterthought for the Ducks. They had clinched a Freedom Bowl berth the week before with a 28-24 comeback win over UCLA, capping their first unbeaten season ever (7-0) at Autzen.

"We sputtered the first three quarters, but the defense kept us in it," Musgrave said of the UCLA game. The Ducks trailed by 11 points early in the fourth period, but Juan Shedrick's two-yard touchdown run and Ngalu Kelemeni's two-point conversion run cut the deficit to 24-21 with 6:10 to play.

Brian Brown's 24-yard punt return with four minutes left set up one of the most dramatic touchdowns in UO history. Musgrave threw to tailback Sean Burwell for a 28-yard gain on a screen pass, and three plays later Musgrave completed a 16-yard touchdown pass to

backup tight end Vince Ferry with 2:01 to play.

"We had run the wide screen to Burwell the whole day," Musgrave said. "On the touchdown, we ran the play the same way, made the pump fake to Burwell, which their safety took, and Ferry just slipped up the sidelines and caught the ball as he went into the end zone."

Oregon's 28-24 victory was also the first time the Ducks had beaten the Bruins in Autzen. "I'm sure Vince will remember that catch the rest of his life," UO Coach Rich Brooks said. "I know I will. And it was pretty nice that Bill's last pass at Autzen went for a touchdown and won the game."

Oregon's season sputtered after that, however. There was the loss to Cal, then a narrow 6-3 win over Oregon State without Musgrave, followed by a frustrating 32-31 upset loss to Colorado State in the Freedom Bowl.

"It was gratifying we could go to a bowl game for the second straight year because Oregon had never done that," Brooks said. "It was gratifying our fans followed us like they did and set a record for the number of tickets we sold [nearly 20,000]. But it was disappointing we could have had a nine-win season and didn't get that done."

Musgrave completed 29 of 47 passes for 392 yards and three touchdowns, but the Ducks lost the ball three times on fumbles and gave up an uncharacteristic 196 yards on the ground. Oregon scored to pull within one point with 1:01 to play, but Musgrave's completed pass to wideout Michael McClellan for the two-point conversion was ruled no good because the ball never crossed the plane of the goal line, even though McClellan was standing just inside the end zone.

As good as Oregon's season was, with a couple of inches at Arizona and another couple in the Freedom Bowl, the Ducks might well have had a 10-2 season and finished in the top 25.

Bill Musgrave had an incredible career at Oregon. He obliterated Oregon's passing and total offense records for single game, season and career. He became the first UO quarterback to throw for more than 3,000 yards when he threw for 3,081 in 1989. His career passing marks of 8,343 yards and 60 touchdowns were far ahead of Chris Miller's 6,681 and 42.

Musgrave was drafted by the Dallas Cowboys in the fourth round of the 1991 NFL draft, but soon was traded to San Francisco, where he earned a Super Bowl ring as a backup to NFL great Steve Young.

a surprising 40-14 rout of Washington State.

He was even better with four touchdown passes and 292 yards in a 28-13 win at Texas Tech the next week. But then the roof fell in. O'Neil played poorly and Oregon was upset 24-17 at Utah. He threw an interception for a touchdown the next week as the Ducks lost to Southern California 30-14 in a forgettable night game on national television.

O'Neil was lost for the season with a dislocated thumb the next week, despite a 29-6 victory over New Mexico State. And then it began, an endless procession of quarterbacks who couldn't produce or stay healthy: Brett Salisbury, Doug Musgrave, Kyle Crowston, Bob Brothers.

Oregon lost its last six to finish 3-8. "I just never thought we'd be that inept again," Brooks said. "I thought those days were behind us. We were back to searching for ways to get first downs again, and that's hard to take because my expectation level is higher, just like everyone else's."

It was similar to the situation in 1988 after the Ducks lost Musgrave following a 6-1 start. They didn't win again and played poorly at positions other than quarterback. "USC didn't have a quarterback that year either, and they went 3-8," defensive coordinator Schuler said. "You can't underestimate the importance of a quarterback to any football team."

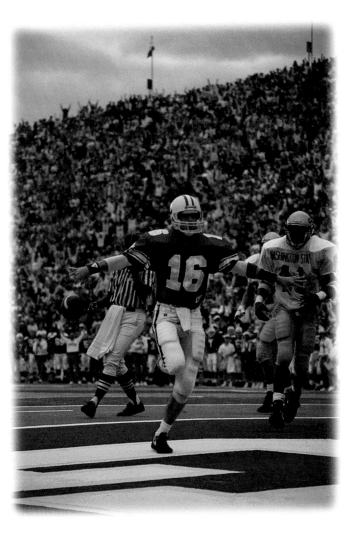

ABOVE: DANNY O'NEIL CELEBRATES HIS TOUCHDOWN AGAINST WASHINGTON STATE IN HIS FIRST OREGON START.

Oregon Football Gets a Facelift

It was during the 1992 season that the facilities for athletics at Autzen were finally improved. With the construction of the Casanova Center next to Autzen Stadium, the Athletic Department had first-class facilities and had gone from the worst amenities in the Pac-10 to the best.

Over and over recruits had been told about the plans to improve the facilities, but it was always someday. With the invitation to the Independence Bowl in 1989 and the Freedom Bowl the following year, UO Athletic Director Bill Byrne could move forward with the improvements.

Included in the changes were sky boxes at Autzen that would be sold to large donors and other enclosed areas that would be available by the seat for a large annual contribution. The press area was drastically improved, and when it

The Roof Caves In

The Bill Musgrave era was still paying dividends at Oregon the following season. The Ducks set an all-time UO attendance record in 1991, averaging 41,514 fans for a five-game home schedule. But the euphoria would be short-lived.

In the beginning, it appeared as though redshirt freshman quarterback Danny O'Neil would replace Musgrave as quickly as Musgrave had Miller. O'Neil threw for two touchdowns and ran for another as the Ducks opened with

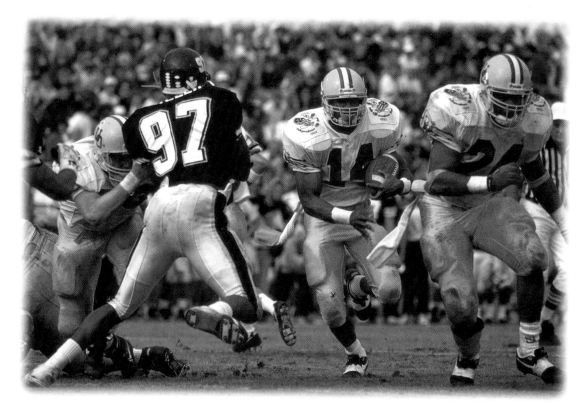

was all completed Autzen Stadium was reformed. It was not unusual to hear fans comment that the Cas Center was the house that Bill built—both Bill Byrne and Bill Musgrave.

To appreciate how expectations had changed at Oregon both inside and outside the program, study the 1992 season. The Ducks blew their opener to Hawaii, 24-21, and were defeated at Stanford 21-7. But they won five of their next seven heading into an important game with UCLA at

Autzen.

Victories over the Bruins and Beavers would give the Ducks a 7-4 record and put them back in bowl business. Yet the UCLA game drew a disappointing crowd of 33,771, only a couple thousand more than watched the Ducks against Long Beach State in 1989 or Utah State in 1990, and fewer than were on hand for New Mexico State in 1991.

This team, on the threshold of a bowl bid or not, clearly had not captured the fancy of UO fans. And it broke the hearts of those who showed up for the UCLA game, as Tommy Thompson missed a 19-yard field goal that would have given Oregon the lead in the final minutes, and instead Louis Perez hit a 40-yarder on the game's final play to give the Bruins a 9-6 upset victory.

Oregon came back to beat Oregon State 7-0 the next week to finish the year 6-5, and wound up with another invitation to the Independence Bowl. To illustrate how times had changed, the UO team's vote of whether to accept the bid wasn't unanimous.

"Coach Brooks heard there were a few key players who didn't want to go," linebacker Joe Farwell said. "I could never understand it. I had no clue why anyone wouldn't want to go to a bowl game. I think that really hurt Coach Brooks

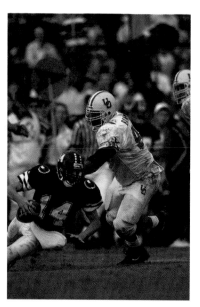

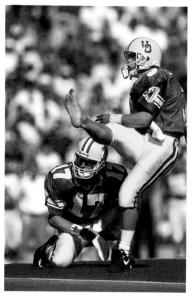

because he takes every game personally and expects the same kind of drive and emotion from his players. To have some who didn't want to go, I'm sure that shook him up."

The only thing that could have put a positive spin on the season was a win over Wake Forest in the Independence Bowl. Had only five years passed since Oregon celebrated a 6-5 season in 1987? Rather than win, though, the Ducks broke to a 29-10 lead in the third period and then fell apart in losing a 39-35 decision to Wake Forest.

"You look at the whole picture and it wasn't a great season," Farwell said. "But it wasn't bad. [Offensive tackle] David Collinsworth and I were the only two guys to play in all three bowl games, and I'm proud to have done that. But 1992 was a lot different than 1989."

Disappointing Decline

Rich Brooks had been through some discouraging football seasons, but the 1993 campaign might have been his toughest. "Of all the years I was there, that was the one I thought we underachieved," Brooks said. "We had a much better team than our record showed, and I was personally devastated by that." The Ducks wound up 5-6, but it clearly should have been 7-4 or 8-3.

Disgruntled Oregon fans had even more ammunition to fire at Brooks than in past seasons, because he had taken over the athletic director's duties as a favor to UO Vice President of Administration Dan Williams, following the departure of Bill Byrne to Nebraska in 1992. As the only Division I coach to also serve as his school's AD, many felt he was too preoccupied to fully concentrate on coaching.

Indeed, Willams' decision to make the athletic director's position a part-time job rather than seek out a full-time replacement was widely criticized. Brooks would receive a mere $20,000 for filling the AD seat, and some saw it as a potentially disasterous cost-cutting move. Yet, while Brooks was athletic director, the athletic budget was balanced, record revenues were raised from UO donors and several Oregon sports were substantially upgraded.

Oregon never got over one particular loss in 1993, a 41-42 defeat at California, in which the Ducks led 30-0 in

ABOVE: LINEBACKER JEREMY ASHER WAS A DEFENSIVE MAINSTAY FOR THE DUCKS, STARTING EVERY GAME IN 1993-94.

the first half. Cal quarterback Dave Barr completed one of the most amazing comebacks in NCAA history with a 26-yard touchdown pass to Iheanyi Uwaezuoke with 1:05 to play, and then a two-point conversion pass to Mike Caldwell.

The Bears' comeback was a Pac-10 record and came within one point of the NCAA record. It came after Oregon had begun the season successfully with wins over Colorado State, Montana and Illinois. A victory over Cal would have made the Ducks 4-0.

Oregon split its next four games, beating Arizona State and Washington State, losing to Southern Cal and Washington. But the Ducks weren't the same team after the loss to Cal. "I think the Cal game impacted us more than just the loss," Brooks said. "It took a lot out of our team mentally in terms of confidence and the whole thing."

The Ducks were still 5-3 and postseason candidates until they were dominated 31-10 by Arizona, then upset 38-34 by Stanford and 15-12 by Oregon State. The collapse took the luster off a tremendous passing performance by Danny O'Neil, who became the fourth Pac-10 quarterback to throw for more than 3,000 yards during the regular season. He finished with 3,224 yards and equaled Musgrave's record with 22 touchdowns.

But that didn't pack it with Oregon's disgruntled fans. They wanted victories. They wanted Brooks' scalp. Oregon had not come from behind to win a game in the second half since UCLA in 1990. They hadn't had a major upset victory since beating fourth-ranked BYU in 1990.

RIGHT: QUARTERBACK DANNY O'NEIL (TOP), CENTER TOM CURRAN (57) AND ANOTHER TEAMMATE CELEBRATE A SCORE.

BELOW LEFT: NOSE TACKLE SILILA MALEPEAI (50) DRAWS A BEAD ON MONTANA'S QUARTERBACK.

BELOW RIGHT: TAILBACK SEAN BURWELL BURSTS THROUGH A HOLE AGAINST CAL.

"We're not back down to the level we were in 1984 or 1985," Brooks said. "But we may get there if we don't get some wins that impress people. We have to do that if we want to keep the stadium full, and we need to do that to support 14 sports and do the things we want

to do."

The Ducks needed to do something quickly to keep Brooks employed. "This will be a critical year for the head football coach," Brooks said in August 1994 as he gave up his duties as athletic director to focus on the football program. "There's a fine line between winning five or six games and winning a whole bunch. Usually, the team that gets to 9-2 wins all the games they can. That didn't happen to us in 1993, and it hasn't happened very many years."

The feeling among Oregon's disenchanted fans was that the Ducks were getting closer to their 2-9 days than the 9-2 that had always eluded them. The atmosphere was getting as ugly as any time during Brooks' 17 years in Eugene.

Brooks refused to step aside after the 1993 season, but a lot of people would have been willing to bet he wouldn't be at Oregon after 1994. They would turn out to be right, for all the wrong reasons. Brooks finally got the Ducks into the Rose Bowl and was lured away to the National Football League as head coach of the Los Angeles Rams.

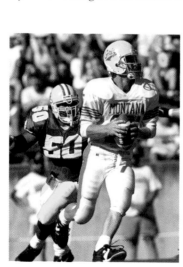

OREGON'S FOOTBALL PROGRAM COMES OF AGE

An Oregon football program that had not been to a bowl game in 26 years made four postseason appearances in the six seasons between 1989 through 1994. What happened?

Former Oregon Coach Rich Brooks has said he believes the Ducks put themselves in a position to be competitive on the field when they made the commitment to be competitive off it. The key was the improvement of athletic facilities to bring UO up to the level of other members of the Pac-10 Conference.

Brooks gives the credit to former UO Athletic Director Bill Byrne, who began pushing for facility improvements when he took the job in 1984. By the time Byrne left to become AD at Nebraska in 1992, UO had completed nearly $16 million in facility improvements, including the new Casanova Athletic Center.

"The most difficult thing we had to overcome with the players when I came to Oregon in 1977 was to change the belief that we couldn't win," Brooks said. "The ability to think beyond the status quo was the key, and Bill brought that vision and the message that we had to get off the dime and do something with respect to facilities."

This was a battle Brooks had fought since taking the UO job. In fact, he rejected a contract extension in 1979 because no progress had been made toward facility improvement. "I don't want to leave Oregon," Brooks said then. "But we talked three years ago about the need to improve our facilities, the administration recognized the need and said it would be taken care of. I want to wait and see if that happens. Some people are happy with what we're doing right now and are content with that. But if we want to improve, we've got to make some changes in our facilities."

Oregon's Athletic Department

offices on University Street were an embarrassment. Coaches worked four to an office, with no room for meetings, and certainly no aura about the place to suggest UO was a successful, competitive enterprise.

The first major facility improvement since the construction of Autzen Stadium in 1967 took place in 1981, when a $650,000 Stadium Club was opened on the east rim of the stadium. Finally, the football program was provided meeting rooms, and the University had a facility suitable for entertaining boosters at pre- and postgame gatherings. In the mid-80s, the

Ducks finally got a grass practice facility next to Autzen Stadium, when two full-size fields were developed across from the stadium on Centennial Boulevard .

The *big* breakthrough came about the time when Byrne came forward with a plan to dome Autzen Stadium, both to protect the Ducks and UO attendance from the weather and to provide a new home for UO basketball. The dome never materialized, but the idea for it was the seed that generated the construction of a new press box and skysuites in 1988 (at a cost of $4.1 million) as well as the 101,477-square-foot Casanova Athletic Center, which was completed in 1991 at a cost of $11.8 million.

The improvements had a major impact on football recruiting even before construction started. The

1986 UO football press book featured a model of the proposed dome on its back cover, and inside the list of 1986 recruits included such important players as quarterback Bill Musgrave, running back Derek Loville, wide receiver Terry Obee, wide receiver Tony Hargain and others crucial to Oregon's bowl appearances in 1989 and 1990.

"They used to joke with me when we had to practice in the rain," Brooks said. "They'd say, 'Where's that dome you promised?' Before they were done, at least we provided first-class training and dressing facilities. Bill Byrne was

very positive, always supportive, very talented and he found ways to overcome the history of procrastination that was ingrained here," Brooks added. "The result is facilities everyone can be proud of, and which are being paid for primarily with income from the skysuites."

When the Casanova Center was completed in 1991, Byrne said, "Our facilities are now as good as most in the Pac-10. That's coming a long way, because we were the worst."

EPILOGUE

Brooks Passes the Torch to Bellotti

The football off-season of 1995 wasn't different from a lot of others; veteran Oregon Coach Rich Brooks was rumored to be considering another job. Brooks had a standard line he always used when asked about such rumors. "It must be recruiting season," he would say. "I'm either being fired, hired or retired." Except this time it turned out to be true.

Not fired. That would have been anyone's guess in September, when the Ducks were 1-2 and seemingly headed nowhere. Not retired. Going to the Rose Bowl in his 18th season at UO wasn't enough to quench Brooks' thirst for coaching. Hired, yes; by the St. Louis Rams on February 10, just one week after the Ducks had signed a promising recruiting class and it appeared to be business as usual in the UO football office.

"The ultimate in coaching is being a head coach in the National Football League," Brooks said. "I think I'm qualified and I'm thrilled to have the opportunity."

Spanning nearly two decades of Oregon football, the Brooks Era will always be viewed in two different lights. Even though Brooks had taken the Ducks to bowl games in four of his final six seasons, some were critical of his overall record of 91-109-4 and anxious for a coaching change.

Others, obviously including people in professional football, felt Brooks had successfully battled long odds at Oregon. They considered his 67-60 record over the previous 11 seasons an outstanding accomplishment, crowned by the 1994 Pac-10 title and Rose Bowl berth.

Brooks weathered the criticism and seldom stood up to defend himself while on the job. But after choosing to join the Rams, he left no doubt he felt his accomplishments were underappreciated. "I leave with this program in a heck of a lot better shape than it used to be," he said. "When I got the job, nobody else wanted it. But we turned things around, even though it staggered up and down a couple of times; we brought excitement and competitiveness back to Oregon football. I think there are a lot of people now who would like to coach the fine young men we have at Oregon."

The one who would get that chance was Mike Bellotti, the offensive coordinator at Oregon since 1989. He was personally endorsed by Brooks and hired just three days after Brooks' resignation. Brooks found it easier to plead for patience and realistic expectations for Bellotti than he did for himself when he sat in the hot seat.

"I really believe that people need to be realistic and patient with Oregon football," Brooks said. "I believe Oregon football will continue to be strong, but let's keep it in perspective. Oregon can't win the Pac-10 or go to a bowl game every year. That would be nice, but it doesn't happen even at schools a lot bigger than Oregon.

"We went to bowl games four of the past six years, but UCLA went to only two during that period. That's not supposed to happen. I really hope that people who didn't like me, now that I'm gone, will rally around Mike and not get down on a good coach and good players who will continue to do everything they can to win games at Oregon."

Brooks' endorsement of the 44-year-old Bellotti, a graduate of UC-Davis who had head coaching experience at Cal State-Chico, was based on two factors. First, the UO offense had enjoyed unprecedented success since Bellotti was hired, faltering only in 1991 when the Ducks went through five quarterbacks due to injury. Second, Bellotti represented continuity, something both Brooks and UO administrators prized after the Rose Bowl season.

Dan Williams, UO Vice President of Administration and Interim Athletic Director, interviewed several candidates from outside the program, but found none better-suited than Bellotti to continue Oregon's winning ways.

ABOVE: NEW HEAD COACH MIKE BELLOTTI.

"My hiring is an affirmation of the hard work by the staff and players on the Oregon football team," Bellotti said. "I'm proud and pleased the administration has the confidence in me to lead the program into the 101st year of Oregon football. I want to maintain the continuity of the program, and our objectives will be the same as before: a winning season, beating Oregon State and our Northwest rivals, a bowl game and winning the conference championship. It's hard to get to the top, but it's harder to stay there. I look forward to the challenge."

Bellotti spoke confidently of handling the challenge. "There are other coaches out there probably just as qualified as I am," Bellotti said. "But the fact I am here makes me more qualified. I believe some people expect us to go back to the Rose Bowl, and others believe there's a better coach out there somewhere. But I believe in what I've accomplished, I know what it takes to recruit here and how to go about it, and I know what we need to do to win."

Everyone at UO talked about continuity, while at the same time knowing there would be staff turnover following Brooks' departure. Bellotti went about selecting replacements with an eye toward maintaining the system that had been in place under Brooks. That philosophy embodied a balanced offense, but one in which the pass usually sets up the run; and an aggressive defense that relied on quickness rather than strength.

Less than two weeks before the start of his first spring practice, Bellotti had a staff in place and his program was ready to move forward. So much had happened, it almost seemed like the 1994 season had never ended. But it had, and a new era was under way as the Ducks embarked on their 101st year (and 100th season) of intercollegiate football.

PARTNERS IN EXCELLENCE

Over the years, numerous companies and individuals have made generous contributions of their time and money to ensure the on-going success of University of Oregon athletics.

In doing so, they have become "Partners" with the UO Athletic Department. Many of these partners provided the funding or work-in-kind required to bring this book to fruition. Others sponsored "Great Moments" or helped out by purchasing quantities of pre-publication books.

You'll read the stories of the primary sponsors of this project in the "Partners in Excellence" chapter which follows. A complete list of the book's benefactors, and levels of contribution, appears below:

Founders Corporate Sponsors: *Beall Trailers of Oregon, Chambers Communications/KEZI-TV, Pepsi Cola Bottling Company of Eugene, McCann Communications Corp.*

Major Corporate Sponsors: *Moshofsky Enterprises, Farwest Steel Corporation, Romania Dealerships, Taylor Electric Supply Inc.*

Special Corporate Sponsors: *RSG Forest Products, Koke Printing, Bi-Mart, KPNW Radio, Wildish Construction Co.*

Pre-Publication Book Buyers: *Patrick J. Kilkenny, Bashor's Team Athletics, Re/Max Real Estate, Bob DeArmand, Southern Oregon Credit Service, Inc., Cascade Empire, Transmission Exchange, Burger King.*

BEALL CORPORATION: RIDING A WINNING STREAK

Sarasota, Syracuse, San Antonio, Sioux Falls, Sacramento, Spokane. Beall's bulk hauling tank trailers travel throughout the nation carrying the products you use every day—fuel, chemicals, milk, flour, and more. Beall is more than a corporate logo, however. It's a proud family name that for almost a century has stood for premium quality.

The Beall story begins in 1905, when John S. Beall founded Beall & Company, a road-building equipment distributor in Portland, Oregon.

His firm later manufactured culvert pipes and became Coast Culvert & Plume. With the addition of steel water pipe and petroleum storage tank manufacturing in the 1920s, the name changed once again, this time to Beall Pipe & Tank Corporation. In the mid-twenties, Beall hired two of his nephews to work for the firm. One of them, John E. Beall, started as a nightwatchman.

As the 1920s progressed, the firm became known for its functional design, automotive styling, and premium quality, as it moved into the manufacturing of truck tanks and tank trailers for the petroleum industry.

In 1932, John E. Beall became president of the company. His uncle John S. passed away the next year. In the hard times of the 1930s, the company continued to grow, adding logging and lowboy trailers to its line.

The war efforts of the 1940s offered opportunities to build a variety of pipe and automotive products. The drive and ability of John E. was a

prime source of the company's growing success. He developed a plethora of products himself, such as the first frameless steel tank-pull trailer and the first successful aluminum truck tank-pull trailer.

The firm moved to a new plant in the 1950s, then added plants in Billings and Boise. By the next decade, Beall Pipe & Tank was an acknowledged leader in the pipe and automotive fields and had added plants in Denver and Oakland.

Throughout the 1970s and 1980s and on into the 1990s, the firm has continued to expand its holdings in the West. Its markets are spreading across the globe, as Beall regularly delivers its top-of-the-line equipment to countries such as Canada, Korea, Kuwait, and Venezuela.

Current president Jerry E. Beall, the son of John E., champions the same philosophy held by his forerunners: offer custom-built design of premium quality at a fair price. He and his employees are proud to place the Beall name on every tank and trailer they sell.

From its corporate headquarters in Portland, Beall directs three production factories and three specialized equipment factories strategically located throughout the Western states. Beall produces trailers for the leading transportation companies in the gasoline, chemical, milk, dry bulk, and construction industries. The company also operates a series of Beall-owned sales, services, and parts centers throughout its marketing area to better service its customers wherever they travel.

Growing up in an environment where quality was of prime consideration, the University of Oregon was the obvious choice for Jerry's business education. He has since been an avid supporter of the school's athletic programs, working to raise funds and serving on the Oregon Duck Club's board of directors. To make it a family affair, three of his five children also chose to attend the University of

Oregon. They help comprise a fourth generation team of Bealls geared to pioneer trucking industry products and services into the next century.

1936 Texaco Tanker: In 1936, Beall Pipe and Tank was already a major supplier of truck tanks throughout the West. Texaco and their jobbers were steady customers. The 3-year-old cowboy perched atop the tanker is Jerry E. Beall, who grew up to become Beall Corporation chairman.

Two contemporary models: Beall's 10,000-gallon aluminum semi-trailers (above) are pulled by major oil and trucking companies throughout the United States. Having pioneered their use in 1949, Beall specializes in lightweight aluminum tankers. Beall's famous aerodynamically designed cement trailers (left) are used for hauling dry bulk products.

CHAMBERS COMMUNICATIONS CORP.: COMMUNICATING SUCCESS

Armed with a BA in accounting from the University of Oregon and a loan from her parents, Carolyn Chambers launched KEZI television in 1957 to offer viewers an alternative to the single television station then available in Eugene.

The station, an ABC affiliate, went on the air for the first time in 1960, and this mother of nine soon began purchasing cable television properties. Her Liberty Communications, Inc., became the 19th largest cable company in the United States before being sold to the Denver-based Tele-Communications, Inc., in 1983. Forming Chambers Communication Corp., Carolyn maintained ownership of KEZI-TV and four cable properties in Washington and California. Chambers Communications Corp. has since grown to include three broadcast stations, six cable television systems, a state-of-the-art video production facility, and a direct mail center. Under the same management for 35 years, KEZI-TV seeks to provide well-balanced programming, objective news, and community participation. The station delivers signals to 56 cable systems, and its 22 translators benefit viewers in four Oregon counties. In addition to a strong commitment to local and national stories, KEZI's Eyewitness News crews have gone on assignment around the world.

The firm has also established itself as a multiple systems operator on the West Coast, with cable television systems spread across Washington, Oregon, Idaho, and California, serving more than 92,000 subscribers.

Chambers Communications is characterized by a "customer-first" attitude, progressive employment practices, prudent use of resources, and active involvement in the communities where they operate.

KEZI has initiated a partnership with local businesses, called Earth Smart, to focus attention and action toward environmental concerns. Carolyn has served as vice president and president of the University of Oregon Foundation, president of the Eugene Area Arts Foundation, and as a board member of Sacred Heart Hospital and the Eugene-Springfield Metropolitan Partnership. Her commitment to her industry and community have won her many accolades, including the Eugene Chamber of Commerce First Citizen award, the

National Cable Television Association's Vanguard Award for Leadership, the University of Oregon Pioneer Award, and the University of Oregon President's Medal.

Not only has her television station been promoting Oregon football over the years with game highlights and telecasts, but the Chambers family takes a personal interest in the Ducks. Three generations of Carolyn's family have attended the University. From enthusiastically cheering for the home team to generously funding positions for prominent visiting faculty, Carolyn Chambers continues to use her University of Oregon education to tally success for her business and the community.

PEPSI-COLA BOTTLING COMPANY OF EUGENE: GENERATIONS OF SUCCESS

Prominently displayed in the lobby of Pepsi-Cola Bottling Company of Eugene's corporate office is a sculpted wood mural depicting generations of Pepsi emblems. The work was not commissioned by a professional artist but was crafted by a talented Pepsi Eugene line employee, Robert Wood.

Robert is typical of the Pepsi Eugene team spirit, dedicated to providing superior products and services to this community and its employees in an environment of trust and fun.

As head coach of this team, president J. Peter Moore forges ahead from an impressive history of success and support in the beverage industry.

Pete's father, William R. Moore, a University of Oregon graduate, started in the business 60 years ago, as a route salesman for a Portland soft drink business. In 1969, the Moore family purchased the Pepsi plant and distribution center in Bend. Pete, who had earned his MBA from the University of Oregon, was the natural choice for managing the operation. Under his leadership, the plant saw tremendous growth.

In 1988, the Moore family and LeFevre family of Roseburg jointly purchased the Pepsi Eugene plant. Pete's brother Craig, also a University of Oregon alum and a UO Foundation trustee, assumed responsibilities for the Bend operation, so Pete could move to Lane County. Pete was happy to move closer to his alma mater and hit the ground running.

Located on a 10-acre lot just off the Glenwood exit of Interstate 5, Pepsi Eugene is the only soft drink producing facility in the Eugene/Springfield area. It serves all of Lane County and 250 miles of Oregon coastline from Lincoln City to California - a total population of 440,000 potential customers. Over 2.5 million cases of bottles are filled here each year for its own operations and most of the other Pepsi plants in Oregon.

Pepsi Eugene provides family wage jobs to 165 men and women in its franchise area, generating a significant payroll in an atmosphere of trust and integrity. Peter believes in reinvesting both in his business and in his people. They, in turn, are encouraged to contribute to the community.

Pepsi Eugene distributes a product line of drinks that includes Pepsi, Mountain Dew, Orange Slice, Mug Root Beer, 7-Up, Dr. Pepper, Squirt, Schweppes, Hawaiian Punch, EARTH2O, Country Time Lemonade, All Sport, Ocean Spray juices, and Lipton Tea drinks—all refreshments that go hand-in-hand with good, clean fun.

Three years ago, in an effort to improve their environmental performance, the Pepsi bottlers of the Northwest made a multimillion dollar investment in a state-of-the-art plastic bottle manufacturing plant in Olympia, Washington. They manufacture all of their own plastic bottles, made from recycled plastic soft drink bottles, and Pete is currently chairman of the board.

The canned soft drinks that Pepsi Eugene distributes are all produced in Mt. Angel, Oregon, where Peter sits on the board of Mt. Angel Beverage Co., a cooperative of Oregon Pepsi bottlers.

Almost every product Pepsi Eugene sells is packaged in reusable or recyclable containers. Because it is good for the community and for business, Pepsi Eugene is constantly looking for new ways to improve its environmental record.

With a winning line-up of great national brands, the Pepsi-Cola Bottling Company of Eugene provides a healthy and refreshing way to celebrate 100 years of Oregon Ducks.

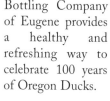

BACKGROUND: To commemorate the many faces of Pepsi over the generations, employee Robert Wood sculpted this collage for the new Eugene corporate office that opened in 1992.

LEFT: The Pepsi Eugene team thrives under the leadership of J. Peter Moore, president *(center)*, with the assistance of Kelly F. Reed, vice president sales and marketing *(left)*, and Tim Luck, vice president finance *(right)*.

McCANN COMMUNICATIONS CORP.: A SPORTING MEDIA SUCCESS

When Michael McCann left his management job with a national magazine publisher to become a sportswriter in 1989, his friends and associates shook their heads. Entry-level sports journalists are among the lowest-paid communications professionals. They couldn't know that Michael's decision would lead him to establish Oregon's most innovative and successful sports communications company.

Buoyed by the unwavering support of his wife, Jennifer, Michael convinced a suburban San Diego newspaper to let him cover high school football games as a free-lancer. At $35 per game, he knew he would have to move up quickly or abandon his childhood dream—but Michael never considered failure as an option.

Eight months later, he was covering the NBA finals as a full-time columnist for a newspaper in Phoenix, Arizona. Later, at a larger paper in Southern California, he would cover the National Football League, Major League Baseball, professional golf and tennis, and world championship boxing.

Despite his success, Michael still dreamed of covering the Ducks, having grown up in Eugene and attended the University of Oregon. In his 12 years away from Oregon, he noted how little news and information was available about the Ducks outside the state. So in 1991, he left his newspaper job and returned to Oregon with his wife and two children, Megan and Scott, to launch McCann Communications Corp. and the *Fighting Ducks Review*.

The *Fighting Ducks Review* began as a four-page weekly sports newsletter, available by subscription only, for out-of-town Oregon alumni and fans. Word of the publication spread fast, and the *Review* gained subscribers throughout North America.

In its fourth year of publication, *Fighting Ducks Review* grew into a four-color tabloid newspaper with statewide newsstand distribution and an even more expanded base of subscribers. A full-time editor, an art director and a marketing director were added, freeing Michael to tend to his growing duties as president of McCann Communications.

The company has since become recognized as an authoritative media resource and a sports marketing leader. Michael was invited to speak at the inaugural James H. Warsaw Sports Marketing forum at the University of Oregon's Charles H. Lundquist College of Business. He is also a frequent guest expert on radio talk shows, including KUGN's weekly "Duck Talk," and provides regular pregame and postgame reports during Oregon sports broadcasts.

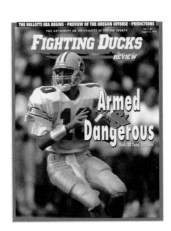

McCann Communications also publishes hardcover books, produces event programs for the University of Oregon and other organizations, provides editorial and design services, and creates custom on-line multimedia sports programming.

Through its commitment to satisfy the sports cravings of targeted sports audiences—wherever they live—McCann Communications Corp.

continues to break new ground in the development of innovative sports media.

ABOVE TOP: THE *FIGHTING DUCKS REVIEW*, A FOUR-COLOR NEWSPRINT MAGAZINE, IS THE ONLY WEEKLY PUBLICATION DEVOTED ENTIRELY TO UNIVERSITY OF OREGON SPORTS.

ABOVE BOTTOM: THE MCCANN COMMUNICATIONS LEADERSHIP TEAM INCLUDES *(left to right)* DARIN J. WEISS, MARKETING DIRECTOR, RONALD L. RICHMOND, EDITORIAL DIRECTOR, MICHAEL C. MCCANN, PRESIDENT, JENNIFER B. MCCANN, VICE PRESIDENT, AND DAVID O'TOOLE, ART DIRECTOR.

MOSHOFSKY ENTERPRISES: THE SPIRIT OF SUCCESS

On a dairy farm in Cedar Mills, Oregon, Edward and Sophie Moshofsky raised their seven children in the midst of the Depression. Farming a large homestead, they never really felt poor. They had land, and an indomitable spirit they inherently instilled in their children.

After an early education in a one-room schoolhouse, every one of those seven children graduated from the University of Oregon. Eldest son Edward was the first, graduating with a business degree. He also played tackle for the Ducks football team. His vision of playing pro ball, however, was cut short by his country's call to arms during WWII.

His brothers Richard, Arthur and Gerald Moshofsky followed in his footsteps, also graduating from the U of O with degrees in business. William received a law degree, and graduated at the head of his class. Evangeline and Betty earned education degrees and became school teachers.

After the war, Ed returned to home turf and a promising start in wholesale lumber. In 1951, Ed formed Whipple & Moshofsky Wholesale Lumber Company with another U of O graduate, E.J. (Jerry) Whipple. Shortly, younger brother Art brought his lumber background and accounting expertise into the company, and then became a partner. Less than a decade later, the brothers purchased a sawmill known as Fort Hill Lumber Company, near Grand Ronde, Oregon.

During 30+ years with their company, the two Moshofsky brothers took calculated risks in timber purchases and mill expansion. They quadrupled the size of the business. Ed led the way with the marketing side of the specialty mill, while Art carefully handled the management, planning and cost control of their two-shift operation.

Most of their products were for the home construction industry, but they broadened their base by producing lumber for door manufacturers and venturing into foreign markets. Innovative development of varied and better wood products and cutting items also kept them ahead of the competition.

In 1975, Ed and Art formed another company, Moshofsky Enterprises, to tackle home construction projects in Iran, and roll their successes into new investment opportunities. In 1988, amid changing government regulations for the timber industry, they sold their mill. In retirement, the two brothers still enjoy managing their investments, and supporting the Ducks, continuing to build on the family's spirit of success.

ABOVE: WHAT HAD ONCE BEEN THE MOSHOFSKY FAMILY HOMESTEAD IS NOW PART OF A GROWING INDUSTRIAL CORRIDOR OFF OF PORTLAND'S SUNSET HIGHWAY. ED MOSHOFSKY *(second from right, standing)* AND HIS BROTHER ART MOSHOFSKY *(fourth from left, standing)* GATHERED WITH OTHER FAMILY MEMBERS AT THE ORIGINAL SITE OF THEIR PARENT'S DAIRY FARM.

BACKGROUND: AN AERIAL PHOTO FROM 1987 SHOWS THE 30-ACRE FORT HILL LUMBER COMPANY (NEAR GRAND RONDE, OR) DURING ITS PEAK PRODUCTION YEARS.

FARWEST STEEL CORPORATION: STRONG SUPPORT FOR THE HOME TEAM

Farwest Steel Corporation supports Duck football from the ground up. The seats of Autzen Stadium, scoreboard, and goal posts are all constructed with Farwest Steel materials, donated in a spirit of commitment to the University of Oregon's outstanding athletic programs.

Farwest Steel Corporation was founded in 1956. Richard Jones, President and CEO, has been with the company more than 30 yeras and is part owner with Wan Koo Huh of South Korea. The owners have maintained the business philosophy of customer service, long-range planning, and technological innovations as interrelated. They call it "partnering for success."

Farwest Steel today, by combining employee excellence, advanced technology, and applied imagination, benefits from high productivity and enviable precision that allows them to consistently deliver superior products at competitive prices.

Farwest Steel currently has steel and rebar warehouse facilities in Medford, Boise, Seattle, and Salt Lake City, with sales offices in Bend, Portland, and Sacramento. In addition to the University of Oregon's athletic facilities, Farwest Steel's products range from intricate parts for motor homes to the vast structural basis of waste water treatment plants. San Francisco's Bay Area Rapid Transit System, NASA cranes at Cape Canaveral, the Honolulu National Airport, and the African Rain Forest of Portland's Washington Park Zoo were all constructed with Farwest Steel materials.

After 40 years and countless changes in the industry, the current owners uphold those traditions that propelled the company into the forefront of the region's steel industry.

Many outstanding graduates from the University of Oregon continue to join the Farwest Steel family and have significantly contributed to its success. When they fill the company's 500-seat rooting section in Autzen Stadium on the corporation's family day, it's obvious that Farwest Steel has a strong foothold in University of Oregon football history.

LEFT: CHEERING FOR THE DUCKS FROM THEIR 500-SEAT ROOTING SECTION AT AUTZEN STADIUM IS JUST ONE OF THE WAYS CIVIC-MINDED FARWEST STEEL ENJOYS BEING A GOOD CORPORATE NEIGHBOR.

ROMANIA ENTERPRISES:
KEEPING AN EYE ON THE SCORE

Father and son, Joe and Steve Romania, seem to have always known the score, in both the transportation industry and Oregon Ducks' football. Joe's 40+ years of experience and caution, paired with Steve's business savvy and aggressiveness have made them an unbeatable team in Eugene car, truck, and RV sales.

Joe, a coal miner's son, began his career in the automotive industry with a full-time job selling tires and auto accessories in a Billings, Montana, department store. After World War II, he sold tires at the local Sears, Roebuck & Co. store before landing a job selling cars for Lew Williams Chevrolet, also in Billings.

In 1957, his boss bought the Silva Chevrolet dealership in Eugene and offered Joe a 25 percent partnership in Lew Williams Chevrolet. Twelve years later, Joe had completed the buyout of Williams' interest and bought a new sign: Joe Romania Chevrolet.

Steve was only four years old when his family moved to Eugene. He literally grew up in the business. Steve spent the summers of his early teen years sorting nuts and bolts in the parts department of his father's business. In 1976, Steve graduated from the University of Oregon with a bachelor's degree in business management. He had already spent two summers selling cars for his father, and it was in his blood. Steve was ready to apply the business lessons he had learned at the U. of O., including "diversify to minimize risk," and "don't be afraid to make mistakes."

These insights were infused with his father's lore of "don't be fair-weather fans" to the University and "support the team unconditionally." Thus, Romania Chevrolet has sponsored the basketball scoreboard in Mac Court since 1969, provided vehicles for various coaches, and actively raised funds for Autzen Stadium and other capital events.

Business was good for the Romanias, and 1978 was the best sales year yet. Then came 1979, when the oil crisis, high interest rates, and sharp rise in import sales sliced the market share of domestic cars and trucks. Joe and Steve took their lumps and applied their earlier lessons. Diversification became the name of the game.

Even though in 1981 they had regained their footing as the largest Chevrolet dealer in Oregon, the Romanias opted to diversify beyond the Eugene economy.

Tapping potential for regional and national sales, they added recreational vehicle sales and service.

To reach the import market, Steve and his wife Lori opened the Hyundai dealership in Eugene in 1989. Then, in 1992, the operation underwent major restructuring. Steve Romania's dealership, Romania Imported Motors, bought out Vic Alfonso Toyota. Then Steve's dealership merged into Joe's Chevrolet Inc. to create one of the top 50 private companies in Oregon. Today, Steve manages the day-to-day operations, as President, while Joe has retired.

From five locations throughout Eugene, the Romanias offer new and used domestic and import cars, trucks, sports utility vehicles, and recreational vehicles, plus service for them all. The Romanias still know the score, and they will maintain their dominance in the Northwest auto retail market by continuing to meet the region's ever-changing transportation needs.

ABOVE: SUCCESS IS A FAMILY AFFAIR FOR ROMANIA ENTERPRISES. STANDING *(left)* IS JOE ROMANIA, FOUNDER OF ROMANIA CHEVROLET, CONGRATULATING HIS SON, STEVE ROMANIA, ON BECOMING PRESIDENT OF THEIR COMBINED AUTOMOTIVE DEALERSHIPS IN JANUARY 1992. THE UPCOMING GENERATION OF ROMANIA ENTREPRENEURS IN LANE COUNTY, YOUNG RYAN ROMANIA, APPEARS IN THE SMALL FRAMED PICTURE AT THE RIGHT.

TAYLOR ELECTRIC SUPPLY: SUCCESS BEYOND THE BOTTOM LINE

As a farm boy in Oregon's rural Washington County . . . as a street corner newspaper salesman in north Portland . . . as a "112-pound dripping wet" quarterback of Estacada High School's football team . . . and as the owner the largest single-house independent electrical-supply wholesale distributor in the United States, Harold Taylor has been characterized by persistence.

Harold worked for the U.S. Forest Service in the 1930s, then at the Kaiser shipyard in Vancouver, Washington, during World War II. After the war, he worked for two electrical-supply companies before striking out on his own and founding Taylor Electric Supply in 1959.

According to his son Bill, Harold's persistence led him to start his own company after several attempts to purchase a former employer. That employer is no longer in business.

Taylor Electric started operations in a rented warehouse with two employees. Shortly thereafter, Harold hired an aspiring young man named Bill Klein to work in the office. Today, with Harold as CEO, Bill Klein is president of the company and Bill Taylor is executive vice president. The company employs 130+ people in three buildings, utilizing more than 100,000 square feet of office and warehouse space on Portland's East Side.

Harold and Margaret Taylor have been married for more than 50 years and Margaret has accompanied Harold on many of his trips with the Ducks. Although Harold never attended any college or university, he became interested in University of Oregon athletics during the Len Casanova era of the late 1950s.

"I think it's just something that reached out and grabbed him," Bill explained. "And they haven't let go of each other since."

Harold has been honored many times for his contributions to the University through the years, by the University and by the Oregon Club of Portland. Recently, he and Margaret were inducted into the UO Athletic Hall of Fame, and in 1993 he received the prestigious President's Award for meritorious service to the University.

BELOW TOP: TAYLOR ELECTRIC SUPPLY HAS BEEN LOCATED IN ITS MAIN BUILDING AT THIRD AND MARKET IN PORTLAND SINCE 1971.

BELOW BOTTOM: TAYLOR ELECTRIC, WHICH NOW ENCOMPASSES THREE CITY BLOCKS, PURCHASED THE BUILDING AT THIRD AND CLAY IN 1993

Harold's ties to Ducks football date back to the Len Casanova era of the late 1950s. Bill remembers going to games with his Dad at Multnomah Stadium and Hayward Field during those successful seasons.

"But he's been there in the lean years as well," Bill said. "That's the way he is, not one to jump ship in times of adversity. I think it says as much for the University and the program as it does for him."

RSG FOREST PRODUCTS: LEGACY OF SUCCESS

Like many who grew up in the tiny harbor town of Charleston, Oregon, Bob Sanders went to work in the local lumber mills as a boy. It was just a job; never did he envision himself as a lumber mill owner.

After graduating from high school, Bob left Charleston and the mills to attend the University of Oregon. While earning a bachelor of arts degree in business, Bob played football for the Ducks. He was known as a fierce competitor, a smash-mouth fullback who backed down to no one. In 1948, Bob and his team went all the way to the Cotton Bowl.

To him, competitiveness is a character trait—something you either have or you don't. Breaking through the line for the Ducks, Bob Sanders knew he had what it takes to make sure his team forged ahead.

"You have to compete to be successful," Bob says. "Not just in sports and in business, but in everything."

Bob built a second mill on the Kalama site, RSG Forest Products. Then he purchased two more mills: Beaver Lumber Co. in Clatskanie and Estacada Lumber Co. Completing his portfolio in 1987, Bob purchased three mills in Molalla, Oregon, all of which he bought from the Smurfit Company, a supplier of Times-Mirror Publishing.

Bob and his wife Jane, who is also an Oregon graduate, have worked

During his heady college days, Bob began forming a vision of himself as more than a mill worker. Years of scrimping and hard work paid off when, in 1971, he signed the papers on his own mill—Olympic Forest Products in Mist, Oregon.

Not long afterwards, he purchased Gram Lumber Co., in Kalama, Washington, ironically, from the man who had served as the manager for his 1949 Ducks football team.

Bob quickly determined that to gain an edge in the lumber industry, he would have to develop new ways to manufacture lumber.

"Some people call that innovation," Bob explains, "but I did it because I knew that's what it would take to be successful. We had to come up with something better, and we did."

hard for the legacy they will leave their two sons, two daughters, and 11 grandchildren. Bob is a major contributor to the Duck Athletic Fund, crediting his University of Oregon education and Duck football experience for providing him with the self-confidence he needed to achieve his business successes.

ABOVE: AN AERIAL VIEW OF THE RSG FOREST PRODUCTS PLANT IN KALAMA, WASHINGTON.

LEFT: THE GRAM LUMBER COMPANY IN KALAMA, WASHINGTON.

BI-MART MEMBERSHIP DISCOUNT STORE: A WINNING STRATEGY

One morning 40 years ago, Jack Phelan and a group of his friends sat around a coffee shop discussing a new membership discount department store that one of them had read about in the Wall Street Journal. The appealing idea was to buy merchandise in volume at a discount and then pass the savings on to member customers. They decided to send two from their group to learn more. A cut from a deck of cards determined that Jack would lead the scouting party, and the men each put up $50 to fund the trip.

Their hunch paid off. And before long, those first 11 stockholders had opened up a little store in Yakima, Washington — the first Bi-Mart Membership Discount Store. Five evenings a week, their wives helped them stock shelves and serve customers. Because they each held full-time day jobs, the store was open only from 6 to 9:00 in the evening.

Things changed fast, though, as Jack and his pals developed the business around a winning strategy that worked well in 1955 and still works today: "Offer the best possible merchandise at the lowest possible prices."

Jack was appointed company president, and in 1962 Bi-Mart was ready to open its second store. They chose Eugene, Oregon, on the corner of 18th & Chambers.

Another five years and three stores later, Bi-Mart moved its corporate headquarters to Cleveland Street on Eugene's industrial west side, where they could be near the greatest concentration of volume and on the main West Coast route for major suppliers.

Jack and friends at first concentrated expansion of their chain in smaller cities with local newspapers. This low-key strategy, combined with targeting their message to a known membership base, saved on advertising costs and provided invaluable insight for growth plans.

Space in the original corporate

headquarters eventually became too cramped, Bi-Mart decided to reaffirm its commitment to the community it had called home for 24 years and in 1986 moved into a new Eugene headquarters located on 220 Seneca Street.

Bi-Mart purchases all merchandise from a central office, distributing from the same place (a 200,000 square-foot distribution center in Eugene), unifying advertising, and keeping prices as low as possible.

Each Bi-Mart store carries televisions and stereos; top-of-the-line fishing, hunting and camping goods; consumer

housewares and hardware; automotive, lawn and garden supplies; food, candy, and toys; health and beauty products, and more. The stores also pride themselves on complete pharmacies that have adapted to customers' prescription drug needs by including "easy access" drive-up/walk-up pharmacy windows.

With 44 stores, the still-growing chain now stretches across Oregon and Washington with over a million family memberships. Three of those stores are in Eugene, and seven are in Lane County.

Bi-Mart's commitment to Eugene includes generous support for the University of Oregon. They consider themselves a "home team" store, proudly sponsoring radio broadcasts of the University's football and men's basketball games on the Ducks Sports Network.

LEFT: THE TINY BUR BEE BUILDING IN YAKIMA, WASHINGTON, WAS HOME TO THE FIRST BI-MART MEMBERSHIP DISCOUNT STORE IN 1955. MORE THAN FORTY YEARS AND 44 STORES LATER, BI-MART'S 30,000-SQUARE-FOOT MODERN STORES *(Above)* STILL PROVIDE NAME BRAND PRODUCTS AT LOW PRICES.

KPNW RADIO:
THE VOICE FOR OREGON SPORTS

Never mind the rolling sand dunes or the crashing whitecaps or the clear skies reflected in the blue Pacific. J. Hobart "Hobie" Wilson was too distracted to enjoy his visit to the Oregon coast on a certain autumn afternoon over 30 years ago. He had left his teenage son back home in Eugene to play football and was annoyed that he couldn't listen to the game on any radio station—not even the one he owned.

This die-hard sports fan made a decision that day which resulted in a major coup for regional radio reception. Already a partner in KPIR, a 10,000-watt radio station in Eugene, Hobie applied on behalf of Emerald Broadcasting Corp. to the Federal Communications Commission for a 50,000-watt clear channel commercial radio license.

After years of maneuvering and waiting, in July 1967, Governor Tom McCall finally smashed a phonograph record with a gold hammer at a dedication ceremony marking the beginning of construction of the megastation's transmitter. When completed, four 444-foot tall radio towers broadcast the most powerful radio station in the Pacific Northwest, one of only 25 clear channel stations in the country. Only one other station in the US (in St. Louis, Missouri) would share the allocated AM 1120 spot on the radio dial.

To win the license, Hobie had to overcome stiff competition from neighboring California. His application prevailed because his station would serve thousands more people who did not have access to adequate radio reception, and the radio signal from the Eugene location would also cover the greatest number of miles.

At that time, Hobie's son Charles was president of Emerald Broadcasting Corp., which then changed its name to Pacific Northwest Broadcasting Corp. When

the radio station went on the air in December 1967, its new KPNW call letters were publicized in every corner of Eugene: "KPNW, Key to the Pacific Northwest, with 50,000 watts of broadcasting power."

In 1975, after Charles moved to Boise to run his own 50,000-watt radio station there, Dave Woodward became vice president and general manager of KPNW. Operating at full power 24 hours a day, KPNW radio features news, talk, and sports. The familiar voices of Jerry and Mike in the morning, Ray Martin with traffic, Leon Hunsaker with the weather, and Dan and Tom in the afternoon keep their listeners informed up to the minute.

Joining the local team are the

ABC Information Network, Paul Harvey with his news commentary, and popular talk radio hosts like Rush Limbaugh and Ken Hamlin.

A 1932 University of Oregon graduate himself, Hobie was naturally pleased with his station's eight-year run as "The Voice of the Ducks." KPNW also broadcasts Eugene

Emeralds, Portland Trailblazers, and Seattle Seahawks games.

ABOVE: AT THE 1967 DEDICATION OF THE KPNW TRANSMITTOR SITE, GOVERNOR TOM MCCALL *(center)* WAS THE HONORED GUEST WHO "BROKE A RECORD" BY SMASHING A VINYL ALBUM WITH A GOLD HAMMER. POSING WITH THE GOVERNOR ARE CHARLES WILSON, THEN PRESIDENT OF PACIFIC NORTHWEST BROADCASTING *(left)*, AND J. HOBART WILSON, CHAIRMAN OF THE BOARD *(right)*.

LEFT: A DISC JOCKEY'S POINT OF VIEW IN THE LATE-1960S STUDIO OF KPNW-RADIO.

WILDISH CONSTRUCTION: LAYING THE GROUNDWORK FOR SUCCESS

It's virtually impossible to go anywhere in Eugene without passing on, over, or by something built by a Wildish construction crew.

For six decades, the Wildish group of sand and gravel and construction companies has been shaping the community's civic landscape. Wildish lays underground utilities, pours foundations and driveways, surfaces streets, smooths out the highway system, and builds bridges and landmarks. The company provides family wage jobs for hundreds of workers. Its people contribute time, energy, materials, and money to community organizations. And Wildish continues to construct projects that improve the community's quality of life.

The organization's history begins with the Great Depression, when T.C. Wildish migrated to Eugene from North Dakota with his wife and 10 of their 12 children. After they arrived in 1935, T.C. traded the family pickup for a dump truck and started delivering sand and gravel. By 1941 he owned a dozen trucks.

With the advent of World War II, the family began doing underground utility work, and by the end of the war, the T.C. Wildish Company had bought its first sand and gravel site. By 1947, the company was crushing bar run material, and four years later, it began producing asphalt concrete.

Throughout the 1950's, business volume expanded, thanks to city street and subdivision contracts. The 1960's saw a steady increase in the firm's ability to bring manpower, skill and materials to bear on its jobs, culminating in the award of a number of major projects, including the rebuilding of the Mahlon Sweet Airport runway.

The Wildish organization grew again in the 1970's and 80's both operationally and geographically. As its capabilities in concrete construction evolved, its market expanded throughout the state and into Washington, California, and Arizona. And as Wildish developed expertise in large-scale commercial construction, the company took on numerous

high-profile projects, most notably, the University of Oregon's Willamette Hall, with its four-story atrium, and the Chiles Business Center. The Barker Stadium Club Facility atop Autzen Stadium and Hayward Field's 400-meter oval and infield event area

were also built by Wildish.

Today, the Wildish management team extends through three generations, all of whom have spent time in the trenches. They each feel personally responsible to Wildish employees and clients, alike, and take great pride in honoring commitments.

In addition to fulfilling their obligations to customers, the Wildish companies also take care to protect the natural environment. As a result, Wildish has been recognized with numerous awards from industry groups and has been a recipient of the Governor's Award for Corporate Excellence.

The rock-solid values of hard work and pulling together have carried the Wildish group of companies

through the 20th Century. This ethic, coupled with an eye toward identifying new and challenging opportunities, is paving the way toward the next century, as the organization continues to build quality projects in Eugene and the Pacific Northwest.

THE WILDISH FAMILY HERITAGE OF EXCELLENCE IS WOVEN THROUGHOUT EVERY PHASE OF THEIR CONSTRUCTION PROJECTS. THE CURRENT MANAGEMENT GROUP CONSISTS OF: *(seated, left to right)* JAMES A. WILDISH, PRESIDENT; WILLIAM R. WILDISH, VICE PRESIDENT; *(standing, left to right)* NORMAN E. WILDISH, VICE CHAIR; STEVEN J. WILDISH, VICE PRESIDENT; THOMAS E. WILDISH, CHAIRMAN OF THE BOARD; MICHAEL C. WILDISH, VICE PRESIDENT.

THE COMPLEX, ARTISTIC DESIGN OF THE UNIVERSITY OF OREGON'S 128,000-SQUARE-FOOT WILLAMETTE HALL WAS A SPECIAL CHALLENGE THAT WILDISH CONSTRUCTION MET SUCCESSFULLY. AT THE TOP OF THE HALL'S FOUR-STORY ATRIUM IS A METAL STRUCTURE WITH 1800 LASER-CUT STARS,

REPRESENTING THE FIELD OF ASTROPHYSICS. INSIDE ITS OFFICES, CLASSROOMS, AND LABORATORIES, STUDENTS PURSUE THE PHYSICAL SCIENCES .

OREGON CENTENNIAL FOOTBALL RECORDS

OREGON FOOTBALL COACHES IN THE FIRST 100 YEARS

YEAR	COACH	WIN/LOSS RECORD	YEAR	COACH	WIN/LOSS RECORD
1894	Cal Young/J.A. Church	1-2-1	1924	Joe Maddock	4-3-2
1895	Percy Benson	4-0-0	1925	R.S. Smith	1-5-1
1896	J.F. Frick	2-1-0	1926-29	John McEwan	20-13-2
1897	Joe Smith	1-1-0	1930-31	C.W. Spears	13-4-2
1898-99	Frank Simpson	6-3-1	1932-37	Prink Callison	33-23-2
1900	Lawrence Kaarsberg	3-3-1	1938-41	Tex Oliver	16-18-2
1901	Warren Smith	3-4-1	1942	John Warren	2-6-0
1902	Marion Dolph	3-1-3	1943-44	No Football	—
1903	Warren Smith	4-2-1	1945-46	Tex Oliver	7-10-1
1904	R.S. Smith	5-3-0	1947-50	Jim Aiken	21-20-0
1905	Bruce Shorts	4-2-2	1951-66	Len Casanova	82-73-8
1906	Hugo Bezdek	5-0-1	1967-71	Jerry Frei	22-29-2
1907	Gordon Frost	5-1-0	1972-73	Dick Enright	6-16-0
1908-09	Robert W.Forbes	8-4-0	1974-76	Don Read	9-24-0
1910-11	BillWarner	7-3-0	1977-94	RichBrooks	91-109-4
1912	Louis Pinkham	3-4-0	1995-	MikeBellotti	—
1913-17	Hugo Bezdek	25-10-3	Totals	35 coaches	442-409-46
1918-23	Shy Huuntington	26-12-6			

ALL-TIME ASSISTANT COACHES

COACH	YEAR	COACH	YEAR	COACH	YEAR	COACH	YEAR
Nick Aliotti	1988-1994	Jerry Frei	1955-1966	Jack O'Brien	1930-1931	Bart Spellman	1919-1924
Dick Arbuckle	1974-1976	Steve Greatwood	1982-1994	Tom Osborne	1995	Vern Sterling	1952-1954
John Becker	1977-1979	Willard Hammer	1953-1957	Don Pellum	1993-95	Lon Steiner	1956
Mike Bellotti	1989-1994	Gene Harlow	1951	Chris Petersen	1995	Ron Stratten	1968-1971
Carl Blackburn	1974	Carl Heldt	1947	John Ramsdell	1983-1994	Bob Sullivan	1948-1949
Al Borges	1995	Ron Hudson	1977-1978	Don Read	1972-1973	Bill Tarrow	1977-1995
Bill Bowerman	1948-1952	Charles "Shy" Huntington	1918	Richard Reed	1927-28,36-37,45-46	Howard Tippett	1977-1978
Jesse Branch	1972-1973	Milt Jackson	1977-1978	Bill Reinhart	1924-25,29-31	Bob Toledo	1983-1988
Gary Campbell	1983-1995	Ed Johns	1963-1969	Frank Riggs	1929	Manny Vezie	1941-1942
Norm Chapman	1967-1971	John Kitzmiller	1932-1935	Sam Robertson	1972-1973	Eugene Vidal	1926-1928
Andy Christoff	1977-1982	Jerry Lillie	1949-1950	John Robinson	1960-1971	Fred von Appen	1972-1976
Reanous Cochran	1957	Fred Malone	1979	Jack Roche	1951-70,75-76	Joe Wade	1972-1974
Ralph Cole	1938	John Marshall	1969-1976	Joe Schaffeld	1974-1995	Dave Walker	1980-1984
Max Coley	1959-1968	Robert Martz	1926-1927	Denny Schuler	1986-1992	John Warren	1935-41,45-48
Vaughn Corley	1939-41,45-46	Bill Maskill	1983-1987	Ray Segale	1942	Charlie Waters	1995
Anson Cornell	1942	Bob McClure	1949-1950	George Seifert	1967-1971	Erik Widmark	1979-1982
Don Cortez	1975-1976	Bob McCray	1977-1981	Willie Shaw	1979	Boz Williams	1924-1925
Gene Dahlquist	1974-1976	Phil McHugh	1958-1968	Eugene Shields	1929-1937	Ben Winkleman	1946
Brad Ecklund	1958-1959	Johnny McKay	1950-1958	Jim Skipper	1980-1982	Frank Zazula	1947-1948
Harry Ellinger	1926	Mike Mikulak	1937-1940	Bruce Snyder	1967-1971	Neal Zoumboukos	1980-1995
Dick Enright	1970-1971	Dick Miller	1947-1948	Steve Sogge	1972-1976		

INDIVIDUAL - GAME RECORDS

COACH	DATE			
Most Rushing Attempts		38	Bobby Moore vs. USC	1970
Most Net Yards Rushing		249	Bobby Moore vs. Utah	1971
Longest Scrimmage Run		92	Bob Smith vs. Idaho	1938
Most Passes Attempted		61	Danny O'Neil vs. Penn State	1995, Rose Bowl
Most Passes Completed		41	Danny O'Neil vs. Penn State	1995, Rose Bowl
Best Pass Completion Percentage		.833 (10-12)	Earl Stelle vs. UCLA	1949
Longest Pass-Run Play		95	Tom Blanchard-Bob Newland vs. Illinois	1970
Most Yards Passing		489	Bill Musgrave vs. Brigham Young	1989
Most Total Offense		498	Bill Musgrave vs. Brigham Young (56 plays 9 rush 489 pass)	1989
Most Touchdown Passes		6	Danny O'Neil vs. Stanford	1994
Most Passes Had Intercepted		6	George Shaw vs. Washington	1952
			Danny O'Neil vs. Washington	1993
Most Points		52	Charles Taylor vs. Puget Sound	1910
Most Points (Modern Record)		24	Derek Loville vs. Idaho State	1988
Most Touchdowns Running		7	Charles Taylor vs. Puget Sound	1910
Most Touchdowns Running (Modern Record)		4	Derek Loville vs. Idaho State	1988
Most Offensive Plays		74	Danny O'Neil vs. Penn State	1995, Rose Bowl
Most Pass Receptions		11	Bob Newland vs. Air Force	1970
			Greg Bauer vs. Stanford	1976
			Derrick Deadwiler vs. California	1993
			Cristin McLemore vs. Stanford	1993
			Josh Wilcox vs. Penn State	1995, Rose Bowl
Most Touchdown Pass Receptions		3	Bobby Moore vs. Utah	1969
			Bobby Moore vs. Idaho	1969
			Terry Obee vs. Arizona	1988
			Cristin McLemore vs. Stanford	1993
			Cristin McLemore vs. Stanford	1994
Most Yards Gained Pass Receiving		234	Derrick Deadwiler vs. California	1993
Longest Punt Return		92	Woodley Lewis vs. Oregon State	1949
Longest Kickoff Return		102	Woodley Lewis vs. Colorado	1949
Longest Fumble Recovery Run		99	Jim Smith vs. Oregon State	1966
Longest Pass Interception Return		99	Ken Klein vs. Air Force	1966
Longest Punt		78	Mike Preacher vs. Nebraska	1986
Highest Punting Average (5 minimum)		49.7	(6 punts)Mike Preacher vs. Nebraska	1986
Longest Field Goal		57	Roy Geiger vs. Washington State	1977
Most Field Goals		5	Kirk Dennis vs. Washington State	1988
			Tommy Thompson vs. Arizona State	1992
Most Conversion Kicks		14	Charles Taylor vs. Puget Sound	1910
Most Conversion Kicks (Modern Record)		8	Ken Woody vs. Idaho	1969
Most Pass Interceptions		4	Shy Huntington vs. Pennsylvania	1917, Rose Bowl

TEAM - SEASON RECORDS

CATEGORY	RECORD	YEAR	CATEGORY	RECORD	YEAR
Most Yards Rushing	2,527	1955	Fewest Rushing Yards Allowed	834	1938
Most Yards Passing	3,270	1993	Fewest Passes Attempted	97	1936
Most Yards Total Offense 4,630 (1, 530 rush 3,100 pass)		1970	Fewest Passes Completed	36	1936
Most Passes Attempted	441	1970	Fewest Passing Yards Allowed	458	1936
Most Passes Completed	240	1986	Most Interceptions	25	1947, 1949 and 1968
Most First Downs Rushing	141	1979	Most Touchdown Passes	25	1993 and 1994
Most First Downs Passing	151	1970	Most Passes Had Intercepted	29	1952
Most First Downs	256	1989	Undefeated Season		1895 (4-0-0)
Most Points	379	1989			1906 (5-0-1)
Fewest Points Allowed (since 1916)	34	1936 (9 games)			1916 (7-0-1)
	50	1958 (10 games)	Most Victories	9	1928 (9-2)
Most Touchdowns	45	1994			1933 (9-1)
Most 1-Point PATs	38	1994			1948 (9-2)
Most 2-Point PATs	6	1970			1994 (9-4)
Most PATs Total	40	1989	Longest Winning Streak	10	(last 7 games, 1915
Most Consecutive PATs	36	1990			and first 3 games,1916
Most Field Goals	24	1989			last four games 1963
Most Field Goals Attempted	34	1992			and first six games 1964)

INDIVIDUAL - SEASON RECORDS

CATEGORY	RECORD	PLAYER	YEAR
Most Running Attempts	265	Derek Loville	1988
Most Net Yards Rushing	1,211	Bobby Moore	1971
Top Rushing Average (50 carries or more)	8.09	Don Reynolds	1971
Most Passes Attempted	401	Bill Musgrave	1989
Most Passes Completed	231	Bill Musgrave	1989
Most Yards Passing	3,224	Danny O'Neil	1993
Top Completion Percentage	619	Danny O'Neil	1993
Most Touchdown Passes	22	Bill Musgrave	1989
		Danny O'Neil	1993
		Danny O'Neil	1994
Most Total Offense	3,087	Danny O'Neil	1993
Most Offense Plays	457	Danny O'Neil	1993
Highest Average Per Play	7.27	Tom Blanchard	1970
Most Passes Had Intercepted	24	Dan Fouts	1970
Most All-Purpose Yards	1,613	Sean Burwell	1990
Most Pass Receptions	67	Bob Newland	1970
Most Yards Gained Pass Receiving	1,123	Bob Newland	1970

CATEGORY	RECORD	PLAYER	YEAR
Most Touchdown Receptions	10	Bobby Moore	1969
		Cristin McLemore	1993
Most Points	109	Gregg McCallum	1989
Most Touchdowns	15	Bobby Moore	1969
Most PAT's	37	Gregg McCallum	1989
		Matt Belden	1994
Most PAT's Without Miss	37	Gregg McCallum	1989
Most Pass Interceptions	13	George Shaw	1951
Most Yards Interception Returns	202	Jake Leicht (10 interceptions)	1945
Most Field Goals Made	24	Gregg McCallum (32 attempts)	1989
Most Field Goals Attempted	34	Tommy Thompson (21 made)	1992
Most Punts	81	Kevin Hicks	1982
Most Punts Returned	46	Ronnie Harris	1992

INDIVIDUAL - CAREER RECORDS

CATEGORY	RECORD	INDIVIDUAL	YEAR
Most Rushing Attempts	814	Derek Loville	1986-89
Best Average Per Carry	6.1	John McKay	1948-49
Most Passes Attempted	1,132	Danny O'Neil	1991-94
Most Passes Completed	636	Danny O'Neil	1991-94
Most Passes Had Intercepted	54	Dan Fouts	1970-72
Most Touchdown Passes	62	Danny O'Neil	1991-94
Highest Completion Percentage	573	Bill Musgrave (634-1,106)	1987-90
Most Plays	1,449	Danny O'Neil	1991-94
Most Yards Total Offense	8,140	Bill Musgrave	1987-90
Highest Average Per Play	6,38	Bill Musgrave (1,275-8,140)	1987-90
Most Pass Receptions	131	Bobby Moore	1969-71
Most Yards Gained Pass Receiving	2,233	Terry Obee	1986-89
Most Touchdown Pass Receptions	20	Cristin McLemore	1992-95
Most Yards Interceptions Returned	298	Jake Leicht	1945-47
Most Touchdowns	45	Derek Loville	1986-89
Most PAT's Attempted	85	Matt MacLeod	1984-86
Most PAT's Made	84	Matt MacLeod	1984-86
Most Consecutive PAT's	74	Matt MacLeod	1984-86
Best PAT Average	988	Matt MacLeod (84-85)	1984-86
Most Punts Returned	124	Terry Obee	1986-89
Most Yards Punts Returned	1,182	Terry Obee	1986-89
Most Field Goals	45	Gregg McCallum	1989-91
Most Field Goals Attempted	62	Gregg McCallum	1989-91

TEAM - GAME RECORDS

CATEGORY	RECORD	YEAR
Most Net Yards Rushing	403 vs. California	1960
Most Net Yards Passing	489 vs. Brigham Young	1989
Most Offensive Plays	95 vs. California	1970
Most Yards Total Offense	667 vs. Brigham Young	1989
Most Passes Attempted	61 vs. Penn State	1995 Rose Bowl
Most Passes Completed	41 vs. Penn State	1995 Rose Bowl
Most Touchdown Passes	7 vs. Stanford	1994
Most Passes Had Intercepted	9 vs. Washington	1952
Most Pass Interceptions	7 vs. Idaho	1949
Most First Downs Rushing	23 vs. Utah	1971
Most First Downs Passing	23 vs. Penn State	1995 Rose Bowl
Most First Downs	33 vs. Utah 1971; vs. Utah State	1990
Most Points	115 vs. Puget Sound	1910
Most Conference Points Scored	58 vs. Washington	1973
Most Conference Points Allowed	66 vs. Washington	1974
Most Points Allowed	71 vs. Texas	1941
Fewest Yards Rushing Allowed	(-47) vs. Brigham Young	1990
Fewest Yards Passing Allowed	(-1) vs. Air Force	1979

A
Abbey, William 1945-46-47
Adams, John 1952
Adolph, D. 1927
Aiken, James Jr. 1948
Aitkenhead, Greg 1984-85
Akerman, Rick 1969-70-71
Albright, Farrell 1952-53
Ale, Leroy 1986-87-88-89
Allen, Derek 1994
Allen, Jeff 1989-90-91
Allison, Michael 1992-93
Allman, Howard 1951
Alstock, Francis 1921
Altenhofen, Greg 1958-59
Amato, Tony 1935-36-37
Anderson, Bob 1948-49-50
Anderson, Christian 1993-94
Anderson, Louis 1923-25
Anderson, Robert 1945
Anderson, Ron 1959-60-61
Anderson, Ted 1951-52-53
Anderson, Jim 1970-71
Anderson Kevin 1978-79
Anderson, Maurice 1971-73
Anderson, Thurman 1969-71
Anderson, Stan 1917-18-19
Anderson, Steve 1937-39
Anderson, Williams 1945
Andrews, Mark 1968-69-70
Angell, H.D. 1898-99
Amunsen, Fred 1914
Arbuckle, Dick 1959-60
Arca, Ron 1979
Archer, Dan 1965-66
Archer, Sam 1986-88
Archer, Woodward 1928-29
Arnold, LeFrancis 1971-73
Arnspiger, O. 1905-06-07
Arriaran, Jim 1978-79
Aschbacker, Darrell 1957-58
Ashcom, Richard 1940-42
Asher, Jeremy 1992-93-94
Ashworth, Robert 1951
Atiyeh, Victor 1942
Austin, Charles 1954-55-56
B
Baack, Steve 1980-81-82-83
Babb, Mike 1978-79-80
Babbs, O.B. 1991-1982
Bachtold, Paul 1977-78
Back, W. 1934
Baguio, Joe 1990-91
Bailey, E.F. 1912
Bailey, Ken 1923-24-25
Bailey Orville 1930-31-32
Bailey, Steve 1970-71
Bailey, Troy 1992-93-94
Bain, Lu 1961-62-63
Baldwin, Bob 1994
Bandison, Romeo 1990-93
Barber, Manning 1952
Barber, Merritt 1952
Barnes, Derrick 1993-94
Barnes, Emery 1950-52-53
Barnes, Eric 1992-93
Barnes, Lew 1983-84-85
Barnes, Mike 1966
Barnett, Steve 1960-61-62
Bartels, Bob 1942
Bartholemy, Wayne 1946-48
Bartlett, Ken 1914-16
Bassett, Bob 1985-86
Bates, Ralph 1930
Bates, Willie 1951
Battle, Larry 1971
Bauer, Greg 1974-75-76
Bausley, Dondre 1989
Bautista, James 1988-91
Bauge, Paul 1959-60-61
Beck, Gary 1977-80-81
Beckett, J.W. 1913-16
Beekley, Bruce 1976-77-78
Belden, Matt 1994
Bell, George 1946-47-48-49
Bennett, George 1974-76
Bentley, Arleigh 1936-37
Berg, Art 1917-18-19
Berg, Ron 1962-63
Berkich, Mike 1978-81
Berrie, Leonard 1952-53
Berry, Bob 1962-63-64
Berry, Chandler 1936

Berry, John 1939-40
Berry, Latin 1986-87-88-89
Berwick, Jim 1946-47-48
Beyer, Tim 1976-77-78
Bidings, E.R. 1898
Billups, Harry 1979-83
Birden, J.J. 1984-85-86-87
Bisharat, Charles 1979-80
Bishop, C.K. 1932-33
Bishop, C.M. 1897-98-99
Bishop, Richard 1934-35
Bjork, Delbert 1934-35-36
Blackman, Thomas 1936
Blackwell, Howard 1990
Blake, Merle 1918-19
Blakey, Mike 1985-88
Blanchard, Tom 1967-69-70
Bland, Todd 1982-83-84-85
Blasher, Willie 1977-78
Blatchey, Ray 1942
Bledsoe, Gordon 1979-81
Blenkisop, Robert 1938
Bliss, Jackson 1923-24-25
Boatright, Scot 1987-90
Bobbitt, Howard 1932-33
Bodner, Steve 1940-41-42
Bolliger, Mike 1971-72-73
Bond, Deane 1945
Bondelie, Ken 1974
Bonney, J. 1895
Boqua, Bud 1948-49
Borba, Tony 1985-86
Borcher, William 1941
Bowie, Bud 1990-91
Bowerman, William 1931-32
Boyd, Frank 1940-41
Bracher, Charles 1936-38
Braddock, Robert 1935-36
Bradley, Chuck 1971
Bradshaw, Robert 1912-13
Brandenberg, Everett 1918-19
Branson, Jeff 1994
Brantley, Peter 1987-90
Brauner, Bill 1968-70
Breaid, Dennis 1937
Brenn, Bruce 1956-57
Brethauer, Monte 1950-52
Briedwell, Paul 1913
Brock, Matt 1985-86-87-88
Brooks, Brady 1989
Brosterhous, Greg 1971
Brosterhous, Jon 1978-81
Brothers, Bob 1988-90-91
Brouchet, Steve 1975-76
Brown, Ben 1960-61
Brown, Brian 1990-91-93
Brown, Dick 1946
Brown, Don 1982-83-85-86
Brown, Donald 1942
Brown, Eugene 1972-76
Brown, John 1955-56
Brown, Mark 1986
Brown, Reggie 1980-81
Brown, Rutherford 1920-22
Brown, Steve 1979-82
Browne, Al 1929
Bruce, Mickey 1960-61
Brundage, Mike 1964-65-66
Bryan, Rudy 1976-77-78
Bryant, Kenny 1977-78
Bryant, Raymond 1913-15
Bryson, R.S. 1895-96
Buettner, Steve 1969-70-71
Buller, John 1966
Bullock, Dennis 1976-77
Bunker, Steve 1964-65-66
Burke, J.O. 1924
Burleson, Paul 1961-63
Burnell, George 1926-27-28
Burnett, Len 1958-60
Burns, Ken 1981
Burwell, Sean 1990-93
Busch, Louis 1946
Bussey, Mark 1981
Butts, Jeff 1974-75-76
Butkovich, Louis 1940
Byler, Horace 1922
Byrd, Desmond 1994
Byrne, John 1982-83-84-85
C
Cabrera, D.J. 1991-94
Cabs, Ed 1991
Cadenasso, Don 1963

Cadenasso, Jim 1938-39
Cafferty, Tom 1976-77
Calderwood, James 1949-50
Callison, Everett 1961
Callison, Prink 1920-21-22
Campbell, Cogs 1922-23
Campbell, Leroy 1951-54
Canfield, Wallace 1913-14
Carey, Robert 1950
Cargill, Duane 1960-61-62
Cartales, Harry 1964-65-66
Carter, Clarence 1925-26-27
Carter, Ken 1972-73
Carter, Ross 1934-35
Carter, Ross 1964-66
Carter, Shirley 1929
Casey, Tim 1963-64-65
Cash, Theodore 1951
Cashin, Carl 1975
Cason, Wendell 1981-84
Castle, Brian 1980-81-82
Castle, Eric 1989-90-91-92
Causey, Don 1963
Cespedes, Jan 1986-87
Chandler, B. 1908
Chandler, Ben 1910-11-12
Chandler, W. 1906
Chapman, Norm 1955-57
Chapman, T.J. 1918-19
Chapman, W.H. 1921-23
Chappell, George 1928
Cherry, Tony 1984-85
Chriss, Mike 1974-77
Christensen, Dave 1983
Christensen, George 1928-30
Chrobot, Ed 1947-48-49
Churchill, Jim 1975-76
Clark, Dan 1977-78
Clark, Jack 1964-65
Clark, Mario 1972-75
Clarke, Dudley 1907-08-09
Clarke, H. 1931-32-33
Clay, Dennis 1980-81-82
Clemens, Delmer 1950
Clerin, Hugh 1921
Clesceri, Joe 1959-60
Clifford, Kealii 1991
Clough, Rich 1977-78
Cobb, Charley 1970
Cochran, Reanous 1954-56
Codding, Clarence 1934-35
Codson, R.M. 1980
Colbert, Austin 1928-29-30
Coleman, Donald 1978-79
Coleman, George 1971-73
Coleman, J.R. 1895-96
Coleman, Lionel 1969-70
Coles, LaSalle 1928
Collins, Brian 1992-93-94
Collinsworth, David 1989-92
Conner, Andy 1988-91
Conners, Jack 1972-73
Cook, George 1917-18-19
Cook, Melvin 1975-76-77
Cook, Sam 1913-15
Cooper, Tim 1985-86-87
Core, Grant 1983
Corey, Buck 1961-62-63
Cornell, Anson 1913-15-16
Cosgrove, Chris 1978-79-81-82
Cossman, Jim 1914-15-16
Cota, Chad 1991-92-93-94
Couch, Ray 1917-18-19
Countryman, Jack 1950
Covington, Jerome 1978-79
Crabtree, Jack 1955-56
Crabtree, Tom 1955-56
Cramer, Mark 1974-77
Cress, Scott 1965-66-67
Crish, Tony 1940-41-42
Crites, Ronald 1945
Crowell, Dean 1914-15-16
Crowley, Dick 1967
Crowston, Kyle 1991-92
Cuffel, Hal 1950
Culligan, Kevin 1973-74-75
Culp, David 1983-84
Culwell, Val 1940-41-42
Cummins, Jeff 1990-92
Cunningham, Gunther 1966-68
Cuppoletti, Bruno 1932-33
Curran, Tom 1991-92-93
Currie, George 1930

Curtis, Lynn 1951
Cusano, David 1986-89
Cuttrell, Dave 1994
D
Dairy, Rory 1988-89-90
Dale, Derrick 1976-77-78
Dalgleish, D. 1918-19
Daly, Dan 1977
Daly, Seaton 1994
Dames, George 1966-67-68
Daniels, Chester 1948
Daniels, Roger 1956-59
Daniels, Samuel 1949-50
Daugherty, Richard 1950
Davenport, Richard 1951
Davis, Don 1977-80-81
Davis, Gary 1964-65
Davis, Keith 1971-72-73
Davis, Robert 1940-41-42
Davis, Todd 1970
Day, J. 1923
Deadwiler, Derrick 1992-93
Dean, Lowell 1962-63-64
DeBisschop, Bobby 1983-86
DeCourcey, Keith 1947-48
Deeds, Cameron 1942
DeGroote, Tim 1992
Del Biaggio, Bill 1960-62
Delegato, Mike 1978-81
DeLeon, Pat 1989
Dennis, Kirk 1986-87-88
Denton, Carl 1911
Devaney, Dan 1983-86
DeVarona, Dave 1965
Diederichs, George 1950-52
DiFonzo, Mike 1992-93
Dills, W. 1925
Dion, Terry 1977-78-79
Dixon, Dick 1960-61-62
Dixon, Homer 1925-27-29
Donahue, John 1928-29-30
Donnell, Gerald 1935
Donnelly, Steve 1972-73-74
Donnerberg, Joe 1994
Donovan, Dennis 1937-39
Donovan, Walter 1945-46
Dorning, Dale 1983-84
Dotur, Steve 1947-48-49
Doughterty, Lee 1949-50
Douglass, Doug 1988-91
Dozier, Eric 1989-90
Drake, Bill 1969-70-71
Dresser, James 1978-79
Drougas, Tom 1969-70-71
Dudley, G. 1917
Duffy, E.J. 1982-83-84-85
Dugan, George 1942-46
Duman, Les 1974-75-76
Dunham, Harold 1950-52
Dunlap, William 1941-42
Dunning, Elliott 1984-87
Durando, Tim 1977-78-79
Durbin, Dan 1973
Dyer, Roy 1939-40-41
Dykes, Curt 1988-89
E
Eagle, Alex 1932-33-34
Eaglin, Ray 1965
Earl, V.D. 1901-05
Earle, Garrett 1978-80
Eastburn, Greg 1976
Ecklund, Brad 1946-47-48
Edmundson, J. 1896
Edwards, Alfred 1950
Edwards, F.A. 1899
Edwards, H. 1945
Edwards, Terrell 1990-91-92
Edwards, Thomas 1950-51
Ehret, Frank 1974
Eichinger, Jon 1986-87
Eldart, Don 1950
Ell, Roy 1940
Elliott, Charles 1941-42-46
Elliott, Eric 1984-85-86-87
Elliott, Thomas 1952
Ellis, Tim 1980-81-82
Elms, Arlan 1964-65-66
Elshire, Neil 1978-79
Emmons, Frank 1937-38-39
English, Pat 1978-79-80
Engstrom, John 1935-36
Erdley, John 1929-39-31

Erickson, Leroy 1942
Ermini, Larry 1975-76
Ervin, Carl 1950
Estes, W. 1934-35-36
Eustace, Alan 1971
Evenson, Jim 1967
F
Farmer, Teddy 1974
Farrar, Edward 1934-35-36
Farris, J.R. 1912
Farwell, Joe 1989-90-91-92
Fell, Bill 1959
Fenton, Carl 1910-11
Feola, Craig 1976-77
Ferry, Vince 1990-91
Ficco, Randy 1977-78
Figoni, Jim 1970-71-72
Figueras, Jaiya 1994
Figures, Joe 1978-79-80-81
Finicle, Tim 1979-80
Fish, Dave 1957-58
Fitchet, Monte 1961-63
Fitzgerald, John 1987-90
Fitzgerald, Paul 1985
FitzPatrick, Devin 1985-88
Fletcher, Stephen 1929-30
Fluke, Dave 1963
Ford, Dwight 1979-82
Ford, J. 1899
Forsta, Eril 1929-30-31
Foskett, Bob 1965-66
Foskett, William 1936-38
Fouts, Dan 1970-71-72
Fouts, Mike 1976
Francis, Russ 1973
Franklin, Jim 1967-68-69
Frary, Howard 1946
Fraser, Sandy 1957-58-60
Frease, Don 1969-70-71
French, Gilbert 1929
Freeman, Dave 1972-73-74
Freissel, F.M. 1905
Frizzle, P.T. 1902-03
Frye, Garder 1932-33-34
Fury, Con 1933-34
Fury, Patrick 1936
G
Gaechter, Mike 1961
Gaffney, Walter 1953-54
Gagnon, Roy 1932-33-34
Gaiser, Rich 1982-83-84
Gammon, David 1936-38
Garrett, Dobie 1914-15-16
Garrett, Tommy 1974-75
Garza, Dan 1946-47-48
Gassner, Dennis 1967-68-69
Gaulden, Richard 1949
Gebhardt, Ted 1937-38
Gee, Leighton 1931-32-33
Geiger, Roy 1976-77
Gibbs, Ross 1980-81
Gibilisco, Jack 1949
Gibson, Cliff 1980-81-82
Gibson, Dave 1948-49-50
Gibson, Greg 1974-75
Giesecke, Ted 1932
Gilbert, Gary 1986-87-88
Gillis, G. 1945
Giovanini, Nello 1936-38
Gipson, Ronnie 1994
Glass, Leland 1969-70-71
Gleason, Jack 1967-68-69
Goldsmith, Vince 1977-80
Golka, Darrin 1985-86
Goodin, F. 1935
Gooding, Bert 1924
Gould, Cotter 1926-27-28
Gould, Ron 1987
Gragg, Jon 1976-77
Graham, Tom 1969-70-71
Gram, H.B. 1921-22
Grant, Reggie 1975-76-77
Gray, Michael 1981-82
Graybeal, Jay 1937-38-39
Grayson, Dave 1958-59-60
Graziani, Tony 1994
Greatwood, Steve 1977-79
Green, Bob 1969-70-71
Green Bobby L. 1972-75
Green, Rod 1986-87
Greenley, Charles 1952-54
Greer, Tony 1927
Gregg, Mark 1993-94

Griffin, Clifford 1941-42-46
Griffin, Damon 1994
Grossi, Tony 1984
Grosz, Dave 1958-59-60
Grote, Kent 1966-67-68
Grottkau, Bob 1956-57-58
Grover, Paul 1957-58
Gunther, Keith 1977
Guy, Tim 1971-72-73
Gydesen, Todd 1989-90-91

H

Haake, Chris 1974-76
Hagen, Lester 1948-49
Hagen, M.C. 1926-27-28
Hagerty, Ed 1978-79-80-81
Haggerty, Ancer 1963-64-65
Haliski, Chester 1939-40
Hall, Collin 1989-90
Hall, Elmer 1910-12-13
Hall, Marion 1930
Halt, Earl 1951
Halverson, Brad 1968-69
Hammond, R.B. 1905
Hammond, T. 1899
Hampton, Kwante 1982-83
Hamstreet, Matt 1977
Hanable, Brian 1988-89
Harden, Harold 1926-27
Hardin, Steve 1991-94
Hardy, Ron 1990-91-92
Hargain, Tony 1987-90
Harper, James 1984-87
Harrington, John 1967-69
Harris, Hymie 1939-46
Harris, Jim 1939-40
Harris, Ronnie 1990-91-92
Harter, Scott 1986
Haskins, Robb 1964-65
Hathaway, M. 1945
Hatton, H. 1929
Haugum, Dan 1970-71
Hawk, Bob 1969
Hawkins, Brian 1987
Hay, Duncan 1967
Hay, Kirk 1968-69
Hayden, Henry 1931
Hayes, Liam 1989-90
Haynes, David 1976-77
Haynes, Gerald 1979-81
Heard, Bob 1957-58
Hearn, Stan 1968-69
Heberlein, Jim 1972-74
Heckman, Rob 1989
Hedgepeth, Donald 1951-53
Hedges, Keith 1967-68
Helfrich, Pat 1965-66
Henderson, Jack 1975-76-77
Hendrickson, Lynn 1966-67
Herd, Greg 1971-72-73
Herman, Doug 1981-84
Heron, Lachlan 1965-66
Herr, Steve 1971
Heusner, William 1912
Hickey, Chuck 1976-77
Hicks, Clifford 1985-86
Hicks, Kevin 1982-83
Hickson, Dave 1973
Higbee, Jeff 1972
Hilbert, Steve 1967-68
Hildreth, Omri 1966-67-68
Hilfiker, John 1955
Hill, Dana 1982
Hill, Francis 1929
Hill, Larry 1961-62-63
Hill, Tony 1982-84-85
Hillstrom, Spike 1955-56
Hines, Burton 1949
Hinkle, Bryan 1977-80
Hirbolt, F. 1894-96
Hodgen, Beryl 1925-26-27
Hodges, Cecil 1951-52-53
Hoffman, Bill 1976-77-78
Hogensen, Greg 1978-80-81
Holcomb, Ben 1947-48
Holden, William 1913
Holeman, Emile 1950
Holland, Barney 1952-53
Holand, Marlan 1957-58
Holman, Scott 1984-85
Holmes, Garrett 1985-86
Holt, Donald 1952-54
Holub, Thad 1990
Honeycutt, Michael 1978-79

Hoopaugh, Michael 1990
Horne, Richard 1939-40
Horton, Derek 1986-89
Horyna, Larry 1963
Hosey, Devon 1990-92
Howard, Martin 1920-21
Howington, Heath 1991-93
Hudetz, Bob 1980-82-83-84
Hudnell, Ricardo 1976-78
Hudson, Jim 1975-76
Hug, C.W. 1904-05-06
Hughes, Bernie 1931-32-33
Hulbert, Ed 1983-84-85-86
Hull, Howard 1949-50
Hunt, John 1917-18-19
Hunt, Rick 1987-88-89
Hunt, Ron 1972-73-74-75
Hunter, Eric 1987
Huntington, C.A. 1914-16
Huntington, Hollis 1916-19
Hurd, L.C., 1905-06-10
Hurney, Andrew 1934-35
Hurst, Bill 1974-75
Husk, Ronald 1937
Husko, Chris 1986-87-88
Huston, Joseph 1935-36-37
Huston, O.B. 1910

I

Imwalle, Dick 1961-62-63
Inman, Jerry 1964-65
Isberg, Leonard 1939-40
Iverson, Duke 1940-41-42
Ivory, Jim 1970

J

Jackson, Alan 1983
Jackson, Bryant 1993-94
Jackson, Curtis 1978-79-80
Jackson, Dennis 1961
Jackson, Eugene 1991-92-93
Jackson, Morris 1940-41
Jacobberger, Francis 1918-20
Jacobberger, Vince 1919
Jacobson, Erling 1938-39-40
Jacobson, Leif 1935-36
Jacques, James 1952
Jakway, B.S. 1899-1900
James, Dick 1953-54-55
James, Mark 1980-81
Jamison, Homer 1910
Jaraczeski, Jeff 1981
Jelks, A.J. 1994
Jensen, Bjarne 1986-89
Jensen, Bruce 1975-76-77
Jensen, Paul 1992-93-94
Jensen, Roy 1937-38-39
Jenson, Steve 1983-84
Jesse, N. 1929
Jessie, James 1991-92
Jodoin, Mike 1971-72-73
Johannsen, Eric 1994
Johnson, Ben 1952
Johnson, Bruce 1970-71
Johnson, Carl 1924-27
Johnson, DeWayne 1945-49
Johnson, Don 1972-75
Johnson, Harry 1953-54-55
Johnson, Jim 1976-78
Johnson, Ladaria 1980-83
Johnson, Michael 1981
Johnson, Mike 1968-69-70
Johnson, Pat 1994
Johnson, R. 1929
Johnson, Ray 1962-63
Johnson, Roger 1940
Johnson, Ron 1983-84-85
Johnson, Steve 1980-81-82
Johnson, Terry 1922
Johnson, Ward 1921-22
Johnson, Wayne A. 1974-75
Johnson, Wayne 1951-52
Jollymour, Doug 1979-80-81
Jones, Anthony 1989-92
Jones, Buddington 1933-35
Jones, Cleveland 1959-60
Jones, Dwayne 1991-94
Jones, Ernest 1990-91-92-93
Jones, J.E. 1912
Jones, Lynn 1925-26-27
Jones, Ron 1961-62-63
Jones, Steve 1966
Jones, Terrance 1979-82
Jordan, Lin 1922
Jordan, Reggie 1993-94

Jorgensen, Mike 1981-84
Josephson, Jim 1960-61-62
Judge, Doug 1982-83-84-85
Jumper, Brandon 1988-91
Jurich, Jerry 1976

K

Kaanapu, Todd 1987-90
Kaminski, Dale 1976-77-78
Kane, Rick 1973-74
Kanehe, Milt 1962-63
Kantola, Steve 1967-68-69
Karnofski, Raymond 1949-51
Kauffman, John 1945-46-47
Kaumeyer, Thom 1987-88
Kaylor, Craig 1981-82-84
Kearns, Bert 1924-25-26-27
Kearns, Mark 1986-89
Keele, Tom 1957-58-59
Keene, C.W. 1895
Keeney, Robert 1926-27
Keeter, Mike 1990
Kelemeni, Ngalu 1989-90
Keller, Dennis 1962-63-64
Keller, John 1954
Kellogg, Jeff 1975-76
Kellogg, R.N. 1909-12
Kennedy, Donald 1936-37
Kennedy, Michael 1978
Kent, Jerry 1991-92
Kemp, Steve 1989-90
Kerr, Johnny 1974
Kerron, S.M. 1904-05
Kershner, Jerry 1955-56
Kesler, Michael 1978-79
Kessler, Shane 1990
Kimbrough, Alden 1957-59
King, Eugene 1982-83
King, George 1920-21-22
Kirtley, E. 1923
Kish, John 1966-68-69
Kitzmiller, John 1928-29-30
Kleffner, Steve 1976-77-78
Klein, Ken 1965-66
Klews, Michael 1994
Knickrehm, Gus 1949-50
Knox, R.R. 1896-98-99
Koch, Robert 1941-46-47
Koker, Tony 1991-92
Kollias, Louis 1951
Kollman, Jim 1964-65-66
Kostka, Stan 1932
Kozak, Kyle 1987-89
Kozak, Scott 1985-86-87-88
Kubitz, Jeff 1979-80
Kufferman, Merritt 1941-42
Kuykendall, D. 1896-97
Kunzman, Todd 1987-88-89

L

LaBounty, Matt 1988-91
Lacau, Jean 1936
Lackaff, Fred 1975-76
Lainhart, Porter
Laiolo, Kim 1969-70
Laird, Charles 1952-53
Lance, Larry 1937-38
Lane, Jack 1954
Lassalle, Dale 1935-36-37
Latham, Hugh 1920-23
Latourette, E.C. 1910-11-12
Latourette, J.H. 1904-05
Laudenslager, Don 1957-59
Laudenslager, Gayle 1962
Laughlin, Barkley 1922
Laughlin, Pete 1977-78
Lawler, Ken 1978
Lawrence, Bob 1965-66-67
Lawson, Russell 1987-88-89
Leavitt, H. 1925
Lee, Clyde 1941
Lee, Todd 1982-83
Leicht, Jake 1945-46-47
Leighton, Tim 1973-74-75
Lemons, Brent 1975
Leslie, Earl 1919-20-21
Leslie, Keith 1917-18-19
Leupold, Chris 1986-87-89
Lewis, Danté 1993
Lewis, Delton 1970
Lewis, Reggie 1972-73
Lewis, Tom 1968-69
Lewis, Woodley 1948-49
Lightfoot, Dave 1971
Lillie, Jerome 1928-29-30

Linden, Jim 1956-57-58
Lindsey, Greg 1968, 72-73
Lloyd, Harold 1944
Lombardi, Mike 1976-77
Londahl, John 1929
Lopez, Ray 1934-35
Loughlin, Bart 1921
Loumena, Henri 1955-56
Love, Hank 1974
Loville, Derek 1986-89
Lowder, Bill 1979-80-81-82
Lowe, George 1954
Lowe, Rourke 1978-80-82
Lucas, P. 1929
Luger, John 1967-68
Luna, George 1959
Lung, Raymond 1949-50
Lusk, Kevin 1980-81-82
Lyman, Ronald 1950-51-52
Lyon, Thomas 1951-52

M

Mabee, Donald 1938-39-40
Macey, Glen 1917-18
MacLeod, Jack 1952
MacLeod, Matt 1984-85-86
MacRae, Jeff 1965-66-67
Mack, Alex 1983-84-85
Maddock, C.R. 1917-18
Main, W.S. 1910-11-12
Maison, H.G. 1917-18
Malarkey, Leo 1913-16
Malarkey, Robert 1915-16
Malepeai, Pulou 1993-94
Malepeai, Silila 1990-94
Malepeai, Tasi 1994
Maley, Dave 1983-84-85-86
Maloney, Dennis 1963
Manerud, C.R. (Skeets) 1919
Mangum, Harold 1926-27
Mansfield, Joe 1984-85-86
Manuel, Fred 1970-71
Markulis, Nick 1954-55-56
Marshall, Greg 1968-69-70
Marshall, Rob 1984-85-86
Martin, George 1972-73-74
Martin, Henderson 1972-74
Martin, Matt 1991-92
Martin, Ron 1962-63-64
Martinez, Raul 1975-76
Mason, David 1927-28-29
Massey, David 1990-93
Mathews, F. 1894-95
Mathews, Jamey 1978-79-80
Matson, Pat 1963-64-65
Mattson, Riley 1959-60
Maule, Gerald 1955
Maurer, Andy 1967-68-69
Maust, Don 1965
Mautz, C.V. 1918-19
Mautz, Robert 1923-24-25
Mayther, William 1942
McCalister, Danny 1981-83
McCallum, Gregg 1989-91
McCall, Kevin 1983-84
McCarty, Mike 1984-85
McCauley, Donald 1950-51
McClain, C.A. 1904-05
McClellan, Michael 1989-90
McClonahan, E. 1898-99
McCowan, James 1947-50
McCready, Lynn 1917-18
McCredie, H. 1934
McCutchan, Everett 1927-28
McConnell, Mike 1970
McDougall, Pat 1976-79
McEnroe, Joe 1974
McGee, Jasper 1954
McGill, Kevin 1978-79-80
McHugh, Phil 1954-55-56
McIntryre, J. 1904-05-10
McJunkin, Tim 1974-75
McKay, John 1948-49
McKean, John 1969-70-71
McKinney, Herm 1958-60
McKinney, H.H. 1905
McKinney, Oliver 1963-64
McLean, Rob 1972
McLemore, Cristin 1992-93
McNally, Pat 1973-74
Meade, Dan 1992-93-94
Means, A.G. 1910
Mecham, Curtis 1940-41
Medley, D. 1917-18-19

Meerten, Joe 1986-87-88-89
Mehl, Darrell 1974-75-76
Meister, Herm 1965
Meland, Ted 1946-47-48
Mellum, Darrell 1975-76
Mettler, Rich 1976
Meyer, Bill 1971-72-73
Mezzera, Steve 1945
Michek, Frank 1933-34-35
Mikels, Jerry 1981-82-83-85
Miklancic, Fred 1955-56
Mikulak, Michael 1931-33
Milburn, Ted 1988
Miller, Charles 1964-65
Miller, Chris 1983-84-85-86
Miller, Dave 1976
Miller, Frank 1986
Miller, Peter 1946-47
Milligan, J. 1933
Milne, Art 1946-49
Mimnaugh, George 1924-26
Missfeldt, Charles 1949-50
Mitchell, Brick 1915-18
Mitchell, Dan 1990-91
Mitchell, G.J. 1908--11
Mobley, Richard 1953-54
Mock, Gerald 1951
Moeller, Edward 1929-31
Molden, Alex 1992-93-94
Molter, Cam 1965-66-67
Mondale, Harry 1951-55-57
Montgomery, LaRoy 1986
Montieth, Orville 1914-16
Moore, Bobby 1969-70-71
Moore, Curtis 1994
Moore, Daryl 1975
Moore, Donovan 1991-92
Moore, Keith 1950
Moore, Vernon 1935-36-37
Moores, G.C. 1904-07
Morfitt, Neil 1920-21
Morgan, Dave 1972-75
Morgan, William 1930-32
Morin, William 1945
Morris, Clifford 1937
Morris, Jack 1955-56-57
Morris, Raymond 1932-34
Morris, Reggie 1969
Morse, Raymond 1934
Moser, Greg 1979-80-81-82
Moshofsky, Ed 1940-41-42
Moshofsky, Gerald 1949-51
Moullen, F.C. 1908-09
Murphy, H.D. 1962-63
Murphy, Kory 1992-93-94
Murphy, William 1946
Muse, Joe 1970-71
Musgrave, Bill 1987-90
Musgrave, Doug 1991-92
Mutscher, George 1953

N

Nado, Steve 1977
Needham, Harry 1958-59
Nehl, John 1974-75
Nelson, C.E. 1917-18
Nelson, Gerald 1954
Nelson, Pete 1986-87-88-89
Nelson, Stuart 1940
Nestor, Bud 1938-39
Neuman, Daniel 1945
Nevills, Sam 1948-49
Newland, Bob 1968-69-70
Newman, Anthony 1984-87
Newquist, James 1941-46-47
Nicholson, James 1936-38
Nickerson, Carl 1972-74
Nicolaisen, Jim 1966-67-68
Nilson, Henry 1936-37-38
Nilsson, E. 1931-32-33
Nolan, Mike 1978-79-80
Nolan, Virgil 1912
Novacio, Anthony 1946
Novikoff, Tom 1951-52
Nowling, Russell 1941-42
Nutt, James 1979-80
Nutting, Kim 1975-76-77

O

Oas, Robert 1946-47-48
Obee, Terry 1986-87-88-89
O'Berry, Herman 1991-92-94
Obertauffer, R. 1907-08-09
O'Brine, Rod 1986
O'Connor, Grady 1992-93

O'Connor, Steve 1987-90
Ogburn, Reggie 1979-80
Okken, Jon 1990
Oldham, Chris 1987-88-89
Oldham, Hugh 1965
Oliphant, Kenneth 1941-42
Oliver, Muhammad 1990-91
Olson, Eric 1967-68
Olson, Monte 1981
O'Neil, Danny 1991-94
O'Neill, Donald 1941
Ord, Arthur 1926-27-28
Ording, Mickey 1960-61-62
Orick, Brent 1984
O'Rouke, Pat 1918
O'Rourke, Randy 1981-82
Osborne, Charles 1955-57
Osterkamp, Rich 1970-71
O'Toole, Bill 1964-65
Otto, Dean 1984-85
Overall, Timothy 1975
Owens, Michael 1981-83
Oxman, Thomas 1941

P

Page, Andrew 1979
Page, Ken 1977-78
Palm, Bob 1972-73-74
Palm, Les 1964-65-66
Palm, Ray 1963-64-65
Pamplin, Rocky 1968-69
Park, Ted 1929
Parke, Robert 1932-33-34
Parke, William 1930-31
Parker, Tim 1984-85-86-87
Parks, Henry 1975-76
Parson, Charles 1921-22
Parsons, Jerry 1964
Parsons, John 1913-14-15
Patera, Jack 1951-52-53-54
Patrick, Richard 1949-50-51
Patton, Herschel 1940-41
Paxton, Richard 1949
Payne, C.A. 1899
Pellum, Don 1982-83-84
Penso, Marc 1989
Pepelnjak, George 1932-34
Perry-Smith, Ryan 1993-94
Persons, Tom 1972
Peters, Merle 1937-38-39
Peterson, Bob 1957-58-59
Peterson, Keith 1952
Peterson, Kent 1959-60-61
Pettingell, Ralph 1968-70
Pew, Jeff 1981-82
Pheister, Ron 1952-53-54
Phelps, Leroy 1956-57
Philbin, Dave 1915
Phillips, Greg 1990-91
Phillips, Joe 1967-68-69
Philyaw, Dino 1993-94
Pica, Wilson 1978
Pieper, Dave 1970-71
Pinkham, Louis 1908-09
Pitcaithley, Alan 1967-68-69
Pittard, William 1935
Plath, Robert 1975-76-77
Pocock, Jack 1955-56
Pope, O. 1931-32
Pope, Theodore 1926-27-28
Popovich, Mike 1972-73
Post, Doug 1961-63-64
Potter, James 1954-55
Powell, Dave 1958-59
Powell, Lloyd 1952-54
Powrie, James 1915
Pozzo, Anselmo 1931-33-34
Preacher, Mike 1984-85-86
Price, Rick 1977-79-80-81
Prozinski, Dennis 1960-62
Pulver, Mike 1971
Putzier, Rollin 1984-87

Q

Quillan, Fred 1975-76-77

R

Rach, William 1937
Radcliff, Ed 1977-78
Ralph, Dan 1982-83
Ramey, Sam 1946
Ranstad, Terry 1968-69-70
Roventos, John 1955-56
Read, Len 1956-57-58
Reed, Daryl 1988-89
Reed, Dick 1922-23-24

Reed, John 1951-53
Reed, John 1973-75-76
Reedal, Tom 1978
Reeve, Harold 1951-54
Reeve, Will 1956-57-58
Reeves, Ray 1970
Reginato, Victor 1937-38-39
Regner, William 1939-40-41
Reid, Eric 1993-94
Reina, Steve 1965-66
Reinhardt, Matt 1994
Reinhart, Bill 1919-20-21
Reiton, Harold 1945
Reitzug, Joe 1988-89-90
Rekofke, Brian 1974-75-76
Renfro, Mel 1961-62-63
Rennie, Steve 1969-70-71
Renstrom, Curt 1970
Reynolds, Don 1972-73-74
Reynolds, I. 1925
Reynolds, Robert 1942-46
Rhea, Floyd 1940-41-42
Rhone, Ed 1980-82-83
Richards, Mark 1963-64-65
Richmond, Rock 1979
Rickert, Rodney 1975-76
Ricketts, Dameron 1993-94
Ridings, E. 1899
Rieschman, John 1934-35
Rife, Willy 1993-94
Riffle, Laird 1974-75
Riggs, Frank 1927-28
Riordan, Stanley 1934-35
Risley, Jake 1914-15-16-17
Risley, Victor 1923
Rivera, Edmund 1983-84
Roback, Ryan 1979-80
Roberson, Dave 1968
Roberts, Bob 1947-48-49
Robertson, Andre 1983
Robertson, Dwight 1978-80-82
Robertson, Ernie 1938-39
Robertson, Gary 1985-88
Robertson, Leonard 1936-38
Robinson, Darrell 1947-49
Robinson, John 1957
Robinson, Kerrell 1987-90
Robinson, Louis 1948-49
Robinson, Robert 1927-29
Roblin, Thomas 1940-41-42
Roche, John 1967
Rockwell, Bryon 1991-93
Rodriguez, Paul 1989-92
Rose, Larry 1953-54
Rose, Mike 1959-60-61
Rosette, John 1975-76
Rotenberg, Sam 1930
Rowe, Paul 1937
Ruhl, Rich 1992-93-94
Rushlow, John 1930
Rust, Jack 1966-67-68

S

Salcido, Mike 1972
Salisbury, Brett 1991
Samuelson, Albert 1938-39
Sanborn, Paul 1980-81-82
Sanders, Robert 1947-48-49
Sax, Moe 1923
Schaffeld, Joe 1957-58
Schmidt, Mark 1993-94
Schneider, Bruce 1967
Schneiders, Bill 1976
Scholer, Gunner 1974-77
Scholl, Marc 1965-67
Schuler, Denny 1967-68
Schultz, Irvin 1929-30-31
Schwab, Greg 1983-84-85
Schwab, Rich 1962-63
Schwabe, Paul 1980-83
Schwartz, Rick 1977-80
Segale, Ray 1939-40-41
Setterlund, Scott 1977-80
Shaffer, Don 1946
Shanley, Jim 1955-56-57
Sharpe, C.A. 1915
Shattuck, E.P. 1894-95
Shaw, George 1951-54
Shaw, Wayne 1950-51
Shea, Terry 1967
Shearer, W. 1929
Shedrick, Juan 1990-93
Sheehy, J.S. 1918
Sheldon, Dean 1949

Shepard, Scott 1980-82-83
Shephard, James 1941-42
Sherman, Jeff 1991-94
Sherman, Keith 1966-67-68
Shields, Archie 1920-21-22
Shields, Floyd 1921-22
Shields, Gene 1923-24-25
Shields, M. 1928-29
Shur, Nic 1967-68
Siegner, Mitch 1992-93-94
Sikora, Michael 1951
Siler, Fred 1958-59
Simmons, Harold 1950-52
Simpson, Ron 1967
Sinclair, Albert 1923-25-26
Sinclair, Cam 1967-68-69
Singleton, Daryl 1987-89-90
Singleton, Herb 1973
Skinner, Kenyon 1935-36
Slapnicka, Tim 1972-73-74
Slauson, Edgar 1926
Slender, George 1955
Sloan, Donald 1950-51-52
Slymen, Mark 1991-93-94
Smetana, Drew 1983-84-85
Smith, Bill 1965-66
Smith, Brad 1983-84-85-86
Smith, Dane 1967-69
Smith, Daryle 1990-91
Smith, Jim 1965-66-67
Smith, Robert 1937-38-39
Smith, Roger 1966-67-68
Smith, R.S. 1896-97-98-99
Smith, Sherman 1924-25-26
Smith, Tim 1978-79
Snidow, Ron 1960-61-62
Snyder, Bruce 1960-62
Snyder, W.C. 1914-15-16
Sovoreign, Jack 1963-66
Spaulding, J. 1899
Spear, Charles 1929
Spear, Mark 1987-88-90
Spear, William 1922
Specht, Greg 1970-71-72
Speetzen, Rodney 1937
Spellman, Bert 1914-15-16
Spence, Blake 1994
Spencer, C.A. 1905
Stadelman, George 1927-29
Stahlhut, Roger 1965-66
Stambaugh, Jack 1968-70
Stanton, Don 1946-47-48
Starck, Justin 1992-93
Starr, Bob 1982
Starr, R. 1898-99
Steber, Bill 1969-70-71
Steepin, Matt 1993
Steers, Henry 1942
Steers, W.H. 1917-18-19-20
Stefanick, Jeff 1984-87
Stensland, Garry 1961
Stenstrom, Marsh 1938-40
Stelle, Earl 1948-49-50
Stewart, Marcell 1994
Still, Walace 1947
Stiner, Alonzo 1953-54-55
Stipanovich, Will 1983-86
Stoeven, Laurence 1947
Stokes, Clark 1947
Stokes, Tim 1970-71
Stone, Don 1970-71
Stone, Jack 1959
Stone, Kamil 1993
Stoutt, Richard 1952
Stoutt, Robert 1951
Stover, Ron 1956-57-58
Strait, Kyle 1994
Stratten, Ron 1961-63
Stringer, Ed 1982-83
Stuart, Jim 1938-39-40
Sullivan, Corkey 1963-64
Sullivan, Dennis 1951
Sullivan, Donn 1954
Sunia, Andy 1987-88-89-90
Surles, Leonard 1941-42
Swain, Bill 1959-60-61
Swanson, C. 1932-33
Sweitzer, Ken 1951-52-53

T

Talbot, Tom 1984-85-86-87
Tapley, Terry 1985
Tarbell, E. 1929
Tarr, Jerry 1960

Tarrow, Bill 1955-56
Tate, Willy 1991-92-93
Tattersall, Jon 1989-92
Tatum, Doug 1982
Taumoepeau, John 1990-93
Taylor, C.M. 1909-10
Taylor, Ernest 1980
Taylor, G. 1916
Taylor, Joe 1985-86-87-88
Taylor, Johnny 1988-89-90
Tefft, Kolya 1988-89
Temple, Mark 1931-32-33
Temple, Tim 1964-65-66
Templeton, C.L. 1898-99
Templeton, F.M. 1896-97-1905
Templeton, H.S. 1894-95
Templeton, J.H. 1894
Tergilgas, Harold 1917-18
Terjeson, Jens 1923-24
Terjeson, Ralph 1932-33-34
Terry, Thomas 1941-42
Thayer, F.V. 1903
Thomas, Aaron 1986-88
Thomas, Bill 1967
Thomas, Charles 1973-75
Thomas, Ed 1961-62
Thomas, Lance 1989
Thomas, Osborn 1981-83
Thomason, Jeff 1988-91
Thompson, Laurence 1947
Thompson, Tommy 1990-93
Tichenor, Carrol 1960
Tobey, Dave 1963-64-65
Tommeraason, Cary 1962
Torchia, Peter 1942-46-47
Tourville, Charles 1956-58
Travis, L.M. 1894-85-96
Trovato, Tom 1965-66
Trowbridge, J.F. 1918
Tucker, Keith 1953-54
Tuerck, W.P. 1915
Turner, Norval 1972-73-74
Tyler, Tim 1979-80-81-82

U

Urell, Dave 1958-59-60

V

Vaccher, Lino 1983-84-85
Van Brocklin, Norm 1947-48
Van Leuven, Dean 1952-53
Van Pelt, Goerge 1940-41
Van Vliet, Maurice 1933-34
Vaughan, Chris 1978
Verdon, Zeth 1985
Veres, Ron 1961
Vernier, Donald 1941
Verutti, Pat 1968-69
Vincent, William 1976-77
Vitus, Otto 1923-24-26-27
Vobora, Andy 1978-81
Vonderahe, Karl 1921-22-23

W

Waldon, Cecil 1937-38-39
Walk, Rich 1986
Walker, Dave 1968-69-70
Walker, D.H. 1909-12
Walker, Isaac 1992-93-94
Walker V. 1934
Walter, Mike 1979-82
Wanner, C.E. 1899
Warberg, Dale 1945
Ward, E.L. 1902
Ward, Rick 1979
Warner, Ken 1982-83-84-85
Warren, John 1926-27
Warren, Scott 1928-29
Wathey, Jim 1967-68-69
Watts, Don 1929-30-31
Watts, H.J. 1901-02
Weaver, John 1985
Webb, Art 1971-72-73
Webb, Tom 1977-78
Weber, Arthur 1954-55
Webster, Devall 1979-81-82
Weems, Thomas 1927-28
Wegner, Ken 1987
Weigel, Al 1959-60-61
Weist, Oscar 1913-15
Welch, Claxton 1966-67-68
Welch, Pete 1957-58
Welch, Todd 1982-83-84
West, M. 1929
West, S. 1929
West, Willie 1957-58-59

Wetzel, Victor 1925-26-27
Wheatley, Ray 1983-84
Wheaton, Kenny 1994
Wheeler, J.C. 1955-56-57
White, Jo Jo 1973-74-75
White, Stewart 1957
Whitney, Scott 1987-88
Whittle, Ricky 1992-93-94
Widlund, C.E. 1910
Wiggins, Paul 1993-94
Wilchuck, Kurt 1985
Wilcox, Dave 1962-63
Wilcox, Dave G. 1973
Wilcox, John 1958-59
Wilcox, Josh 1993-94
Wilcox, Robert 1951
Wilken, Dan 1981-83-85
Wilkins, Dick 1948
Willener, John 1957-58-59
Willener, Greg 1960-61-62
Willhite, Kevin 1983-86
Willhite, Randy 1985-87-88
Williams, Andre 1986-88-89
Williams, B.T. 1917-18-19
Williams, Chad 1994
Williams, Charles 1927-29
Williams, Emmett 1951-52
Williams, Gary 1990-93
Williams, Jarrod 1950
Williams, Jeff 1981-84
Williams, Larry 1976
Williams, Mike 1970
Williams, Mike D. 1974
Williams, Rob 1994
Williams, Vince 1977-79-81
Williamson, Bill 1923
Wills, Chuck 1973-74-75
Wilson, Alan 1934
Wilson, Dale 1963-64-65
Wilson, L. Dow 1917-18-19
Wilson, Elliott 1940-41
Wilson, F. 1898-99
Wilson, G.E. 1921
Wilson, Gordon 1923-24
Wilson K. 1931
Wilson, Lerry 1982-83-84
Wilson, Michael 1987
Winetrout, Art 1939
Winn, Dick 1964-65
Winn, Eric 1994
Winn, Harvey 1970-71
Winn, Mark 1988
Winter, Lawrence 1931
Wise, Tim 1982
Wishard, Charles 1931-33
Wolf, John 1984-85-86
Wong, Warner 1966-67-68
Wood, Harry 1927-28-29
Wood, Jeff 1977-78-79
Woodfill, Stan 1974-75
Woodle, Ira 1926-27-28
Woods, LaMont 1993-94
Woods, Marcus 1988-89-90-91
Woodward, Hugh 1972-73
Woody, Ken 1968-69-70
Wooton, Tom 1966-67-68
Wynne, Patrick 1941

Y

Yaru, Tom 1973-74-75
Yatsko, Stuart 19780-81
Yerby, John 1936-37-38
Young, Brett 1986-87-88
Young, Eugene 1980-81-82
Young, Reggie 1978-79
Young, S.A. 1898-99
Youngblood, Terry 1981-83
Youngmayr, Bill 1963

Z

Zaharie, Geno 1987
Zeigler, F. 1896-99-1900-01
Zemp, Ron 1983-84-85
Zimmerman, Gary 1980-83
Zinke, Ryan 1980-81-82-83

About the Authors

Michael C. McCann, 36, is the publisher of the *Fighting Ducks Review* and the president of *McCann Communications Corp.* He has worked as a sportswriter, columnist and radio commentator, and has been covering *University of Oregon Sports* since 1991. He resides in Eugene, Oregon.

John Conrad, 50, is the sports editor of *The Register-Guard,* where he has worked for much of his adult life. He is a frequent contributor to national college football magazines and has been covering *University of Oregon* sports since 1981. He resides in Eugene, Oregon.

Bob Clark, 45, is a sportswriter for the *The Register-Guard,* as well as the paper's former sports editor. He also has worked as an assistant sports editor for the Oregonian, and has been covering *University of Oregon* sports since 1980. He resides in Eugene, Oregon.

Paul Buker, 44, is a sportswriter for *The Oregonian* and the former sports editor of the *Oregon Daily Emerald.* He is a frequent contributor to national sports magazines and has been covering *Univeristy of Oregon Sports* since 1989. He resides in Portland, Oregon.

Ron Bellamy, 46, is a columnist and sportswriter for *The Register-Guard,* where he has worked since 1975. Now in his ninth year as Eugene's most read columnist, he has been covering *University of Oregon* sports since 1983. He resides in Eugene, Oregon.

Michael F. Sims, 37, is a free-lance writer and government-relations consultant. He formerly worked as the managing editor of the *Oregon Daily Emerald* and the *Tillamook Headlight-Herald,* and as a reporter for newspapers in Lake Oswego and West Linn. He resides in Salem, Oregon.

Bill Mulflur, 69, is a free-lance writer and the former sports editor of the *Oregon Journal.* He has covered a wide variety of college and professional sports in Oregon for more than 35 years. He resides in Portland, Oregon.